THE SHELTERED LIFE

ELLEN GLASGOW

THE
SHELTERED
LIFE

 Afterword by Carol S. Manning ₹

The University Press of Virginia
Charlottesville and London

THE UNIVERSITY PRESS OF VIRGINIA
Copyright © 1938, 1932 by Ellen Glasgow
Copyright renewed 1966, 1960 by First and Merchants
National Bank of Richmond, Executor

Afterword copyright © 1994 by the Rector and Visitors
of the University of Virginia
Expanded Paperback Edition

First University Press of Virginia printing 1994

Published by arrangement with Harcourt Brace & Company

Library of Congress Cataloging-in-Publication Data

Glasgow, Ellen Anderson Gholson, 1873–1945.
  The sheltered life / by Ellen Glasgow : with an afterword by Carol S.
Manning.—Expanded paperback ed.
    p. cm.
  ISBN 0–8139–1514–7 (paper)
    1. City and town life—Virginia—Richmond—Fiction. 2. Southern
States—Social conditions—Fiction. 3. Young women—Virginia—
Richmond—Fiction. 4. Family—Virginia—Richmond—Fiction.
5. Richmond (Va.)—Fiction. I. Title.
PS3513.L34S5 1994
813'.52—dc20   93–41095
                                                                          CIP

Printed in the United States of America

For

ARTHUR GRAHAM GLASGOW

*Whose affection is a shelter
without walls*

NOTHING, EXCEPT the weather report or a general maxim of conduct, is so unsafe to rely upon as a theory of fiction. Every great novel has broken many conventions. The greatest of all novels defies every formula; and only Mr. Percy Lubbock believes that *War and Peace* would be greater if it were another and an entirely different book. By this I do not mean to question Mr. Lubbock's critical insight. *The Craft of Fiction* is the best work in its limited field, and it may be studied to advantage by any novelist. In the first chapters there is a masterly analysis of *War and Peace*. Yet, after reading this with appreciation, I still think that Tolstoy was the best judge of what his book was about and of how long it should be.

This brings us, in the beginning, to the most sensitive, and therefore the most controversial, point in the criticism of prose fiction. It is the habit of overworked or frugal critics to speak as if economy were a virtue and not a necessity. Yet there are faithful readers who feel with me that a good novel cannot be too long or a bad novel too short. Our company is small but picked with care, and we would die upon the literary barricade defending the noble proportions of *War and Peace*, of *The Brothers Karamazov*, of *Clarissa Harlowe* in eight volumes, of *Tom Jones*, of *David Copperfield*, of *The Chronicles of Barsetshire*, of *A la Recherche du Temps Perdu*, of *Le Vicomte de Bragelonne*. Tennyson was with us when he said he had no criticism to make of *Clarissa Harlowe* except that it might have been longer.

The true novel (I am not concerned with the run-of-the-mill variety) is, like pure poetry, an act of birth, not a device or an invention. It awaits its own time and has its own way to be born, and it cannot, by scientific methods, be pushed into the world from behind. After it is born, a separate individual, an organic structure, it obeys its own vital impulses. The heart quickens; the blood circulates; the pulses beat; the whole body moves in response to some inward rhythm; and in time the expanding vitality attains its full stature. But until the breath of life enters a novel, it is as spiritless as inanimate matter.

Having said this much, I may confess that spinning theories of fiction is my favourite amusement. This is, I think, a good habit to cultivate. The exercise encourages readiness and agility while it keeps both head and hand in practice. Besides, if it did nothing else, it would still protect one from the radio and the moving picture and other sleepless, if less sinister, enemies to the lost mood of contemplation. This alone would justify every precept that was ever evolved. Although a work of fiction may be written without a formula or a method, I doubt if the true novel has ever been created without the long brooding season.

I have read, I believe, with as much interest as if it were a novel itself, every treatise on the art of fiction that appeared to me to be promising. That variable branch of letters shares with philosophy the favourite shelf in my library. I know all that such sources of learning as Sir Leslie Stephen, Sir Walter Raleigh, Mr. Percy Lubbock, Sir Arthur Quiller-Couch, Mr. E. M. Forster, and others less eminent but often more earnest, are able to teach me, or I am able to acquire. Indeed, I know more than they can teach me, for I know also how very little their knowledge can help one in the actual writing of novels. If I were giving advice to a beginner (but there are no beginners nowadays, there is only the inspired amateur or the infant pathologist), I should probably say something like this: "Learn the technique of writing, and having learned it thoroughly, try to forget it. Study the principles of construction, the value of continuity, the arrangement of masses, the consistent point of view, the revealing episode, the careful handling of detail, and the fatal pitfalls of dialogue. Then, having mastered, if possible, every rule of thumb, dismiss it into the labyrinth of the memory. Leave it there to make its own signals and flash its own warnings. The sensitive feeling, 'this is not right' or 'something ought to be different' will prove that these signals are working." Or, perhaps, this inner voice may be only the sounder instinct of the born novelist.

The truth is that I began being a novelist, as naturally as I began talking or walking, so early that I cannot remember when the impulse first seized me. Far back in my childhood, before I had learned the letters of the alphabet, a character named Little Willie wandered into the country of my mind, just as every other major character in my novels has strolled across my mental horizon when I was not expecting him, when I was not even thinking of the novel in which he would finally take his place. From what or where he had sprung, why he was named Little Willie, or why I should have selected a hero instead of a heroine —all this is still as much of a mystery to me as it was in my childhood. But there he was, and there he remained, alive and active, threading his own adventures, from the time I was three until I was eight or nine, and discovered Hans Andersen and *Grimm's Fairy Tales*. Every night, as I was undressed and put to bed by my coloured Mammy, the romance of Little Willie would begin again exactly where it had broken off the evening before. In winter I was undressed in the firelight on the hearth-rug; but in summer we moved over to an open window that looked out on the sunset and presently the first stars in the long green twilight. For years Little Willie lasted, never growing older, always pursuing his own narrative and weaving his situations out of his own personality. I can still see him, small, wiry, with lank brown hair like a thatch, and eyes that seemed to say, "I know a secret! I know a secret!" Hans Andersen and the brothers Grimm were his chosen companions. He lingered on, though somewhat sadly, after I had discovered the Waverley Novels; but when I was twelve years old and entered the world of Dickens, he vanished forever.

In those earliest formative years Little Willie outlined, however vaguely, a general pattern of work. He showed me that a novelist must write, not by taking thought alone, but with every cell of his being, that nothing can occur to him that may not sooner or later find its way into his craft. Whatever happened to me or to Mammy Lizzie happened also, strangely transfigured, to Little Willie. I learned, too, and never forgot, that ideas would not come to me if I went out to hunt for them. They would fly when I pursued; but if I stopped and sank down into a kind of watchful reverie, they would flock back again like friendly pigeons. All I had to do before the novel had formed was to leave the creative faculty (or subconscious mind) free to work its own way without urging and without effort. When Dorinda in *Barren Ground* first appeared to me, I pushed her back into some glimmering obscurity, where she remained, buried but alive, for a decade, and emerged from the yeasty medium with hard round limbs and the bloom of health in her cheeks. Thus I have never wanted for subjects; but on several occasions when, because of illness or from external compulsion, I have tried to invent, rather than subconsciously create, a theme or a character, invariably the effort has resulted in failure. These are the anæmic offspring of the brain, not children of my complete being; and a brood whom I would wish, were it possible, to disinherit.

It is not easy to tell how much of this dependence upon intuition may be attributed to the lack of harmony between my inner life and my early environment. A thoughtful and imaginative child, haunted by that strange sense of exile which visits the subjective mind when it is unhappily placed (and always, apparently, it is unhappily placed or it would not be subjective), I grew up in a charming society, where ideas were accepted as naturally as the universe or the weather, and cards for the old, dancing for the young, and conversation flavoured with personalities for the middle-aged, were the only arts practised. Several members of my family, it is true, possessed brilliant minds and were widely and deeply read; but all despised what they called "local talent"; and my early work was written in secret to escape ridicule, alert, pointed, and not the less destructive because it was playful. There is more truth than wit in the gibe that every Southern novelist must first make his reputation in the North. Perhaps this is why so many Southern novelists write of the South as if it were a fabulous country. When a bound copy of my first book reached me, I hid it under my pillow while a cousin, who had run in before breakfast, prattled beside my bed of the young men who had quarrelled over the privilege of taking her to the Easter German, as the Cotillion was called. Had I entered the world by way of Oxford, or even by way of Bloomsbury, I might now be able to speak or write of my books without a feeling of outraged reserve. And yet, in the very act of writing these words, my literary conscience, a nuisance to any writer, inquires if ideas were really free at Oxford, or even in Bloomsbury, at the end of the century, and if all the enfranchised spirits who babble of prohibited subjects nowadays are either wiser or better than the happy hypocrites of the nineties.

From this dubious prelude it might be inferred that I consider the craft of fiction merely another form of mental inertia. On the contrary, I agree with those writers who have found actual writing to be the hardest work in the world. What I am concerned with at the moment, however, is the beginning of a novel alone, not the endless drudgery that wrung from Stevenson the complaint, "The practice of letters is miserably harassing to the mind; and after an hour or two's work, all the more human portion of an author is extinct; he will bully, backbite, and speak daggers." For being a true novelist, even if one's work is not worth the price of a cherry to public or publisher, takes all that one has to give and still something more. Yet the matter is not one of choice but of fatality. As with the enjoyment of music, or a love for El Greco, or a pleasure in gardening, or the taste for pomegranates, or a liking for Santayana's prose, the bent of nature is either there or it is not there.

For my own part, and it appears, however far I stray, that I must still return to "the highly personal statement," the only method I have deliberately cultivated has been a system of constant renewal. If novels should be, as Sir Leslie Stephen has said, "transfigured experience," then I have endeavoured, whenever it was possible, to deepen experience and to heighten what I prefer to call illumination, to increase my understanding of that truth of life which has never become completely reconciled with the truth of fiction. I do not mean by this that life should necessarily be eventful or filled with variable activities. Profound emotion does not inevitably bear "the pageant of a bleeding heart." Several of the most thrilling lives in all literature were lived amid the unconquerable desolation of the Yorkshire moors. Yet it is doubtful if either the exposed heart of Byron or the brazen trumpet of D. H. Lawrence contained such burning realities as were hidden beneath the quiet fortitude of Emily Brontë.

Because of some natural inability to observe and record instead of create, I have never used an actual scene until the impression it left had sifted down into imagined surroundings. A theme becomes real to me only after it is clothed in living values; but these values must be drawn directly from the imagination and indirectly, if at all, from experience. Invariably the characters appear first, and slowly and gradually build up their own world and spin the situation and atmosphere out of themselves. Strangely enough, the horizon of this real or visionary world is limited by the impressions or recollections of my early childhood. If I were to walk out into the country and pick a scene for a book, it would remain as flat and lifeless as cardboard; but the places I loved or hated between the ages of three and thirteen compose an inexhaustible landscape of memory. Occasionally, it is true, I have returned to a scene to verify details, though for freshness and force I have trusted implicitly to the vision within. And just as my scene is built up from fragments of the past, whether that past existed in fact or in a dream, so the human figures, though not one of them has been copied from my acquaintances, will startle me by displaying a familiar trait or gesture, and I will recognize with a shock some special blending of characteristics.

Frequently these impressions had been buried so long and so deep that I had entirely forgotten them until they floated upward to the surface of thought. Yet they were not dead but living, and recovered warmth and animation after the creative faculty had revived them. In the same way, half-obliterated images, events, or episodes, observed in moments of intense experience, will flash back into a scene or a figure; and this is equally true of the most trivial detail my memory has registered. For example, in one of the tragic hours of my youth I looked out of a window and saw two sparrows quarrelling in the rain on a roof. Twenty years or more afterwards, a character in one of my novels looks out of a window in a moment of heartbreak and sees two sparrows quarrelling in the rain. And immediately, light streamed back, as if it were cast by the rays of a lantern, into the unlit recesses of memory, and I felt the old grief in my heart and saw the rain fall on the roof and the two sparrows quarrelling there.

Because everything that one has seen or heard or thought or felt leaves a deposit that never filters entirely through the essence of mind, I believe that a novelist should be perpetually engaged in this effort to refresh and replenish his source. I am confident, moreover, that nothing I have learned either from life or from literature has been wasted. Whatever I have thought or felt deeply has stayed with me, if only in fragments or in a distillation of memory. But the untiring critic within has winnowed, reassorted, and disposed the material I needed.

Not until the unconscious worker has withdrawn from the task, or taken a brief holiday, and the characters have woven their own background and circumstances, does the actual drudgery of moulding the mass-substance begin. Even now, after the groundwork is completed and the subject assembled, I still give time and thought (brooding is the more accurate term) to the construction. I try to avoid hastening the process, and to leave the invisible agent free to flash directions or warnings. The book must have a form. This is essential. It may be shaped like a mill-stone or an hour-glass or an Indian tomahawk or a lace fan—but a shape it must have. Usually a novel assumes its own figure when it enters the world, and the underlying idea moulds the plastic material to its own structure. More deliberately, the point of view is considered and selected, though this may, and often does, proceed naturally from the unities of time and place, or from one completely dominant figure. In *Barren Ground*, a long novel, I felt from the moment Dorinda entered the book that here could be but one point of view. From the first page to the last, no scene or episode or human figure appears outside her field of vision or imagination.

In *The Sheltered Life*, where I knew intuitively that the angle of vision must create the form, I employed two points of view alone, though they were separated by the whole range of experience. Age and youth look on the same scene, the same persons, the same events and occasions, the same tragedy in the end. Between these conflicting points of view the story flows on, as a stream flows in a narrow valley. Nothing happens that is not seen, on one side, through the steady gaze of the old man, seeing life as it is, and, on the other side, by the troubled eyes of the young girl, seeing life as she would wish it to be. Purposely, I have tried here to interpret reality through the dissimilar mediums of thought and emotion. I have been careful to allow no other aspects to impinge on the contrasting visions which create between them the organic whole of the book. This convention, which appears uncertain, when one thinks of it, becomes natural and even involuntary when the work grows, develops, pushes out with its own energy, and finds its own tempo.

Patiently, but without success, I have tried to trace the roots of *The Sheltered Life*. The background is that of my girlhood, and the rudiments of the theme must have lain buried somewhere in my consciousness. But I can recall no definite beginning or voluntary act of creation. One moment there was a mental landscape without figures; the next moment, as if they had been summoned by a bell, all the characters trooped in together, with every contour, every feature, every attitude, every gesture and expression complete. In their origin, I exerted no control over them. They were too real for dismemberment; but I could, and I did, select or eliminate whatever in their appearances or behaviour seemed to conflict with the general scheme of the book. It was my part to see that the unities were recognized and obeyed.

It is only logical to infer that when a group of imaginary beings assembles, there must be a motive, or at least an adequate reason, for the particular gathering. I knew, or thought I knew, that no visitor had ever entered my mind without an imperative purpose. These people were there, I felt, according to a design, for a planned attack upon life, and to push them out of the way would only spur them to more intense activity. It was best to ignore them, and this, as nearly as possible, was the course I pursued. Sooner or later, they would let me know why they had come and what I was expected to do. For me, they were already alive, though I could not as yet distinguish the intricate ties that bound this isolated group into a detached segment of life. So this state of affairs continued for several years. Another novel, *They Stooped to Folly*, engaged my attention, while some distant range of my imagination was still occupied by the Birdsongs and the Archbalds.

Then, at last, *They Stooped to Folly* was finished, was over. Presently it was published; and in company with all my other books that had gone out into the world, it became a homeless wanderer and a stranger. It had ceased to belong to me. I might almost say that it had ceased even to interest me. The place where it had been, the place it had filled to overflowing for nearly three years, was now empty. Were there no other inhabitants? What had become of those troublesome intruders I had once banished to some vague Siberia of the mind?

It was at this crucial instant that the Birdsongs and the Archbalds, under their own names and wearing their own outward semblances, escaped from remote exile. While I waited, in that unhappy brooding season, which cannot be forced, which cannot be hurried, the vacant scene was flooded with light and animation, and the emerging figures began to breathe, move, speak, and round out their own destinies. I knew instantly, as soon as they returned, what the integral drama would be and why it had occurred. The theme was implicit in the inevitable title. Beyond this, I saw a shallow and aimless society of happiness-hunters, who lived in a perpetual flight from reality and grasped at any effort-saving illusion of passion or pleasure. Against this background of futility was projected the contrasting character of General Archbald, a lover of wisdom, a humane and civilized soul, oppressed by the burden of tragic remembrance. The stream of events would pass before him, for he would remain permanently at the centre of vision, while opposing him on the farther side he would meet the wide, blank, unreflective gaze of inexperience.

In a sudden wholeness of perception, one of those complex apprehensions which come so seldom yet possess a miraculous power of conviction, I saw the meaning not only of these special figures, but of their essential place in this theme of age and youth, of the past and the present. They had been drawn together by some sympathetic attraction, or by some deeper sense of recognition in my own consciousness. My task was the simple one of extracting from the situation every thread of significance, every quiver of vitality, every glimmer of understanding. The contours were moulded. I could see the articulation of the parts, as well as the shape of the structure. I could see, too, the fragile surface of a style that I must strive, however unsuccessfully, to make delicate yet unbreakable. I could feel the peculiar density of light and shadow. I could breathe in that strange symbolic smell which was woven and interwoven through the gradually thickening atmosphere of the scene.

As at least one critic has recognized, the old man, left behind by the years, is the real protagonist of the book; and into his lonely spirit I have put much of my ultimate feeling about life. He represents the tragedy, wherever it appears, of the civilized man in a world that is not civilized. And even the title, which I have called inevitable, implies no special age or place. What it implies to me is the effort of one human being to stand between another and life. In a larger sense, as this critic perceives, the same tragedy was being repeated in spheres far wider than Queenborough. The World War was beginning and men were killing each other from the highest possible ideals. This is the final scope of the book's theme. The old man, his point of view, his thwarted strong body, saw the age pass by him. Not in the South especially; it was throughout the world that ideas, forms, were changing, the familiar order going, the beliefs and certainties. The shelter for men's lives, of religion, convention, social prejudice, was at the crumbling point, just as was the case with the little human figures in the story. . . .

While I am at work on a book I remain, or try to remain, in a state of immersion. The first draft of a novel, if it is long, will take two years, and still another year is required for the final writing. All this time the imaginary setting becomes the native country of my mind, and the characters are seldom out of my thoughts. I live with them day and night; they are more real to me than acquaintances in the flesh. In our nursery copy of *Gulliver's Travels* there was a picture which seems, when I recall it now, to illustrate my predicament in the final draft of a novel. Gulliver lies bound in threads while the Lilliputians swarm over him and hamper his struggles. So words swarm over me and hamper my efforts to seize the right one among them, to find the right rhythm, the right tone, the right accent. But here again intuition, or perhaps only a flare of organized memory, will come to my aid. Often, when I have searched for hours for some special word or phrase, and given up in despair, I have awaked with a start in the night because the hunted word or phrase had darted into my mind while I was asleep.

Nevertheless, it is the act of scrupulous revision (the endless pruning and trimming for the sake of valid and flexible prose style) that provides the writer's best solace even while it makes drudgery. Every literary craftsman who respects his work has, I dare say, this same feeling, and remains restless and wandering in mind until in the beginning he has entered the right climate and at the end has tracked down the right word. Although my characters may develop traits or actions I had not anticipated, though scenes may shift and alter in perspective, and new episodes may spring out on the way, still the end shines always as the solitary fixed star above the flux of creation. I have never written the first word of the first sentence until I knew what the last word of the last sentence would be. Sometimes I may rewrite the beginning many times, as I did in *They Stooped to Folly*, and sometimes (though this has actually occurred but once) a shorter book like *The Romantic Comedians*, completely realized before pen was put to paper, may bubble over, of itself, with a kind of effortless joy. Yet in the difficult first chapter of *They Stooped to Folly* I could still look ahead, over a procession of characters that had slipped from my control, to the subdued scene at the end, while the concluding paragraph of *The Romantic Comedians* placed the tone of the entire book and accented the rhythm.

The final words to be said of any activity will always be, I suppose, was it worth what it cost? Well, the writing of fiction is worth, I imagine, exactly what digging a ditch or charting the heavens may be worth to the worker, and that is not a penny more or less than the release of mind which it brings. Although I may not speak as an authority, at least I can speak from long perseverance. I became a novelist before I was old enough to resist, and I remained a novelist because no other enterprise in life has afforded me the same interest or provided me with equal contentment. It is true that I have written only for the biased judgment within; but this inner critic has held up an unattainable standard, and has infused a certain zest of adventure into what may appear on the surface to be merely another humdrum way of earning a livelihood. Still, to a beginner who is young and cherishes an ambition to be celebrated, I should recommend the short cut (or royal road) through the radio and Hollywood; and certainly more than one creative writer, in search of swift economic security, would do well to buy a new broom and to set out for the next crossing. But, incredible as it may appear in this practical decade, there are novelists so wanting in a sense of the best proletarian values that they place artistic integrity above the voice on the air, the flash on the screen, and the dividends in the bank. There are others who possess an unreasoning faith in their own work; and there are yet others endowed with a comic spirit so robust, or so lively, that it can find diversion anywhere, even in our national exaltation of the inferior. To this happy company of neglected novelists, the ironic art of fiction will reveal its own special delights, and may even, as the years pass, yield its own sufficient, if imponderable, rewards.

In looking back through a long vista, I can see that what I have called the method of constant renewal may be reduced to three ruling principles. Obedience to this self-imposed discipline has enabled me to write novels for nearly forty years, and yet to feel that the substance from which I draw material and energy is as fresh to-day as it was in my first youthful failure. As time moves on, I still see life in beginnings, moods in conflict, and change as the only permanent law. But the value of these qualities (which may be self-deluding, and are derived, in fact, more from temperament than from technique) has been mellowed by long saturation with experience—by that essence of reality which one distils from life only after it has been lived.

Among the many strange superstitions of the age of science revels the cheerful belief that immaturity alone is enough. Pompous illiteracy, escaped from some Freudian cage, is in the saddle, and the voice of the amateur is the voice of authority. When we turn to the field of prose fiction, we find that it is filled with literary sky-rockets sputtering out in the fog. But the trouble with sky-rockets has always been that they do not stay up in the air. One has only to glance back over the post-war years to discover that the roads of the jazz age are matted thick with fireworks which went off too soon. To the poet, it is true, especially if he can arrange with destiny to die young, the glow of adolescence may impart an unfading magic. But the novel (which must be conceived with a subdued rapture, or with none at all, or even with the unpoetic virtues of industry and patience) requires more substantial ingredients than a little ignorance of life and a great yearning to tell everything one has never known. When I remember Defoe, the father of us all, I am persuaded that the novelist who has harvested well the years, and laid by a rich store of experience, will find his latter period the ripening time of his career.

Transposed into an impersonal method, the three rules of which I have spoken may be so arranged:

1. Always wait between books for the springs to fill up and flow over.

2. Always preserve, within a wild sanctuary, an inaccessible valley of reveries.

3. Always, and as far as it is possible, endeavour to touch life on every side; but keep the central vision of the mind, the inmost light, untouched and untouchable.

In my modest way, these rules have helped me, not only to pursue the one calling for which I was designed alike by character and inclination, but even to enjoy the prolonged study of a world that, as the sardonic insight of Henry Adams perceived, no "sensitive and timid natures could regard without a shudder."

Ellen Glasgow.

Richmond, Virginia,
December, 1934–1937

CONTENTS

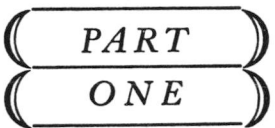

PART ONE

THE AGE OF MAKE-BELIEVE

B Y THE open French window of the dining-room Jenny Blair Archbald was reading *Little Women* for the assured reward of a penny a page. Now and then she would stop to shake her head, toss her smooth honey-coloured plaits over her shoulders, and screw her face into a caricature Aunt Etta's expression. "It isn't safe to skip," she thought. "Grandfather would be sure to find out. Well, even if Mamma did form her character on Meg and Jo, I think they're just poky old things." Poky old things, and yet spreading themselves over five hundred and thirty-two pages! "Mamma may call the Marches lots of fun," she added firmly, "but I'm different. I'm different."

The book dropped from her hands, while her startled gaze flew to the topmost branch of the old sycamore in the garden. Deep pulsations of light were flooding the world. Very thin and clear through the May afternoon, there was the chime of distant bells striking the hour. Somewhere, without or within, a miracle had occurred. At the age of nine years and seven months, she had encountered the second important event in human experience. She was discovering her hidden self as once before, in some long forgotten past, she had discovered her body. "I don't care. I'm different," she repeated exultantly.

From the warm mother-of-pearl vagueness within, a fragment of personality detached itself, wove a faint pattern of thought, and would gradually harden into a shell over her mind. But all she knew was, "I am this and not that." All she felt was the sudden glory, the singing rhythm of life. Softly, without knowing why, she began crooning, "I'm alive, alive, alive, and I'm Jenny Blair Archbald." Ages before, in the time far back beyond the vanishing rim of memory, she had composed this refrain, and she still chanted it to herself when happiness overflowed. For it was all her own. No one, not even her mother, not even her grandfather, knew how she loved it. Jealously, she kept it hidden away with her chief treasure, the gold locket in which somebody had wound a tiny circle of her father's hair after his tragic death in a fox-hunt. Though she was only five at the time, she had had this song even then. When she was alone and happy, she sang it aloud; when she was with her mother or her aunts, the words dissolved into a running tune. Nothing, except the white poodle she had lost and mourned, had ever given her such pure ecstasy. "I'm alive, alive, alive, and I'm Jenny Blair Archbald."

"What are you saying, Jenny Blair?" her mother called from the front window of the library, which looked over the diminished grandeur of Washington Street to the recent industrial conquest of Queenborough. Beyond the open folding doors, the child could see the soft old bronze and ruby red of the library, and the glimmer of light on Aunt Etta's eyeglasses and on her mother's fawn-coloured hair, which was still worn à la Pompadour.

"Nothing, Mamma." How could she tell her mother that whenever this darting joy pierced her heart, she was obliged to burst into song, or skip a rope very fast, or swing high up in the green and gold branches of trees? How could she say in words that she sang or skipped or swung because joy fell apart and broke into splinters of pain? For her mother would never, never understand that joy has no meaning.

Breathing hard, she shut her eyes tight and opened them quickly. This was a magic spell to make the world more surprising; and enchantment worked immediately upon the sky, the sycamore, and the rich bloom of the walled garden. In the garden, which was reached by stone steps from the back porch, splendour flickered over the tall purple iris that fringed the birdbath, and rippled like a bright veil over the grass walks and flower-beds. A small place, but it held beauty. Beauty, and that deep stillness through which time seems to flow with a perpetual rhythm and pause. On the edge of the bird-bath a robin stood drinking. Farther away, two black and yellow butterflies spun round and round, without flight, as if they were attached to invisible threads. Only at long intervals, when the breeze died down and sprang up again, was the tranquil air brushed by a roving taint, a breath of decay, from the new chemical factory near the river. Now rising, now falling, the smell was scarcely more than a whiff that came and went on the wind. Scarcely more than a whiff, yet strong enough, when the houses were open, to spoil the delicate flavour of living.

"Mamma," Jenny Blair called, turning her head from the garden, "that bad smell has come back again."

"I know, my child, but your grandfather says there is nothing to be done about it."

Ever since the War Between the States had transformed opulent planters into eminent citizens, a dozen old country families had clung to the lower end of Washington Street. Here they had lived, knit together by ties of kinship and tradition, in the Sabbath peace that comes only to those who have been vanquished in war. Here they resisted change and adversity and progress and here at last they were scattered by nothing more tangible than a stench. Those who could afford a fashionable neighbourhood fled in the direction of Granite Boulevard. Others retired to modest Virginian farms. Only the Archbalds and the Birdsongs, at the other end of the block, stood their ground and watched the invasion of ugliness. The Birdsongs stayed because, as they confessed proudly, they were too poor to move and the Archbalds stayed because the General, in his seventy-sixth year but still incapable of retreat, declared that he would never forsake Mrs. Birdsong. Industrialism might conquer, but they would never surrender.

One by one, they saw the old houses demolished, the fine old elms mutilated. Telegraph poles slashed the horizon; furnaces, from a distance, belched soot into the drawing-rooms; newspapers, casually read and dropped, littered the pavements;

when the wind shifted on the banks of the river, an evil odour sprang up from the hollow. Still undaunted, the two families held the breach between the old and the new order, sustained by pride and by some moral quality more enduring than pride. After all, they might have asked, were they not defending their homes from a second invasion? Moreover, so long as Mrs. Birdsong remained, Washington Street might decline, but it could not be entirely stripped of its old elegance. As Eva Howard, Mrs. Birdsong had been a famous beauty in the eighteen nineties; and the social history of Queenborough was composed wherever she decided to live that history. As late as the spring of 1906, she was still regarded less a woman than as a memorable occasion. Rumours sped from door to door as she walked down the street; crowds gathered at corners or flocked breathlessly to the windows of clubs. In her middle thirties, and married for twelve years to a man who was unworthy of her, she had already passed into legend. Romantic stories were told of her girlhood. Not only had her beauty delayed wedding processions, but once, it was said, she had even retarded a funeral when she happened to enter Rose Hill Cemetery just as the pallbearers were lowering a coffin into a grave.

"Jenny Blair, are you getting on with your book?" With her hand poised above the coat of blue piqué she was braiding in white, Mrs. Archbald turned her animated glance toward the French window. At thirty-nine, she was still attractive and fresh-coloured, plump, but not too plump to be comfortable in stays of the more liberal Edwardian style.

"Jenny Blair," she called again in an imperative tone, "do you hear me?"

"Yes, Mamma, but I'm thinking."

"Thinking?" repeated Aunt Etta, who was frail and plain and sickly. "What on earth do you have to think about, Jenny Blair?"

"Nothing, Aunt Etta."

"How, my dear, can you think about nothing?"

"Aren't you getting on with your book?" Mrs. Archbald

asked, removing a pin from her mouth and running it into the sleeve of the piqué coat. "I hope it isn't too old for you. Are you sure you understand what you're reading?"

"Oh, Mamma, it is so dreadfully poky."

"Poky? Why, I could never have too much of *Little Women* when I was a girl. I remember I tried to form my character on Meg—or it may have been Jo. But I can't understand children to-day. I don't know what they're coming to."

"How soon may I stop, Mamma?"

"Finish that chapter, and then we'll see what time it is."

"But I've just begun a new chapter."

"Well, finish it anyhow. Your grandfather will be sure to ask how much you've read."

"Do you think he will pay me when I'm half through? I need a new pair of roller-skates more than anything in the world. There is a very nice pair in Mrs. Doe's window for a dollar and a half."

After thirty years of disfavour, roller-skating had wheeled again into fashion. In the spring of 1906 all the world skated, especially young women of leisure, who admired themselves in the tight fur-trimmed jackets and new ankle-length skirts, which were worn with jaunty little caps in the skating-rinks. Aunt Isabella, who was handsome and bold and dashing, with a figure that looked as if it had been melted and poured into her princess robe of black satin, had attended the opening gaieties in the fine new rink in Broad Street.

"Where is the pair I gave you last Christmas?" Aunt Etta called sharply.

"They're broken, Aunt Etta. One of the rollers won't roll right. It tripped me up yesterday, and I fell down and scraped my knee."

"Perhaps Amos can mend it."

"He did mend it, but it came unfixed right away. Do you think, Mamma, that Grandfather will let me have a dollar and a half when I've read a hundred and fifty pages?"

"I'm not sure, dear." Her mother's tone was softer than Aunt

Etta's. "He may, if he thinks you've read in the proper spirit."
Jenny Blair sighed. "I wish he'd pay me for reading French."
"Didn't he reward you when you finished *A French Country Family?*"

"Oh, I don't mean that. I mean real French, the kind Aunt Etta is always reading." For she was persuaded, after observing Aunt Etta's way with books in yellow covers, that all the really interesting things were written in the French language.

"You aren't far enough advanced for that, dear," Aunt Etta was sympathetic but discouraging, "though you are doing very nicely with your French conversation."

"Come here a minute, darling." Mrs. Archbald raised her pleasant voice in command. "I want to see if I've got the right length for this coat. What I can never understand about Jenny Blair," she added to her sister-in-law, "is the way she is so far ahead in some things and so backward in others."

"Well, we were all that way," Etta said consolingly. "I'm sure she seems very bright when you compare her with Bena Peyton."

"But Bena has a nice plump little figure, and Jenny Blair is as straight as a pole."

Rising obediently, Jenny Blair tripped with reluctant feet into the library, and stood patiently between her mother and Aunt Etta while the coat was slipped over her shoulders and fastened with a safety-pin on her flat little chest. She was a golden wisp of a child, with soft flaxen hair, a shower of freckles over her small snub nose, and a vague rosy mouth which melted into a short dimpled chin. Though she was not pretty, she had inherited the yellow-hazel eyes and the wide, expectant gaze of the Archbalds. While she stood there, she shifted uneasily on her feet, and, because she hated trying on more than anything in the world, desperately invoked the power of pretense.

"Hold still, Jenny Blair, or I can't measure you. What are you mumbling?"

"Oh, nothing, Mamma, but I do hate trying on. I was just making-believe."

"Well, you make-believe entirely too much. That may be one reason you are so stringy and peaked. If you would only stop moping for a while, you might put some flesh on your bones. Have you had your glass of milk after lunch?"

Jenny Blair nodded. "Joseph Crocker gave me a currant bun to eat with it. I was out there when the carpenters stopped to rest, and Aunt Isabella brought them some coffee."

Mrs. Archbald glanced quickly at Etta and then looked away again. "They must have almost finished that work on the stable," she said slowly.

"Oh, they have, Mamma, but I'll be so sorry. I like old Mr. Crocker and Joseph better than—than anybody."

"Well, run away now, and finish your chapter before you go out to skate."

Slipping away quickly, Jenny Blair ran back through the folding doors and sank down on the rug by the French window. Hopefully, she opened her book at the place where Jo and Amy very nearly, but not quite, make a scene. Dejectedly, since nothing happened, she shut the book again and turned her eyes to the garden. An inner stillness pervaded her, and through this stillness, she became aware presently of the faint stirring, of the slow pulse of time—or was it eternity? But when did time end and eternity begin? Nobody knew, not even her grandfather. She had asked him, "When is time?" and he had answered, "Now." Then she had asked, "When is eternity?" and he had answered, "For ever." He didn't know, he said, what time was like, but she knew—she had always known. She had only to shut her eyes very tight and repeat the word, and she saw that time was flat and round and yellow, but eternity was long and pale and narrow and shaped exactly like a pod of green peas. But when she tried to make her grandfather understand, he laughed and told her not to let her fancy run away or she would never be able to catch it again. "They are like that,

Grandfather. I see them," she had insisted; and her mother, who was always repeating herself, had said tartly, "Don't be silly, Jenny Blair. You see entirely too much."

About her the old house stirred and murmured and creaked with a life of its own; and beyond the house there was the world in which factories boomed, steam whistles blew, bad smells sprang up on the wind, and the new red touring cars buzzed through the streets. In the library voices flowed on and stopped and flowed on again, like a brook over pebbles. Beyond the French window, the blows of a hammer rang out, clear as a bell, from the stable where old Mr. Crocker and his son Joseph were repairing the roof. Across the hall, in the back drawing-room, Aunt Isabella was revenging herself on the piano for her broken engagement. In the midst of a vehement passage, she would break off in anguish, pause, with suspended hands, while the piano waited and shivered, and crash down into a discord. Whenever the torrent of false notes splintered about Jenny Blair's ears, she would cower down into the past, down into another room, with blue water and yellow ships on the wall, down into another age when she was having supper while her mother played to her in the firelight.

Like a soap-bubble blown from the bowl of a pipe, the scene wavered for an instant, and then floated outward and upward on Aunt Isabella's wild music. Blue water and yellow ships; the rusty glimmer of firelight; the fresh taste of bread and milk in her mouth; the sound of her mother's playing, which rippled on and on until it was shattered at last by a scream and the steady tramp, tramp, tramp, of feet on the staircase,—all these memories hung, imprisoned and alive, in that globe of air, while Aunt Isabella's discord trembled and moaned and sank, dying, far away in the stillness.

"Oh, Isabella, how can you?" Aunt Etta wailed. "You are spoiling the piano."

A stool was pushed back on a velvet carpet; there was the sound of irregular footsteps in the hall; and Isabella appeared, dark, scornful, with a wine-red colour burning in her cheeks and lips. "I don't care," she answered defiantly. "I want to spoil something."

"Not the piano," Mrs. Archbald implored. "And before Jenny Blair too."

Jenny Blair did not mind, as she hastened to assure her mother, but, without a pause, Aunt Isabella had flown through the French window, and down into the garden where the Crockers were working. In her beauty and anger she was magnificent. Nothing, not even the royal air with which Mrs. Birdsong swept up the aisle in church and sank rustling on her knees, had ever made such delicious thrills flicker up and down Jenny Blair's spine. It might not be conduct, she told herself, but it was splendid. With her genuine gift for imitation, she decided that she would try her best to have a broken engagement, when she grew up, and to be passionate and defiant while she struck false notes on the piano.

"There are times," remarked Etta, who appeared to invite disaster, "when I almost think she is out of her head."

"Be careful." Mrs. Archbald was pursing her lips. "Jenny Blair understands more than you think. But a shock like that," she added, with commiseration, "is enough to unbalance any woman. And, after all, Isabella was not really to blame."

"Not really," Etta assented. "Not for the accident to the horse anyway. But you must admit, Cora," she added primly, "that Thomas Lunsford had reason on his side when he insisted that an engaged girl ought not to go out in a buggy with another young man. I can never understand how Isabella could be so deeply in love with Thomas, and yet carry on her flirtation with Robert Cantrell."

"She is high-spirited," Mrs. Archbald replied in a subdued tone, "but nobody will ever make me believe she has any harm in her. Of course, I can't help feeling that there is some excuse for the way Thomas acted, though, I must confess, I did not expect him to take Isabella at her word when she offered to release him. If I'd dreamed he could behave that way, I should have advised her just to go to bed and stay there until the scandal

blew over. That is what Amy Cross did, and everything turned
out right in the end."

"I begged her to go to bed," Etta rejoined, "but you can't do
anything with a headstrong girl like Isabella. 'You may be as
innocent as a babe,' I reminded her, 'but you must acknowledge
that staying out in the woods until daybreak did not look well.'
After all, you can't expect men not to judge by appearances."

Since this was the very last thing that Mrs. Archbald, being a
reasonable woman, would have expected of men, she merely
nodded, with a look of secretive wisdom, while she whispered,
"Don't speak too plainly, or Jenny Blair might catch on. I have
a feeling that she is trying to hear."

Etta shook her head. "She seems perfectly absorbed in her
book,"—which only proved, as Jenny Blair, who was listening
with all her ears, reflected scornfully, how little grown-up people really know about children. They imagined that she suspected nothing of the broken engagement, though she was skip-
ping rope on the front pavement a year before when Aunt
Isabella, her hat worn very high and her waist pinched in very
tight, had started off in a buggy drawn by a sober horse but
driven by a spirited young man. She suspected, also, that the
accident might never have happened if the buggy of last year
had been one of the new motor cars which were considered so
dangerous. The high hat, of course, would have suffered (for
motoring, in its early years, could be enjoyed by a lady only at
the price of a spoiled appearance), but if Aunt Isabella had selected a young man with a touring car, she might have discouraged his advances with the help of goggles and gauntlet gloves
and a bonnet and veil, to say nothing of a severe linen dust-coat.

This, naturally, was what Mamma would have called Aunt
Isabella's "first mistake"; and her second mistake occurred, as
Aunt Etta made perfectly clear, when she consented to drive
with a sober horse and a spirited young man, instead of safely
reversing the order. If only she had chosen a spirited horse and
a sober young man, how much happier she would have been the
next morning! For the dreadful part was that she had stayed

away until daybreak. Something had happened. Far out in the country, where there were no trains and no travellers, something had happened, and both the sober horse and the spirited young man had apparently lived up to their characters.

After Aunt Isabella's return, things were said that no wakeful ears could avoid hearing, and these remarks, though obscure in sense, were sufficiently eloquent in punctuation. Listening carefully, Jenny Blair had gathered from Aunt Etta's tearful reproaches that Aunt Isabella was blameless in thought and act, but mysteriously tarnished in reputation. Like the silver spoon Zoana, the cook, had left out all night in the grass, poor Aunt Isabella's shining lustre had been impaired by exposure. Immediately, Thomas Lunsford, who appeared to seek brightness alone, had ceased to call in the evenings; and not only Thomas, but all the other gay young men had flown away as swiftly as summer moths when the lamp is put out. A few of these, it is true, returned secretly at twilight, when Aunt Isabella lingered under the rose-arbour at the end of the garden; but after Joseph Crocker began repairing the stable, these twilight lingerings had changed to bolder daylight excursions.

There wasn't the slightest doubt in Jenny Blair's mind that God, who was watching over these occasions, had arranged everything for the best. Certainly, no young man in Aunt Isabella's circle could hold a candle, the child decided, to Joseph Crocker. Not only had she disliked Thomas Lunsford, but she was convinced that plenty of good things to eat improve any love scene on earth; and Aunt Isabella's little trays made her flirtation with Joseph very nearly as nice as a picnic. Besides, though Joseph, as her mother insisted, was far too good-looking for a carpenter, he never pulled Jenny Blair's plaits and never tried to be superior about dolls. Instead, he treated her as an equal, and discussed sensible subjects, like dogs and horses and how to mend things that are broken. Whenever she could spare time from her lessons, she would steal out to the stable and watch the skilful way the two men sorted and handled their tools. It must be wonderful, she thought, to own a basket of tools, or, better still, to have a real tool-chest. If only she had been born a boy, she would choose to be a carpenter instead of a lawyer like Grandfather, who didn't have half so much fun as old Mr. Crocker.

"Jenny Blair!" her mother called in an excited tone. "Jenny Blair, do you wish to see Mrs. Birdsong in her new violet toque?"

Springing to her feet, the child rushed into the library and flung herself between the red damask curtains. "Oh, Mamma, is she coming? Do you suppose she will speak to us?"

RS. BIRDSONG was one of those celebrated beauties who, if they still exist, have ceased to be celebrated. Tall, slender, royal in carriage, hers was that perfect loveliness which made the hearts of old men flutter and miss a beat when she approached them. Everything about her was flowing, and everything flowed divinely. Her figure curved and melted and curved again in the queenly style of the period; her bronze hair rippled over a head so faultless that its proper setting was allegory; her eyes were so radiant in colour that they had been compared by a Victorian poet to bluebirds flying.

She had been, at eighteen, the reigning beauty of Queenborough in an age when only authentic loveliness could hope to be crowned. For the first five years of the eighteen nineties, she had gathered the hearts of men (here the poet speaks again) in her hands. When she appeared every party turned into a pageant. She could make a banquet of the simplest supper merely by sitting down at the table. The Victorian age, even in its decline, worshipped beauty and she was as near perfection in her girlhood as if she had stepped out of some glimmering antique horizon. Moreover, as if form and colour were not sufficient, nature had endowed her with a singing voice so pure in quality that the most famous Romeo of his day had declared her soprano notes to be worthy of Melba. Enraptured by his discovery, he had begged for the privilege of training a new Juliet, and Mrs. Birdsong's family still believed that only an unwise marriage had intervened in the way of a world conquest. For, without warning, to the astonishment and despair of her admirers, Eva Howard had tossed her triumphs aside and eloped with George Birdsong, the least eligible of her suitors. George Birdsong had charm and was unusually well-favoured; but he was nothing more than a struggling attorney, who would be hard pressed to keep a modest roof over her head.

All this had happened twelve years before, and the marriage, so far as one could see, had turned out very well. George, though imperfectly faithful, still adored Eva; and Eva, living on a meagre income and doing a share of her own work, seemed to be happy. Even after George had inherited a modest fortune and thrown it away, the romantic glamour appeared not to diminish. Eva's radiance was so imperishable that, as Mrs. Archbald one remarked, it might have been painted. Happiness looked like that, she added impulsively, but, then, proper pride often flaunted the colours of happiness. "Nobody will ever find out what regrets Eva has had," she had concluded. "Not even if he takes the trouble to unscrew the lid of her coffin."

Now, as she approached the house, Mrs. Birdsong walked buoyantly. The toque of violets on her bronze waves was poised at the correct angle; her puffed sleeves were held back, and her narrow waist was bent slightly; one slender hand, in white kid, grasped the flaring folds of her black taffeta skirt, which trailed on the ground whenever it slipped from her fingers. To a superficial observer, she presented a vision of serene elegance; but Mrs. Archbald was very far indeed from being a superficial observer. "I wonder what is the matter now," she said to herself, pushing aside the curtains and leaning over the window-box of clove pinks and geraniums.

Thinking herself alone in the street, unaware of the row of admiring spectators, Mrs. Birdsong had permitted her well-trained muscles to relax for a moment, while her brilliance suddenly flickered out, as if the sunshine had faded. The corners of her mouth twitched and drooped; her step lost its springiness; and her figure appeared to give way at the waist and sink down for support into the stiff ripples of taffeta. Then, as quickly as her spirit had flagged, it recovered its energy, and sprang back into poise. As the first whisper reached her, her tired features were transfigured by an arch and vivacious smile. Glancing up at the window, she waved gaily. Starry eyes, curving red lips, the transparent flush in her cheeks, even the delicate wings of her eyebrows,—all seemed to be woven less of flesh than of some fragile bloom of desire.

"How adorable she looks," Etta sighed, with an emotion so intense that it was almost hysterical. Leaning out, she asked eagerly, "Eva, can't you come in for a minute?"

Mrs. Birdsong shook her head with a gesture of regret that was faintly theatrical. Her expression, so pale and wistful the moment before, was charged now with vitality. "Not this afternoon, dear. George will be waiting for me." Then, as if she had drained some sparkling delight from admiration, she passed on to the modest house at the other end of the block.

"I can't believe she was ever more beautiful," Etta murmured, without envy. Her long, bleak face, tinged with the greenish pallor of the chronic invalid, broke out into wine-coloured splotches. Several years before, when she had lost faith in men and found it difficult to be romantic about God, she had transferred her emotion to the vivid image of Mrs. Birdsong.

"If you gush over her too much, she will grow tired of you," said Isabella, who looked subdued but encouraged by what she had found in the garden.

"She won't," Etta rejoined passionately, and burst into tears. "You know she will never tire of me." For a few minutes she sobbed deeply under her breath; then, since nobody tried to quiet her, she stopped of her own accord, and picked up the sleeve of Jenny Blair's coat. Her eyes were usually red, for she cried often, while her family looked on in silent compassion, without knowing in the least what to do. She had come into the world as a mistake of nature, defeated before she was born and she was denied, poor thing, Mrs. Archbald reflected, even the slight comfort that Isabella found in attributing her misfortunes to man. Yet the more tenderly Etta was treated, and her poor health dominated the household, the more obstinate her malady appeared to become.

Jenny Blair, who was still gazing after Mrs. Birdsong, cried out abruptly, "Her face looks like a pink heart, Mamma." "Don't be silly," Mrs. Archbald retorted. "You are letting your imagination run away with you again."

"But her face is like a pink heart, Mamma. I mean a pink heart on a valentine."

"I can see what she means," Etta said, pausing to wipe away a tear that trembled, without dropping, on the end of her eyelashes.

"Please don't encourage her, Etta," Mrs. Archbald returned, as coolly as she ever permitted herself to speak to her frail sister-in-law. "Now, run away, Jenny Blair, and play a while out of doors. You don't get enough sunshine."

With a ceremonial sweep, the curtains dropped back into place; Jenny Blair disappeared, and Mrs. Archbald threaded her needle. Presently, before beginning a seam, she let her work sink to her lap. With a sigh, she glanced round the library, where the afternoon sunshine splashed over the ruby leather, over the floral designs in the Brussels carpet, and over the old English calf in the high rosewood bookcases. On the mantelpiece, an ornamental clock of basalt, with hands that looked menacing, divided two farm groups in red and white Staffordshire ware.

General Archbald was a man of means according to the modest standards of the nineteenth century, which meant that he was sufficiently well off to provide for his only son's widow and child, as well as for two unmarried daughters and the usual number of indigent cousins and aunts. His daughter-in-law had been left a penniless widow at an age when widowhood had ceased to be profitable. At first she had made an effort to support herself and her child by crocheting mats of spool cotton and making angel food for the Woman's Exchange. But, after that long lost endeavour, nothing had seemed to matter but rest—the perfect rest of those who are not required to make noble exertions. Still disposed to fill out in the wrong places, she had pulled in the strings of her stays and settled down into security. After all, one could bear any discomfort of body so long as one was not obliged to be independent in act.

Gradually, while the sheltered life closed in about her, she had retreated into the smiling region of phantasy. With much patience, she had acquired the capacity to believe anything and nothing. Her hair was just going grey; her fine fresh-coloured skin was breaking into lines at the corners of her sanguine brown eyes; but when she talked the wrinkles were obliterated by the glow of a charming expression. All her life, especially in her marriage, she had been animated by earnest but unscrupulous benevolence.

Now, as she thrust her needle into the stubborn material upon which she was working, she murmured irrelevantly, "I sometimes wonder——"

"Wonder?" Etta's bloodshot eyes opened wide. "About Jenny Blair or Eva Birdsong?"

"Oh, about Eva. Jenny Blair, thank Heaven, hasn't reached an age when I need to begin worrying about her. But the idea has crossed my mind," she added slowly, "that Eva suspects."

"Who could have told her? Who would be so heartless?"

"There are other ways of finding out."

"I can't believe," Isabella broke in, "that she could look so happy if she suspected."

Mrs. Archbald shook her head while she wound the braid on the edge of a sleeve and prodded it with her needle. "You never can tell about that. I am perfectly sure that if she knew everything, she would never betray herself. When happiness failed her, she would begin to live on her pride, which wears better. Keeping up an appearance is more than a habit with Eva. It is a second nature."

"She adores George," Etta's voice trailed off on a wailing note, "and he seems just as devoted as ever."

"He is." Mrs. Archbald gave a short stab at her work. "He is every bit as devoted. I believe he would pour out every drop of his blood for her if she needed it. Only," she hastened to add, "that is the last thing she is likely to need."

"If he feels like that," Isabella demanded impatiently, "why doesn't he let other women alone?"

Mrs. Archbald shook her head with a reserved expression. "You will understand more about that, my dear, when you are married."

"You mean I shall never understand," Isabella retorted defiantly; and to the distress of her sister-in-law, who had been, innocent of such meaning, and indeed of any meaning at all, she sprang up and flounced into the dining-room and out of the French window.

"Do you think," Etta asked in a breathless whisper, "that she is going too far?"

"With George Crocker? No, my dear, how could she? Why, he wears overalls. She is only amusing herself, poor girl. I suppose it helps to take her mind off Thomas Lunsford."

"That doesn't seem fair to Joseph. Even in overalls, he is far more attractive than Thomas."

"All the same, I don't believe there is any real harm in it." No, there wasn't any real harm in it, she assured herself, glancing through the dining-room and the French window to the dappled boughs of the old sycamore. Though it was true that young Joseph Crocker was dangerously well-favoured, she had convinced herself that he carried a steady, if too classic, head on his shoulders. The Crockers were good people, plain but respectable, the kind of plain people, she had heard the General remark, who could be trusted in revolutions. Even if poor Isabella, desperate from wounded love and pride, should grow reckless, Mrs. Archbald believed that she could rely, with perfect safety, upon the sound common sense of the two Crockers. Surely men who could be trusted in revolutions were the very sort one could depend upon in a love affair. Only, and here doubt gnawed at her heart, could she be sure that her father-in-law meant what he said or exactly the opposite? His opinions were so frequently unsound in theory that there were occasions, she had observed, with tender reproach, when she should have hesitated to rely upon him, not only in a revolution, but even in an earthquake, which, since it is an act of God, seemed to her a more natural catastrophe.

"I sometimes think," Etta was saying, "that it is a mistake for a man to be too good-looking. That is the trouble with George Birdsong. It isn't really his fault, but his charm is his undoing. I wonder why it is that women seem to bear the gift of beauty better than men? Look at all that Eva gave up when she was married. Yet I am sure she would never waste a regret on her sacrifice if only George would be faithful. I was a child when she ran away with him, but I remember that everybody said he was the only man in Queenborough handsome enough to walk up a church aisle with her."

"I saw her the night she eloped," Mrs. Archbald said softly, "and I shall never forget how lovely she was in peachblow brocade, with a wreath of convolvulus in her hair. Her hair, too, was worn differently, with a single curl on her neck and a short fringe on her forehead. But it wasn't only her beauty. There was something brilliant and flashing—summer radiance, Father used to call it—in her look. Every one stopped dancing to watch her waltz with George. Just to look at them, you could tell they were madly in love, though nobody seemed to think Eva's preference would last. But, of course, we were wrong. Passion like that, after it once runs away with you, cannot be bridled. I shall always remember the way she seemed to float in a transfigured light. You could see it flaming up in her smile. It is the only time," she finished sadly, "that I have ever seen what it meant to be transfigured by joy."

"I suppose," Etta sighed hungrily, "that it was a great passion."

"It is." Mrs. Archbald altered the tense with a smile. "She is still, after twelve years, transfigured by joy—or pride."

"But her life hasn't been easy. They can't afford more than one servant, and I've heard Eva say that old Betsey has to be helped all the time."

"Eva has risen above that. She could rise above everything except George's unfaithfulness. I believe," Mrs. Archbald continued shrewdly, "that what isn't love in her is the necessity to justify her sacrifice to herself—perhaps to the world. To have given up all that—and she really believes that she gave up a career in grand opera—for anything less than a great passion would seem inexcusable. That is at the bottom of her jealousy—that and never having had any children. Of course she can't understand that showing jealousy only makes matters worse. Though she has never opened her lips on the subject, I believe she is worrying herself to death now over George's fancy for Delia Barron. Delia isn't bad at heart, but she will flirt with a lamp-post."

Etta wiped her eyes. "Do you suppose it is true that George has been keeping Memoria? Why, Memoria has done their washing for years."

"Oh, Etta, I try not to think of that."

"But wasn't he taken ill in her house, and didn't Eva have to go to him because they thought he was dying?"

"No, that was another woman. She wasn't coloured, but she was worse than Memoria. I don't care what anybody tells me, I always insist that there is good in Memoria. She has had a hard struggle to bring up her three children, and she has taken devoted care of her mother ever since she was paralyzed. I've never seen any sense in trying to put the blame on the coloured women, especially," she concluded crisply, "when they are so nearly white. Memoria has always worked hard, no matter who keeps her, and I never saw a better laundress when she takes pains. Father always complains if I let anybody else do up his shirts."

"I wonder why those mulatto women are so good-looking," Etta sighed again. "It doesn't seem right."

"Well, I don't know. Perhaps it is some sort of compensation. Your father says that Memoria has noble bones. Of course no man would stop to think that she gets her upright bearing from carrying baskets on her head. Jenny Blair, I thought you'd gone out to play," she said in a sharper tone, as her daughter ran in from the hall.

"I was going, Mamma, but I saw Grandfather coming, and I waited to ask if he will pay me for a hundred and fifty pages. Joseph Crocker says I do need a new pair of skates. He can't make this roller roll any better."

"Well, your grandfather is coming in. You may ask him. But, remember, he isn't so young as you are, and I don't wish you to worry him."

"I won't, Mamma. I saw Mrs. Birdsong, too, and her face is like a pink heart. Joseph says it *is* like a pink heart on a valentine."

For an instant Mrs. Archbald appeared almost to give up. While she put one hand to her brow, the artificial smile on her lips trembled and dissolved in a sigh. Then, collecting herself with an effort, she patted the stiff roll of her hair, and adjusted her slightly bulging figure to the severe front of her stays. "I don't know what to do with you, Jenny Blair," she said sternly. "You no sooner get an idea into your head than you run it straight into the ground. Now, ask your grandfather, if you choose, and then run out to play before the sun begins to go down."

CHAPTER 3

✿ ✿ ✿ ✿ ✿ ✿ ✿HE ROOM is too close," General Archbald said, while he stooped to receive the embraces of his daughter and his daughter-in-law. At seventy-five, he was a tall, spare, very erect old man, with features carved into nobility by tragic experience. Beneath the thick, silver-grey hair, the eyebrows were still dark and beetling; the eagle nose was still betrayed by the sensitive mouth under the short grey moustache. Only his eyes, with their far inward gaze, were the eyes of a man who had been born out of his time. In his early years, before the War Between the States, he had lived much abroad; yet everywhere, even in his native Virginia, he had known that he was not a part of his age. The clock was set too far back, or, perhaps, too far ahead. But he could not make himself feel as the people about him felt; he could not bring himself to believe the things they believed.

For thirty years he had been a good husband to a woman he had married by accident, because, after a country dance from which they had stolen away alone, they had been caught out in a sleigh until the end of a snowstorm. How often, he reflected, with sardonic amusement, had poor Isabella's tragedy occurred in the past! To save appearances (what had his whole life been but saving his own or some other person's appearance?), he had proposed the next morning to a comparative stranger; and to save appearances (though she had been in love with another man), she had accepted him. To save appearances, they had lived amicably together, and more in duty than in passion, they had brought three well-appearing children into the world.

The son, a handsome and engaging fellow, had been killed in a fox-hunt; but his widow, a woman with a genuine gift for

24

managing people and events, occupied Richard's room in his father's house and Richard's chair at the table. Though she had been as good as a right hand to him, the General was fond of saying, she was the only person left in the world, since God had removed his wife, whom the old man not only respected but feared. For the last two years, while her presence brightened his home, the hardest battle of his life had been fought to a finish between them. With all his frustrated youth and his aging rebellious soul, he had longed to marry again. He had longed to seek and find his one brief hour of delight, and she had stood in his way. Mild, charming, implacable, with all the secret malice of destiny, she had stood in his way. Even when he had found the love he desired in his age—a slim, nunlike woman, young but not too young to be companionable, smiling up over her Prayer-Book in Saint Luke's Church—he had felt that his longing was hopeless because his daughter-in-law was the stronger.

After a heartbroken youth (for he had known tragic passion), after thirty years of heroic fidelity in an age when marriage was an invisible prison, he had been obliged to sacrifice that fading glimmer of happiness. Supported by his daughters, who demanded that he should be faithful to a wife he had never loved, supported by public opinion, which exacted that he should remain inconsolable for the loss of a woman he had married by accident, his son's widow had stood, small, plump, immovable as the rock of ages, between him and his desire. Thirty years, and God alone would ever know what those years had meant to him! Not that he had wished for his wife's death. Not that he had failed in the obligations of marriage. But in that shared confinement of thirty years, in that lifelong penalty he had paid for an accident, for a broken sleigh, for being caught out in a snowstorm, there had been flashes of impulse in which he had asked himself, "How long shall I be able to live like this?"

Yet he had endured it. For thirty years, day and night, waking, sleeping, in sickness and in health, having children, as married persons are expected to do—for thirty years he had sacrificed his youth, his middle age, his dreams, his imagination, all the vital instincts that make a man, to the moral earnestness of tradition. Well, he had lived through it. He had lived through it until, at seventy-one, just as he had reached the turn in a long life when a man, if he has been prudent, still retains vigour enough for a last flare at the end—just as he had reached this turn in his life, Erminia had died, and release had come like a blow.

She had died, and immediately, so unreasonable are the ways of the heart, he had been overcome by regret. Almost to his astonishment, he had felt her loss, he had grieved for her, he had reproached himself bitterly. Lying in her coffin, with that defenseless smile on her lips and a wisp of tulle hiding her throat, she had appealed to his tenderness more deeply than she had ever appealed to his passion. In the days that followed, he had suffered as a man suffers who loses an aching limb. But regret, he discovered before six months had gone, is not among the enduring realities. "When the year is over," he had told himself, meeting his daughter-in-law's brimming eyes with a shiver of apprehension, "Even if I wait until the year is over, I shall be still young enough to find a little happiness at the end." Already, though he had been a faithful husband, he knew where happiness might be found. He had seen the nunlike figure and the dove's eyes of a joy that was young, and yet not too young to be companionable to restful age. Well, a year, even at seventy-one, is not everlasting.

But at the end of the first year, his two daughters were still shrouded in mourning, and poor Etta's reason was almost despaired of; at the end of the second year, his son's widow failed in her endeavour and came with her only child to live in his house; and at the end of the third year, the fatherless little girl had twined herself about the roots of his heart. Even then, with three women and one little girl making a home for him, he had not relinquished the hope of his Indian summer of happiness— that patient hope of the old, so much less elastic and so much more enduring than the hope of the young.

Yet, in the end, this also was slowly strangled by life. By life, and by the suffocating grasp of appearances. How could he spoil the lives of three women and one fatherless little girl? How could he bring his joy with the dove's eyes into a house which was already filled with these three women and one little girl tenderly making a home for him? If they had not been so devoted, it might have been easier; but love, as marriage had taught him (for his wife also had loved him before the end of their honeymoon), is responsible for most of the complications of life.

Jenny Blair was jumping up and down in his arms. "Grandfather, I've read a hundred and fifty pages. Don't you think you can pay me?"

"Pay you? What's that, darling? Well, we'll see, we'll see." Looking over her head, he said gently, "I hope you've had a pleasant day, my dears. Has your neuralgia troubled you, Etta?"

Etta smiled at him appealingly while she pressed her hand to her sunken temples. "It was bad this morning, but I took a headache powder, and that helped me."

"Poor child," he said, "poor child," for he sincerely pitied her. "Neuralgia must run in our family. Your grandmother used to complain of it when I was a boy. I remember to this day the red marks from mustard plasters on her temples, and then there was poor Margaret——"

He broke off with a sigh, for his only sister had been dear to him, though she had eloped, when he was a boy, with an Italian musician, who had turned out to have a wife somewhere in Europe. After she had run away, Margaret had vanished completely. He could still remember the despairing efforts his father had made to find some trace of her abroad, and the way his mother used to wake in the night crying because she had dreamed that her daughter did not have enough cover to protect her from the cold. In his early twenties, he had looked for her over Europe; but all he ever discovered was that she had died alone in some obscure lodging-house in Vienna. Well, well, poor girl, it was useless to deny that all the Archbalds were subject to intermittent flashes of nature.

There was, for example, the case of his great-aunt Sabina,

who had publicly defied her Creator, in the early years of Virginia, and had escaped suspicion of witchcraft merely because she was related to all the best blood in the Colony. Then, too, there was Rodney, his brother—but Rodney's tragedy was far more modern in character. Instead of defying his Creator, he had quietly resigned from creation. But he was always, the General recalled, a quiet chap, and so, when he had put a bullet in his heart, he had left a scrawl that said only, "Shadows are not enough." Nobody knew what he meant. Crazy, they called him. Crazy, because after twenty-nine years of life, having exhausted alike the pleasures of love and the consolations of religion, he had found that shadows are not enough. Long ago, he might have been forgotten, as most unpleasant recollections are forgotten in the struggle for happiness, if Isabella's features had not preserved the shape of his fine Roman nose, the glowing dusk of his eyes, and the ivory space between the bold black curves of his eyebrows. And then, just as the General had become reconciled to the living memorial of Isabella's countenance, his granddaughter had shot up from an expressionless baby into a wilful child, who combined the doubts of his great-aunt Sabina with the eyebrows of Rodney and the pointed tongue of Erminia.

"Poor girl, poor girl," he murmured again, while he stroked back the straight brown hair from Etta's forehead. Then, in a more natural tone, he inquired, "What's become of William? Has anybody seen William?" For William, his English setter, demanded nothing of him, not even that he should feel a suffocating emotion when he was old and tired.

"I saw him come in," Jenny Blair said, still plunging up and down with her hands on the General's arm. "He must have gone back to ask Zoana for something to eat. He is very fond of Zoana."

"He eats too much." It was a relief to be able to laugh. "He is beginning to look middle-aged before he is six."

One November afternoon three years before (was it really that long ago?) he had met William, trembling and caked with mud, as he was dragged at the end of a dirty rope from his last ignominious encounter with quail. As a cure for gun-shyness, some blundering fool had peppered the dog's legs with bird-shot. That's the way with them still, thought the old man, searching his memory, there are many fools in the world, but the biggest fool of all is the fool sportsman who believes that a load of bird-shot will break a dog of being afraid of a gun. The free end of the rope was in the hand of a small coloured boy. Black as pitch, alert, wiry, nimble, it was queer the way that little negro persisted. William had been given to him, he had explained, and he was going to try some new way of breaking. His Pa knew a heap about curing bird dogs that were gun-shy.

"Wait a minute," the old man had said slowly. What, he wondered immediately afterwards, had made him say that. "Wait a minute," as if he had nothing more to do than stand in the mud of a red clay road and haggle with a negro urchin over a hunting-dog that was not only gun-shy but peppered with bird-shot. Very slowly, he had opened his pocketbook, and very slowly, after unfolding two one-dollar notes, he had handed them to the boy in exchange for the dog and the rope. What on earth—he had muttered under his breath, what on earth—and Cora didn't like dogs. Suddenly the moment had gone flat. Cora didn't like dogs. Long after the boy had pattered off down the red clay road, the General had stood there, with the dirty rope in his hand, waiting, in the midst of the autumn landscape, for a gleam of light to break into his mind. Cora didn't like dogs. And all the time William had looked up at him, from the other end of the rope, defeated, suspicious, utterly disillusioned. "No, I do not love human nature," the old man had thought, without irony and without emotion, while he bent over to ease the strain on the dog's neck.

That was the beginning of a satisfactory, though reticent, association. Unhappy memories had dampened the joy of living and extinguished sentimentality in man and dog. But Cora, who did not like dogs, admired, as she said, their fine qualities, and refused, as usual, to make a point of her prejudices. It may have occurred to her, as a simple way out of her troubles, that a dog, especially one that is gun-shy, is less upsetting in the house than a second wife, especially one that is young. No matter what happened, it is always possible, she had found, to believe the best and to trust that, sooner or later, with the help of a merciful Providence, the best may turn out to be true. As for the General, he had been obliged, for forty years, to bestow perfunctory caresses, and now, in his old age, he asked little more than the companionship that makes no demands. William, more soundly disenchanted, appeared, and perhaps was, contented to lie for hours at peace in the sunshine. Only, whenever he was taken into the country that first autumn, he would begin to tremble again at the sight of fields and woods; and then the General would take him in his arms and stroke his body, while Robert, the coachman, was ordered to return to the city. And again the old man would think, "No, it is true, I do not love human nature." Three years had gone by; yet even to-day the noise of a train or the faint far-off sound of a shot would awaken in William's nerves the old paroxysms of fear.

"And Isabella?" The General's manner was still playful. "Is she in the kitchen too?"

"She was here a minute ago," Mrs. Archbald answered, "but I'm afraid I said something that hurt her feelings. She went out. I think down to the stable." For an instant she hesitated, and then added with a significant look, "Don't you think, Father, it is time the work on the stable was finished?"

The General started, for he never missed a point in his daughter-in-law's strategy. "The Crockers will do the best they can," he replied. "I left it to them."

"I know," Mrs. Archbald assented. Then she said in a severe tone, "Jenny Blair, stop hanging on your grandfather. I told you not to worry him."

"I'm not worrying him, Mamma, but you said I might ask him. Grandfather, will you pay me for a hundred and fifty pages? They are dreadfully poky."

"We'll see, we'll see. If you are in urgent need, I suppose I'll have to do something about it."

"Oh, thank you, Grandfather darling." She took a step toward the door, picked up her skates, and swinging them in her hand, paused to look back over her shoulder. "Did you know the bad smell had come back?"

"Yes, I know, my child, but there's nothing to be done about that. Already it has gone, hasn't it?"

She wheeled round on the threshold. "I wish I could go down to the place it comes from. Do people live down there?"

"Yes, people live there. That is one of the wrongs of our civilization, that some people are obliged to live with bad smells."

"I wish I could go down there. I mean just to look."

"Put that idea straight out of your mind, Jenny Blair," Mrs. Archbald commanded with weary tartness. "I have trouble enough as it is."

O UTSIDE, in the slanting beams of the sun, Jenny Blair strapped on her roller-skates and started dangerously over the sunken bricks of the pavement. Her mother had told her to keep on the sunny side of the street and not to skate beyond the corner, where the bricks were uneven and loose at the edges; but experience had shown her that it was safe to interpret broadly her mother's directions. The other children at school had dared her to walk alone, just before sunset, down Canal Street as far as the edge of Penitentiary Bottom; and though she belonged to that gallant breed which has never, as she told herself proudly, "taken a dare," she decided to keep up appearances by going the longest way round, through the Birdsongs' garden at the end of the block. Three long blocks, divided by three dingy alleys, stretched between Washington Street and the mysterious quarter which began with Canal Street and ended in the crowded hollow known as Penitentiary Bottom; but in upper Canal Street, where white people still occupied some of the old houses, she might be able to look over the hill into the exciting place from which the bad smells sprang up on the wind. Always, until to-day, she had paused at the end of Hickory Street and gazed with the eager eye of adventure past the unpaved alleys, where no skates could roll, to the muddy sidewalks and crumbling fences over which the gleaming white-washed wall of the penitentiary presided. Nobody, least of all her mother, could understand the fascinated horror that drew her, like a tightened cord, toward the unknown and the forbidden. Nobody who had not been born with a rebel heart could share her impulse to skip and dance and flap her arms like fledgling wings as soon as she had broken away from the house and was sure that none of them could run after her because none of them knew where she was going. None of them, not even Grandfather, who was more of a child than the others, would ever suspect that she meant to walk down Canal Street as soon as the sun dipped beyond the walls of the prison. She hadn't told them because it never did any good to tell grown-up people the truth. It simply couldn't be done.

"I'll go and peep in on Mrs. Birdsong," she thought, honourably postponing her excursion until the sun had declined. "It won't take but a minute if I go through her yard."

Something—it may have been the beauty of Mrs. Birdsong—enveloped the small wistaria-mantled house in a perpetual air of surprise. No matter how often she went there, everything was always fresh and dewy and delightful, as if she had never seen it before. The ragged garden at the back, with its untrimmed shrubs and overgrown pool, had seemed to her, even as a little child, far more exciting than the carefully pruned borders and flower-beds of the garden at home. Especially, she loved to be at the Birdsongs' when Uncle Abednego, an ancient negro who lived in the almshouse, was making ineffectual efforts to preserve the dwindling box-trees, the straggling perpetual roses, and the flowering shrubs that had not died in the winter. Sometimes Mrs. Birdsong would come out with a trowel and plant a few flowers in the borders; but she did not like to dig in the earth; even when she wore gloves, she complained, the soil ruined her hands, and there was so much work to do in the house that she preferred to leave the garden to the feeble exertions of Uncle Abednego. The truth was that she knew little of flowers, and loved most the orchids and gardenias that came from florists and were grown only in hothouses. She rarely went into the garden for pleasure, and never walked there except on summer evenings when she was in search of a breeze. John Welch, an orphan cousin, was the only member of the Birdsong family who liked planting, and he had raised a border of what he called "witches' herbs" near the back porch.

Now, as Jenny Blair was taking off her skates in the front

yard, he opened the door and came, whistling rudely, down the steps. He was an overgrown, rather awkward boy of seventeen, with a crest of flaming red hair above attractive pointed features and a lively expression. His curiosity about life was insatiable, and in a few years he would begin the study of medicine. Ever since he had come, as a little boy, to live with the Birdsongs, he had insisted that he meant to be a doctor, not a lawyer like George Birdsong. That first spring, when he was only nine, he had planted, with Uncle Abednego's help, his border of "witches' herbs," and he was always interested in trying to cure animals or birds that were injured. More important still, he kept a pet bullfrog, named Old Mortality, in the sunken pool, which was once a lily-pond, at the far end of the garden. Jenny Blair had welcomed Old Mortality, one May afternoon, when he was brought as a tadpole from an old ice-pond. Several other Old Mortalitys had lived and died in the pool; but the child was sure that she could recognize the face of her acquaintance among them; and she never doubted that the present bearer of the title was the progenitor of the family.

"Where are you going?" she inquired of John Welch, while she stood swinging her skates from her hand.

"You'd like to know, wouldn't you?" he retorted teasingly; for he was at an age that she considered objectionable and he missed no opportunity of proving the fact.

"No, I wouldn't. I just asked."

"Yes, you would."

"No, I wouldn't."

After making an impertinent face at him, she darted away in search of the more agreeable company of Uncle Abednego. But Uncle Abednego had already put away his spade and gone home to the almshouse. The garden, untended and untrimmed, was alone with the delicate green light and the roving whispers of spring. Over the edge of the brick walk there was a froth of wild heartsease; the border of dying box was hollow within but wore a living veil overhead; farther away, beyond the twisted crêpe myrtle, weeds surged round the lily-pond, where Old

Mortality, a green bullfrog with a Presbyterian face, sat on a moss-grown log in the midst of a few faded lily-pads, and croaked prophetically, at twilight, of the evil to come. "I know he is the very same," Jenny Blair thought now, looking down on him. "I remember his face perfectly well."

Before going out by the tall green gate in the alley wall, she ran back to the house and stole up the steps of the porch to the window that looked into the dining-room. Inside, Mrs. Birdsong was moving softly about, preparing supper before her husband's return. Jenny Blair knew that old Aunt Betsey, the cook, had gone to her sister's funeral in Manchester, and that Mrs. Birdsong was alone with the fascinating process of laying the table and stirring up batterbread in the big yellow bowl. Often Jenny Blair had dropped in to help on one of Aunt Betsey's afternoons "off," which occurred only when there was a funeral.

It was as good as a play, the child thought, and far better than improving the mind, to help Mrs. Birdsong at work. How they would laugh together while they arranged a few flowers in the silver loving-cup Mr. Birdsong had won at a shooting-match, or placed the thread-mats and knives and forks as carefully as if they were having a party. All the time Mrs. Birdsong's gay and lovely voice would ripple on in a silver stream, and as a final reward the child would be permitted to stir the batterbread and pour it out, very slowly and evenly, into the muffin-cups. "And this," Eva Birdsong would exclaim, as she closed the door of the oven, "is the true story of the Queen of the Ball!"

This afternoon, it seemed to Jenny Blair, peeping in from the back window, Mrs. Birdsong appeared less happy than usual. But she might look that way merely because she was alone and there was no one to laugh with her. Even in Queenborough, which contained as much laughter as any place of its size in the world, a celebrated belle and beauty could scarcely be expected to laugh by herself. Mirth required company, as Jenny Blair had learned long ago, since even her mother's cheerful twitter was as silent as a wren's in winter when she was left alone in a room.

"I wish I could stop," Jenny Blair thought, vaguely disturbed without knowing why, "but if I don't walk on Canal Street, Bena will make my life a burden to-morrow." Repeating her mother's favourite phrase in the hour of necessity, she slipped away from the porch window, and stole down the flight of steps into the garden. As soon as she had shut the alley gate behind her and reached the brick pavement of Hickory Street, she strapped on her skates and rolled to the end of the block. There, since the street was deserted, she picked her way over the cobblestones and wheeled in long reckless curves on the opposite side.

In the middle of the third block, when she could see the walls of the prison sharply cutting the golden blue of the horizon, she met Uncle Warner, the old negro rag-picker, and stopped to exchange greetings. His figure was bent beneath the weight of his pickings, which he carried in a hempen bag on his back, and he thumped the pavement, as he walked, with the hickory pole he used to poke out scraps from the trash-heaps. Long before she had known Old Mortality, Jenny Blair remembered the stooping figure, the swollen bag, and the thumping stick of Uncle Warner. Twice a week he came to the bag gate for slops, which he carried away in a borrowed cart with a white mule named Posey, and every Saturday night he was given all the cold meat and stale bread that were left over. Whenever the Archbalds had a ham cooked, the bone, with a little of the meat still left on it, was put aside for Uncle Warner. He had always been there, a familiar figure to two generations; yet nobody could recall whether he had been free or a slave in his youth.

"Uncle Warner," Jenny Blair asked now, "have you ever been down yonder where the bad smell comes from?"

Uncle Warner chuckled. "Go way, chile. Whut you wanter know 'bout dat ole stink fuh?"

"I want to see what it is like down there. I want just to look. If I go far out on top of the hill, can I look over and see?"

"Ef'n you does, I'se gwinter tell yo' Ma on you jes' ez sho' ez I live."

"Have you ever been down there?"

"I'se done slept down dar fuh mos' a hunnard year chile, fuh mos' a hunnard year, fuh mos' a hunnard year."

He passed on mumbling and thumping, as if he had forgotten her, while Jenny Blair balanced herself on her skates and lingered to decipher the hieroglyphics left in chalk on the board fence by horrid little boys. "I wonder if there is anything in it," she thought in disgust. "Boys think they know everything."

By the time she reached Canal Street, the sun was going down in a ball of fire, and the deep and thrilling shadows of the penitentiary slanted over the pavement. Suddenly, as if by magic, the spirit of adventure seized her, and she felt that life was thronging with perils. Warlike but ungallant boys were fighting in bands over the cobblestones; from the windows, where soiled lace curtains streamed out on the breeze, women of dubious colour made remarks in a language that Jenny Blair found exciting and unfamiliar. "I don't believe even Aunt Etta could tell what they are saying," she reflected; for it seemed to her that Aunt Etta's education had been the sort that included the misunderstood tongues.

So absorbed was she in watching the combat in the street that she was more astonished than hurt when her skate tripped over a loosened brick, and a sudden shower of stars sprinkled the pavement.

"I s you hurt yo'self, little girl?" asked a warm, husky voice, which brought back to her the scent of earth by the pool in which Old Mortality lived. Opening her eyes, she looked up into a handsome face, very nearly but not quite coloured, and felt herself lifted by hard, smooth arms and pressed against a deep bosom in clean-smelling blue gingham. "Come in and let me wash the blood off yo' head. It ain't nothin' worse than a cut."

"I'm afraid I've knocked out my front tooth."

"There. Let me see. No, you ain't. Just spit out the blood, an' you'll find your tooth is all right. Don't you want to come in an' lie down till you feel better?" Bending down, she unstrapped the roller-skates and examined the fresh scraped place on the child's knee.

"Have I ever seen you before?"

"I'm Memoria. You've seen me bringin' the clothes to Mrs. Birdsong. I wash for the Birdsongs."

Jenny Blair struggled to her feet. Yes, she remembered now. Memoria was the name of the proud-looking coloured woman who carried away a clothes-basket covered with a piece of striped calico and brought it back foaming over with fluted cambric and lace ruffles. She walked with long, graceful strides, and seldom had anything to say to the children. Occasionally, her eldest child, a boy of ten, very light in colour, would accompany her, and then the basket would arrive perched on top of a red wagon. Jenny Blair had always stood a little in awe of Memoria; for she knew that she was what her mother called a superior negro, and had almost dropped the friendly dialect when her "white folks," Mr. Birdsong's parents, had sent her to school.

"Yes, you're Memoria. What are you doing here?"

"I live here. This is Canal Street. What made you come down to Canal Street? It ain't a good place to skate."

"Oh, I came just so. Is this the house you live in?"

"Yes, I live here. I've got Mrs. Birdsong's clothes hangin' out now in the back yard. Are you able to walk home?"

"It's only my head that hurts," Jenny Blair answered, "but that hurts very bad." She tried to take a step forward; but the evening air thickened and grew suddenly cold. Horror seized her lest she be sick out in the street, where all the rude boys and the young women at windows could see her. A sensation more of despair than nausea surged up like a black chill from the pit of her stomach. Hurriedly, with all the politeness she could summon for so dreadful a fact, she said, "I'm afraid I'm going to throw up, Memoria," and did so immediately.

"Don't you bother, honey. I'll take care of you," Memoria said kindly. "You just hold on to me till you feel better." Then, when the worst was over, she picked up Jenny Blair as if she had been a baby, and carried her through the broken gate and into a small frame house with curtains of Nottingham lace at the front windows. Here, after she had been properly sick in private and in a basin, the child was stretched out on a hard sofa, which had once belonged to a good family and was still upholstered in respectable horsehair. Shutting her eyes as tight as she could, she opened them quickly and looked at the pots of begonia on the window-sill, and beyond the flowers to the back yard, where she could see the white and coloured garments swinging on the clothes-line.

The light hurt her head, and she lowered her eyelids again on a flash of red roofs and blue sky. For an instant it seemed to her that she had fallen asleep and wakened in the old nursery, when she was very little, and that her father would presently stoop and lift her over the high sides of her crib. Without surprise, quite as if it were the most natural thing in the world, she discovered that it was not her father but Mr. Birdsong who bent over her and placed his hand on her head. He must have come into the room while her eyes were closed, but he appeared perfectly at home in the midst of all the crazy colours and cheap furniture. Never had he looked so fresh and ruddy and hard and vigorous; and never before had she seen him in his shirt-sleeves, with his grey coat neatly hanging on the back of a chair. "He's forgotten his tie," she thought; but this, she understood after a moment, was not really important. Nothing was important except this queer sense of his belonging here, of his being at home in Canal Street, and in Memoria's house. For he stood there, in the centre of what Jenny Blair thought of vaguely, as "a coloured room," with an unchanged air of physical exuberance, of vital well-being, of sanguine expectancy. He had, indeed, the manner of dispensing happiness that she associated with Sunday after church and mint juleps in silver goblets. Yet she knew, of course, being a wise child, that he must be pretending, just as she herself was pretending in an effort to make Memoria feel that her hospitality was appreciated.

Her first startled wonder faded to friendly recognition before she became aware that he was looking down on her with his clear grey eyes which never, not even when the rest of his face was serious, seemed to stop smiling. Memoria, who was holding a bottle of camphor to Jenny Blair's nostrils, accepted his presence as naturally as she accepted good or bad weather, or the going down of the sun. She gave no sign of astonishment, or indeed of any other sensation, when she handed him the bottle of camphor, and moved with her majestic step into the kitchen. Returning with a towel over her arm and a basin of water in her hand, she washed the blood and dust from the child's face, and lowered her upon the pillows Mr. Birdsong was arranging.

"Do you feel better?" he inquired in his light-hearted voice.

Jenny Blair looked up with eyes that seemed enormous beneath the bandage Memoria had left on her forehead. "Where did you come from?" she asked politely, and then, feeling the necessity to make conversation, she added, "I hope you did not have an accident too."

"Well, rather." He had slipped on his coat while he answered, and he stood now, smooth, supple, instinct with vitality, by the side of the sofa. His parted chestnut hair had been brushed so severely that it must have hurt him, she thought, and his eyes were as bright and sparkling as if they had been left out in the rain.

"Was it a fall?" Puzzled but sympathetic, she gazed up at him.

"Not exactly. I mean it was only a stitch in my side. I got a stitch just as I was passing along the street."

"I didn't know nice people ever walked on Canal Street."

"Maybe I'm not nice, but you are. I'll wager," he concluded gaily, "that your mother doesn't know you are down here."

"Well, it's only three squares away," she answered evasively.

"And you weren't walking," he laughed, "you were skating."

She shook her head while she accepted the brandied peach in a chipped pink saucer Memoria brought to her. Of course he was laughing at her; but she had learned long ago that men only laugh over things that are not really funny. Eating the peach in very small pieces so that the taste would last longer, she remarked sympathetically, "It was a blessing, anyhow, that we were both in front of Memoria's gate."

"That it was. I couldn't have gone on until I felt better."

"What would you have done if the stitch had come sooner."

"I can't think. Dropped on the curb, perhaps, or on somebody's steps."

"There aren't many nice steps around here. Did she have to help you into the house? I don't see how she managed it."

"Oh, well, it was only in one side, you know. I could still keep going with the other."

With her eyes on the saucer, Jenny Blair swallowed the last taste of peach as slowly as possible. "I think Memoria is very kind, don't you?"

"Very. If you want to know the truth, I think Memoria is an unusually capable laundress. Isn't that what your grandfather would say?"

"I don't know, but I'll ask him." She repeated the words with a strained look on her thin little face, because they were hard words to remember. "Did she give you a peach? Mamma thinks a brandied peach is good for a pain."

"No, she wasn't sure I needed one. They are good, aren't they?"

"I think," Jenny Blair replied for Memoria's benefit, as she returned the pink saucer, "that, if anything, they are better than Mamma's." Cautiously slipping off the sofa, she steadied herself before she took an experimental step into the room. "I'm much obliged to you, Memoria," she said, for she lacked politeness only to her superiors, "but I'd better be going home, or Mamma will send out to look for me." Removing the bandage from her forehead, she laid it aside on the table. "I'm not bleeding now, am I?"

"No, you're not bleeding," Mr. Birdsong replied, glancing in the most careless way at Memoria, who stood in silent dignity at the foot of the sofa, "but are you sure you're all right? If you are all right, we might help each other along. You won't mind my leaning on you now and then, will you?"

"I don't mind, but I'm afraid I'm not big enough. P'raps"—there were some words she could never pronounce, no matter how hard she tried—"Memoria might lend you a stick."

"She hasn't one. I've already asked her. But I think I'll be able to manage. Anyhow, there won't be any difficulty about your leaning on me. I'm big enough. How about taking my arm?"

It seemed a strange way of leaning on a person to offer her your arm; but Jenny Blair knew that the intentions and the behaviour of grown-up people seldom accorded completely, and that asking questions when you are in doubt is one of the very worst ways of finding out the truth about things. Though she had never heard of watchful waiting, she was as familiar as other children with the process involved.

"Good-bye, Memoria. Thank you very much," she said slowly and distinctly as they left the room; for she hoped this would be a tactful reminder to Mr. Birdsong that, after all Memoria's kindness, he was leaving without a word of acknowledgment. As he appeared still forgetful, she whispered while they descended the steps, "You've forgotten to tell Memoria goodbye."

"Is that so? Well, good-bye, Memoria, we're both much obliged to you," he called back so indifferently that Jenny Blair wondered if improving the manners of men was always as hopeless as she had found it to be. Then, glancing up at the look of tender protection in his face, she yielded completely to the charm of the moment. Even if nothing really exciting ever happened to her in the future, this one day would be always brimming over with thrills. To have an accident more interesting than painful in front of Memoria's house; to discover that Mr. Birdsong, for all his strength and bigness, had had the same, or almost the same, mishap a few minutes before; to be carried into Memoria's room, which her mother would never have allowed her to enter; to eat a delicious brandied peach in tiny tastes from a pink saucer while she was recovering on Memoria's horsehair sofa; and having come safely through all these adventures, to be walking away from Canal Street at sunset, with Mr. Birdsong's gay voice in her ear and Mr. Birdsong's arm encircling her shoulders,—surely life could never be the same again when she had such recollections stored up for rainy afternoons, or for the middle of the night when she awoke and began to tremble with fear.

Suddenly, in the midst of her pleasant agitation, her companion stopped beside a pile of lumber in a place where a house was torn down, and waved with his free hand to a comfortable seat on one end of a plank. They had reached the top of a gradual ascent, and from where they sat, hand-in-hand, she could look over Penitentiary Bottom and see the dark wings of pigeons in the burnished glow of the sunset.

ET me see, how old are you, Jenny Blair?" Mr. Birdsong asked, with flattering interest, while he settled himself beside her on the pile of lumber.

"Going on ten. I'll be ten years old the twenty-first of September."

"You're old for your age, and you get better looking, too, every day. It won't surprise me if you grow up to be one of the prettiest girls in Queenborough. You have the eyes and hair of a wood-nymph, and when you have eyes and hair, it doesn't matter a bit if God has forgotten your nose and chin. You may take my word for it, I've seen many a beauty who had worse points than yours."

A beauty! She drew in her breath sharply, as if all her thoughts were whistling a tune. Never before had any one held out the faintest hope that she might grow up to be pretty. "Handsome is as handsome does," her mother had replied only yesterday to a charitable visitor, who had remarked in the child's presence that she was becoming more attractive in feature as she grew older. And now Mr. Birdsong (who was one of the most adorable persons she had ever seen) really and truly thought that she might be a beauty. With her enraptured gaze on his face, she nodded as vacantly as a doll, because she felt her heart would burst if she spoke a single word of the torrent of gratitude raging within her.

"So you're nine years old," he said very slowly, as if he were counting.

"Going on ten. I'm nine years and seven months and three weeks." She corrected him as patly as if she were reciting a lesson.

"Well, that's getting on. That's getting on in life."

"Yes, that's getting on," she assented switching one of her plaits over her shoulder and tying the bow of plaid ribbon. Down in Penitentiary Bottom the shadows were thickening. From beneath the fire-coloured sunset, rays of light were spreading like an open fan above a drift of violet-blue smoke.

"I should think," he continued gravely, "that nine years and seven months and three weeks would be old enough to keep a secret."

She looked round quickly, her pride touched. "Oh, I can keep secrets. I've always had to keep secrets of my own. You can't get far in this world," she added, repeating a phrase of Aunt Etta's, "if you tell everything that you know."

With a gay and tender laugh, he leaned over and patted her hand. "If you've found out that, you may go as far as you please. But how about this idea? Don't you think it would be more fun if we kept all this—I mean everything we've done this afternoon—a secret between us?"

What a surprise! What an adventure to fall back upon! "Do you mean everything?" she asked in a whisper of ecstasy. Never had she dreamed of having a secret that belonged to her and Mr. Birdsong and nobody else.

"Everything." His accent was so firm and grave that for an instant she wondered if she could have mistaken his meaning.

"The whole afternoon?" she inquired eagerly.

"The whole afternoon," he repeated even more firmly. "Everything that has happened from the minute you left Washington Street. It has just occurred to me," he explained, "that it would be great fun for us to have a secret between us."

"Oh, great fun!" she echoed.

"Of course," he said, looking more closely at the cut on her forehead, "you will have to tell your mother you had a fall. I suppose you could have a fall anywhere."

"Oh, anywhere." Then she glanced down uneasily. "But I've left my skates at Memoria's."

"You did, eh? Well, I'll bring them up to my yard. I'm going to drive down this way to-morrow, and I'll get your skates and leave them—— Where shall I leave them?"

She thought a moment. "You might put them down by Old Mortality's pool. Are you sure," she asked abruptly, "that you aren't doing it all just to shield me? Mamma says Grandfather shields me too much."

"You needn't bother about that. But it's better not to tell your mother that you had a fall in Canal Street. It might make her feel worse, you know, and I've never found it did any good to make people feel worse. They usually feel bad enough as it is."

With this she was in earnest accord. "No, it never does any good. I always try not to tell Mamma anything I know will make her unhappy."

"You're a sensible child, and very grown up for your years, including the extra months. And it would certainly hurt your mother if you told her that you had run away and skated on that bad pavement. You might so easily have broken your bones."

"She'd feel dreadfully if she knew I'd gone because the children at school dared me. It upset her when she heard me tell Grandfather I wanted to see where the bad smell comes from."

"Well, she's right about that. You'd better keep away from that smell. But you're like me. You're too plucky ever to take a dare, or ever," he continued pointedly, "to tell a secret after you've crossed your heart."

"Oh, I wouldn't, not if—not if——"

"I know you wouldn't. That's why it will be such jolly fun having a secret between us. We must both be careful not to let anybody know that we've seen each other this afternoon. It would spoil everything if your mother should suspect."

"Oh, yes, that would spoil everything."

"If you let out so much as a hint of it, I'd feel, of course, that

I could never trust you again. I'd feel, indeed, as if I couldn't trust anybody but Old Mortality."

Without a struggle, drugged with happiness, she yielded herself to his charm. Never had she imagined that a single afternoon (she called it evening in her mind) could be so filled with excitement.

"Then, that's a promise," he said, rising, and held out his hand.

"Yes, that's a promise."

"Cross my heart?" He illustrated the question.

"Cross my heart." She imitated the sign as perfectly as she could.

"Well, I knew you'd be the kind," he said in a caressing voice. "I always knew there was something plucky about you."

Intoxicated by his praise, she blushed over her thin little face and turned her eyes again to the sunset. Instead of moving on, as she had expected him to do, he sank back, still holding her hand, on the edge of the plank. Was it possible, she asked herself, for any one to feel happier than she felt sitting there on the pile of lumber, with Mr. Birdsong beside her? When her blushes had ceased tingling, her eyes wavered back to his face, and she thought what a nice and pleasant face it was when you looked at it closely. He must scrub very hard with soap to make his cheeks so fresh and clear and ruddy, and she was sure that Mammy Rhoda might brush all day long, but she could never, never bring that shining gloss to her plaits. In the paling glow she gazed up at his grey eyes, set well apart beneath eyebrows like dark edges of fur, at his straight, slightly aquiline nose, and his full red mouth, which curved outward beneath the faint shadow on his upper lip. Yes, she had never seen, not even in a picture book, a face she liked better.

"I try," she responded presently because it was the only thing she could think of that sounded serious enough for the occasion.

"Well, you do. It's a comfort to talk to you. The truth is, Jenny Blair, that I am not nearly so plucky as I should like to be. I don't seem able to hold fast to anything very long." He broke into a short laugh. "The trouble is, I was born with a roving nature."

Though she was saddened by the strain of melancholy in his voice and even in his laugh, she had reached at last, she felt, ground that was both firm and safe. "I'm afraid I was born with a roving nature too," she replied consolingly. What, indeed, but a roving nature could have taken her to Canal Street that evening, or have tempted her down to the place from which the bad smell sprang up?

"Well, you'd better bridle your nature, my dear little girl. You'd better bridle it tight before it runs away with you."

"Does it run away with you?" she inquired curiously.

Again he laughed, but this time the melancholy had passed out of the sound. "It is always running away with me."

"Then why don't you bridle it?"

"I'm not strong enough. Unless you bridle a roving nature in the beginning, it is obliged to get the better of you."

"And then what happens?"

"Trouble. That's what happens. Trouble and more trouble and still more trouble."

She sighed deeply, for she felt very sad—almost as sad as she had felt just before she came down with scarlet fever. "If you told Mrs. Birdsong, wouldn't it be a help?" she asked presently. "Aunt Isabella says she is helpful in trouble." Instinct warned her that she had left the firm, safe ground as soon as she had reached it, and was floundering helplessly in some primitive element. Though she had had sufficient experience with ruffled occasions, she felt inadequate to deal with obscure upheavals of conscience.

"Your Aunt Isabella is right," he said after a long silence, and his voice sounded thick and agitated, as if something alive and hurt were struggling inside of him. "I married an angel." Then, abruptly, another and a very different exclamation burst from him, and she watched the genial ruddiness stream back under his smooth, fair skin. "By George, I'm always forgetting that you are only nine years old. There's something so sympathetic about you."

Sympathetic! This was almost too much. While her heart fluttered with joy, she turned her eyes away in an embarrassed glance at the horizon. The last flare of sunset stained the white-washed wall of the prison, and a soft mulberry-coloured dusk floated up from the hollow. Sympathetic! She rolled the long delicious word on her tongue.

"I feel, too, that you can be trusted," Mr. Birdsong continued earnestly, pronouncing each syllable very slowly and distinctly, as if he were trying to impress its importance upon her mind. "I feel that we would never, never give each other away."

"Oh, never, never!"

"Nothing could make us tell, for instance, about this afternoon."

"Nothing. Not—not wild horses."

"Even after you're grown up, we'll still have our secret."

"Always. Nobody shall ever know. Even if I live to be a—a thousand, I'll never tell anybody."

"Well, that's what I call loyal," he answered, and the strain seemed to relax in his voice. "You're a friend worth having, and no man has too many of them at my age. The best part of it is that you are sparing your mother, because she would be distressed to know how near you were to being hurt."

Slipping down from the pile of lumber, Jenny Blair put her hand into his warm and comforting clasp. A wave of adoration surged up, and it seemed to her that she was drowning in a kind of exquisite torment. Never before had she felt this yearning rapture, not for her mother, not for her grandfather, not even for Mrs. Birdsong, who was as beautiful as a dream. No, this was something new in the mingled ways of love and admiration and a strange sort of homesickness. Until this evening, she had always loved Mrs. Birdsong best, but now, she told herself, Mr. Birdsong was first of all, or at least the very next to her mother and grandfather, who were both trying at times, but must be loved because they were unable to be happy without her.

"Well, we'd better be going in now. I'll take you to your corner," Mr. Birdsong said, squeezing her hand.

"I think I'd better slip in the back gate. The alley is right over there."

"We'll cross here, then. If your mother asks you where you've been, what will you tell her?"

"Maybe she won't ask, but I can say I fell down and hurt myself because my roller-skates wouldn't roll right."

"You fell down and hurt yourself. That's right, and it's true."

"Oh, yes, it's true."

The flushed sky was paling into grey, and waves of silver-purple twilight flowed into Washington Street.

"Well, good-night, little girl." The gay and charming smile illumined the dusk for a moment; the grey eyes laughed; the caressing lips brushed her cheek. "You're a trump sure enough, and we'll always stand by each other."

Captivated afresh, she gazed up at him. "Oh, yes, we'll always stand by each other."

The back gate opened and shut, and she ran into the dim garden, where the light from the street drifted down through the faintly stirring boughs of the old sycamore. She could see the silver bole of the tree, and the glimmer of the rose-arbour at the end of the grasswalk. Then, as she sped by, the sound of whispers reached her, and she slackened her pace. "I mean honestly," said a deep voice that she recognized. "You know I mean honestly by you." Then a long, low, despairing sigh, and Aunt Isabella's plaintive notes, "But you don't understand, Joseph. You don't understand——"

Flitting on, while Aunt Isabella called sharply, "Is that you, Jenny Blair? Your mother has been worrying about you," she ran up the back steps and into the house. They might keep their precious secret, she told herself, for she had one now of her own that was far more important. From this evening, as long as she lived, she would have a part in that mysterious world where grownup persons hide the things they do not wish children to know.

"Well, my dear, we were growing anxious about you," remarked her grandfather, who was alone with William, she saw thankfully, in the library.

"My roller-skates tripped me again, Grandfather, and I fell down. You really will give me the money to-night, won't you?"

"I suppose I'll have to, my dear, I can't have you tripping up and bumping your head. Does it hurt?"

"It did dreadfully. And, Grandfather," she asked in a lower tone, "is it true that only bad people live in Penitentiary Bottom? Don't any good people live there?"

"Yes, my child, good people live wherever there are people."

"Is Memoria good, Grandfather?"

"Yes, Memoria is good. She is a good laundress and a good daughter."

"I know who is good too. Mr. Birdsong is good."

"Yes, George is good," the old man answered. "He is a good friend and a good sportsman. Now, you'd better run upstairs. Your mother has been worrying."

LL THAT cloudless June afternoon Jenny Blair watched Mrs. Birdsong make over a satin evening gown from the puffed sleeves and bell-shaped skirt of the 'nineties into the more graceful style of the twentieth century.

"Will you waltz at the party?" she inquired hopefully, while her admiring gaze wandered from the primrose-coloured satin to the rainbow hues of the garden. On Thursday evening there was to be a dance at Curlew, the country home of the Peytons, and Jenny Blair had been invited to spend the night with Bena and watch the illuminated fountain from the upstairs porch of the nursery.

"Only the first and the last waltz with George," Mrs. Birdsong answered, with her brilliant smile, which began in her eyes and wavered in an edge of light on her lips. Beyond her head, with its lustrous waves of deep bronze, the open window framed a climbing pink rose and a border of sky-blue delphinium.

"She is like roses and lilies," the child thought in a singing refrain. "She is like roses and lilies together—roses and lilies." Gliding into prose, she continued, "But I like Mr. Birdsong best. I like him best because we've a secret together." With the thought, an airy bliss was spun like light, like the bloom of pink roses and larkspur, over the bare places within; and a little bird that lived there in a blossoming tree sang over and over, "I know a secret! I know a secret!" She had only to shut her eyelids very tight while she plunged far down into herself, below the whirling specks and gleams that floated before her eyes, and the extraordinary delight of that evening on the pile of lumber, with Mr. Birdsong holding her hand, would rush over her and sink into her depths, as if it were all a part of the sweetness of June. "I know a secret! I know a secret!" piped the strange little bird, flapping its wings, and everything became different, everything became more real and living and splendid.

John Welch had dashed in for a moment to pull her plaits and ask some of the silly questions boys consider amusing. But he had gone out almost immediately to play baseball in a vacant lot; and she was happily alone again with her friend.

"Don't you like John, dear?" Mrs. Birdsong was spreading the width of primrose-coloured satin over her knees, and while she asked the question she picked up a pair of shears from the mahogany sewing-table by her side.

Jenny Blair pondered deeply and decided to be impersonal. "I never could abide boys," she answered.

"I know. They are rather trying, but John is different from most boys. He is very considerate. I sometimes think," she added, with a touch of pride, "that nobody in the world is so considerate of me as John is."

"Not—not more than Mr. Birdsong."

"Oh, George—well, yes, of course I was not thinking of George. But John is an unusual boy. Your grandfather thinks he has a great deal of character."

Grandfather would think that. It sounded exactly like him; but Jenny Blair was not interested in character, and was inclined to skip it whenever she saw it approaching, especially in books, where, she had learned from tedious experience, it was apt to interfere with the love story. So she merely folded her hands and repeated primly, "I never could abide boys."

Yes, it was true, she liked Mr. Birdsong best, she assured herself. For she shared no secret with Mrs. Birdsong, who would never, she felt certain, drop the bright, gauzy veils of her manner. Beautiful as she was, you could never come really close to her. In spite of her deep sparkle, her rippling vivacity, which flashed and glimmered and scattered like the spray of the Peytons' illuminated fountain, she would never in adventure, in any peril, give her secret away. Always, even upon a pile of lumber, gazing with her blue eyes at the sunset, the glow of her loveliness would come, in some strange way, between her and life.

"I'm glad we picked out this yellow satin," Jenny Blair said presently, starting all over again in her company voice. They had searched in the cedar chest for a dress that Mrs. Birdsong could make over to wear to the dance, and after much indecision, they had chosen a gown she had worn to a ball in the 'nineties. Now, while she ripped, turned, cut, basted, and stitched the shimmering folds, she talked more to herself than to the attentive child of the glorious occasions when she had reigned as a belle. Though she was only thirty-four, with the wild heart of youth still unsubdued, her voice borrowed a pensive note, as if the triumphs of the past had receded into the vague brightness of memory. "I wore this dress at a ball given in honour of Lord Waterbridge, the great English general. That was five years after our marriage, just before we lost the money George's father left us. Then I still had my evening gowns made in Paris."

"Did you dance with Lord Waterbridge?"

"We led the march together, and I danced the minuet with him when the ball opened." Lost in reverie, she paused an instant, while the needle with its shining thread trembled above the billows of satin, and her radiance melted into the iridescent bloom of the garden.

Yes, her grandfather was right, Jenny Blair thought, no one was ever so beautiful. No one was ever so beautiful—only—only she still loved Mr. Birdsong (here she shut her eyes very tight) best of all. "And when you waltzed with Mr. Birdsong did everybody stop and watch you?" she asked, clasping her hands in rapture. "Did everybody stop and watch just as Mamma says they used to do?"

"They used to do?" The animated voice dropped so softly that it was like the fall of a leaf. "Yes, they used to watch us when we danced. People had more time then. They were less eager to do things themselves. I was the impatient one, but nowadays they think me too slow and old-fashioned. They tell me I am old-fashioned because I never dance round dances with any one but George. Never since the evening we became engaged, and that was at a ball, have I ever waltzed with another man." She broke off, turned her eyes to the garden and murmured wistfully, "When two people really love each other, they ought to be sufficient to themselves. Nothing else ought to come between, nothing else ought to matter. You don't understand me, but you will some day. You will when you fall in love."

"I do understand," Jenny Blair said eagerly, in an effort to overcome the feeling that more was expected of her than she was able to give.

"Do you, dear? Well, you will understand still better when you are older. You will know then that a great love doesn't leave room for anything else in a woman's life. It is everything."

"Everything," the child echoed faintly. Something, she knew, was required of her; but the exact nature of the demand she could not comprehend. With Mr. Birdsong, she had known immediately that it was nursing he craved, the maternal sort of nursing she gave her doll after she dropped it. So naturally had this response welled up in her heart that it had seemed effortless. In the warmth of her sympathy the years between them had melted like frost, and in spite of his bigness and splendour, he had become, for the moment at least, as dependent upon her protection as the battered doll she had cherished so tenderly because it had lost an eye and the better part of its hair. But vaguely, through some deep intuition, she realized that Mrs. Birdsong's appeal was less easy to satisfy. What Mrs. Birdsong craved was not nursing, was not even sympathy. She demanded more than the child could give, more even than she could grasp.

"I used to think I wanted to be a great singer," Mrs. Birdsong mused aloud in a bright reverie. "But that was before I fell in love. After that, I stopped wanting anything else." The needle flashed into the satin. "It seems absurd now, but when we were engaged, it made me dreadfully unhappy if he so much as looked at another girl. I remember crying half the night because Daisy Wallace threw him a white rosebud from her bouquet, and he stuck it in his buttonhole." A haunted look crossed her face and was gone as swiftly as the shadow of a bird in the air. Then, holding up the primrose-coloured satin, she asked with a smile that brought the glow back into her eyes, "Mother's rose-point bertha will look well on this, don't you think?"

"Lovely," Jenny Blair answered, and she longed to add, though she could not bring herself to form the words with her prim child's mouth, "You are like roses and lilies, you are like roses and lilies."

"I hope it will be becoming, because it has been so long since I went anywhere. I want people to see that I haven't lost my looks."

"Mamma says you are as beautiful as you ever were."

"That's sweet of her." She glanced round at the roses and delphinium and laughed softly. "What else do they say of me, Jenny Blair?"

Gazing up at her, Jenny Blair tried in vain to gather her thoughts, while her mind lay still as the garden pool and waited for the reflection of Mrs. Birdsong's beauty to sink down to its clear depths. And not her beauty alone but all the little graces that made her different from any one else in the world,—the airy fringe on her forehead, the wisp of curls escaping from the knot on the nape of her neck, the way the colour ebbed and flowed in her cheeks, the trick she had of catching her lower lip in her teeth and smiling as if she also knew a secret, the tiny brown mole at the point of her left eyebrow, and above all the flowerlike blue of her eyes beneath the shadowy dusk of her lashes. These were things, the child told herself, that she could never forget. These were things that made Mrs. Birdsong more surprising, more startling to look at than any one else. Everything fresh and lovely in the world was mingled with her image in Jenny Blair's thoughts. If you took her away, something bright and joyous went out of the garden and the June sky and the piping of birds.

"What else do they say of me, Jenny Blair?" Again the needle flashed into the satin.

The child pondered more earnestly while she tried to separate her mother's starched ideas from the soft confusion within. "They say that—that you gave up too much."

"Too much?" There was an edge to Mrs. Birdsong's voice. "But what is too much?"

This was deeper again than Jenny Blair was able to plunge. "Oh, well, everything," she answered, with the comforting vagueness of youth.

"Everything? Do they mean my gifts, I wonder? Yes, I suppose they must mean my gifts." She bit her lip, frowned, and paused over her sewing. "But how do they know that I could have done anything with my voice?" Then, after a brief hesitation, she laughed and said tenderly, "You poor little thing. I am talking to you as if you were your Aunt Etta. When they talk that way they are thinking that I might have made another great Juliet. I once posed as Juliet in some tableaux that were given for charity."

"I've seen the picture," Jenny Blair said eagerly. "Aunt Etta has one in her album. It used to be Mamma's, but she gave it to Aunt Etta because she felt so sorry for her in one of her bad attacks of neuralgia."

Mrs. Birdsong laughed. "Yes, there is one in every old album in Queenborough. That was in 1889, and the photographs look silly enough nowadays. But you may tell them—only, of course, you must not tell them anything—that you can never give up too much for happiness."

Her face was glowing now with that misty brightness. Then, while Jenny Blair watched, the change came in a quiver of apprehension. There was a swift breaking up, a floating away, of the joyful expectancy. She lifted her head; her right hand stiffened and paused; her eyes grew soft and anxious. "George is late again," she said, glancing round at the clock on the mantelpiece. "I wonder what can have kept him?"

Jenny Blair sprang to the defense. "Grandfather is often late. There is always something down at the office to keep him."

"Yes, of course, it is that." Mrs. Birdsong was apparently satisfied with the excuse. "He is working much harder this spring. He works entirely too hard when you think how little he makes."

The last sunbeams quivered and vanished and quivered again over the garden. It seemed to the child that the flowers lost the dryness of light and became dewy with sweetness. Mrs. Birdsong thrust her needle into the satin, carefully folded her work, and replaced the scissors, the spool of silk, and the emery shaped like a strawberry, into the top drawer of her sewing-table. A frown bent her winged eyebrows together, and in the dying light her features lost their vivacity and became as still and pale as if they were spun out of a dream. It was that lonely hour of day when Jenny Blair longed for a friend like Mr. Birdsong instead of a playmate with a sunny disposition like Bena Peyton.

Rising from her chair, Mrs. Birdsong listened attentively to a sound in the street. Then she nodded twice in the spirited way she had when she was pleased. "There he is now," she said, and immediately afterwards Jenny Blair heard a firm, quick step on the porch.

"Where are you, Eva?" a voice called eagerly, while the door opened and shut and a wave of summer floated into the room.

"I am in the library, dear, and Jenny Blair is with me. We've been anxious because you were so late in coming."

"A man stopped me," he answered, as he entered the library. Then the faintest change, scarcely more than a stillness, closed over his features. "You must not worry, Eva," he added. "I can't have you getting lines in your face." After holding her in his arms a minute, he turned his gay and smiling eyes on

Jenny Blair. "So this little girl has been with you. Well, you couldn't find better company."

"She has helped me pick out a dress for the dance." Mrs. Birdsong put her arm round the child's shoulders. "We rummaged in the old chest for hours. I am going to wear that primrose satin Worth made for me in the 'nineties. You don't remember it, of course, but it will do very well with Mother's rose-point bertha and aquamarine earrings."

"You are beautiful in rags, Eva," he answered. "I don't have to remember your dresses. She's beautiful in rags, isn't she, Jenny Blair?"

Jenny Blair, who had turned hot and cold while she hoped and feared he might notice her again, responded with a look of trembling delight. She knew now that, even if he were rude to her, even if he hurt her dreadfully, she should not be able to stop loving him best. "I've never seen her in rags," she replied gravely.

"You haven't, eh? Oh, but she calls anything a rag that hasn't just come from Paris. She says I keep her in rags, you know."

"George, how can you?" Mrs. Birdsong remonstrated. "Jenny Blair doesn't know that you never mean what you say. But you promised that you would go with me to Colonel Bateman's funeral."

"By Jove, so I did! I'm sorry, Eva, but I forgot the old chap was having a funeral. A man came in about a piece of land, and of course I had to attend to him. After all, the funeral wasn't important to anybody but the Colonel, and he will excuse me."

"Of course he will, dear old soul! But I don't like your forgetting."

"Well, it shan't happen again. I promise you it shan't happen again."

"You always say that, George."

"Do I? Then I'll say it differently this time. I'll say it before Jenny Blair. If you forget, she will remember."

"If I forget!"

"Don't you ever forget anything, Eva?"

"Not things like that. Not the funerals of my friends or—or things I have promised you."

"But you're different." He stooped and kissed her lightly, almost carelessly, though he must have seen that he had hurt her. "You have nothing to do but sit at home and remember."

"Nothing to do!" There was a sob in her voice. "Nothing to do, when I've worked harder than Aunt Betsey, when I've worked like a servant to have the house nice for you."

Turning abruptly, he flung his arms about her and crushed her to his heart. "I didn't mean that, darling. I was only laughing. God knows, I would give my right arm if I could keep you from spoiling your hands."

"George, George," she murmured, and the impatience in her tone softened to tenderness. As she lifted her eyes to his there was a luminous vibration in her look. Even the child noticed the change and wondered curiously what could have made her so happy. "George, George," she repeated with a note of passionate longing.

She had drawn slightly away from his clasp, but as she spoke his name, his arms closed more firmly about her. "God knows, too, that I love you, Eva," he added. "I can't help being what I am, but I love you."

"Yes, you love me. Even if you killed me, I'd believe that you love me. If I didn't——"

"If you didn't?" He was still holding her so roughly that he seemed to bruise her delicate flesh.

"If I didn't believe that," something was strained and tearing beneath the tremulous words. "If I didn't believe that, I couldn't —oh, I couldn't bear things as they are."

Without releasing her, he glanced round at Jenny Blair, and his face looked flushed and heavy, the child thought, as it did when he had taken more mint juleps than were good for him. "You'd better run home, little sweetheart," he said in a tone he failed to make light. "Your mother will be wondering what has become of you."

"Be sure to come early in the morning," Mrs. Birdsong added. "I want you to tell me if the aquamarine earrings are becoming."

A few minutes later, running swiftly along the block, Jenny Blair thought passionately, "I don't know why—I wish I didn't, but I can't help loving him best of all."

AKING in the night with a start of fear, Jenny Blair said aloud, "I'm keeping a secret for Mr. Birdsong," and immediately the darkness was slashed by a pearly glimmer. Was that glimmer, she asked herself the next instant, only the edge of light that shone through the crack of the door? And was the noise that had startled her in her sleep the familiar complaint of Aunt Etta on one of her midnight visits to her sister-in-law's room? Whenever Jenny Blair overheard Aunt Etta sobbing because nobody loved her, she would feel a dull ache tightening about her heart, just as Aunt Isabella's stays tightened about her waist when Dolly, her maid, drew the laces. "I'd give poor Aunt Etta anything I have," she thought. "I'd give her my coral necklace if it would make her happy."

"I had to come, Cora, I couldn't help it. I have such a dreadful feeling." Aunt Etta's voice floated in a whine through the door and sank into the blackness of Jenny Blair's room, where it seemed to quiver on and on like wind in the leaves.

"What kind of feeling, dear?" This was the voice of Mrs. Archbald, crisp, benevolent, and faintly ironic. "Here, lie down under the coverlet. You are having a nervous chill. I'll give you a dose of bromide."

"I don't know what kind of feeling." Aunt Etta's teeth chattered as if she were stiff with cold in the warm June weather. "I went to sleep early, and woke up so frightened I couldn't bear being alone. I feel all the time that I am trying to get away from something, but I don't know what it is. Oh, Cora, I am so frightened!"

"But there isn't anything to be afraid of, dear. Take this

bromide, and lie down by me until you feel better. Try not to think of unpleasant things, and you'll go back to sleep."

"Can Jenny Blair hear us?"

"No, she's fast asleep." The voice sank to a whisper. "I never saw a sounder sleeper; but she makes me leave a crack in the door because she is afraid of the dark."

"I am sorry I woke you," Aunt Etta's tone was more a stifled croak than a whisper, "but I felt I'd go wild if I were left by myself. You are so different from Isabella."

"Isabella has her troubles."

"But they aren't like mine. I shouldn't mind having Isabella's troubles."

"Well, they are just as hard for her anyway. All of us have our troubles. God knows, I've had my share, Etta."

"But they weren't like mine. They weren't like mine."

"They're bad enough. The kind of trouble we have always seems worse than others."

"At least you've had love. You've had love, even if you lost it."

Mrs. Archbald sighed. "Yes, I've had love, but love isn't everything."

"It is all I want. It is the only thing in the world I want!" The low wailing sound was like the cry of a spirit in mortal distress. Before it died away into the night, Jenny Blair felt that an iron band was crushing her heart. Oh, why couldn't somebody love poor Aunt Etta? Being sorry for people was the worst pain of all. It was worse than falling down and scraping your knee. It was worse than the sickness that came after eating too much blackberry roll. It was worse even than measles and having to take medicine. "Please, God, don't let me feel sorry any oftener than you are obliged to," she prayed in desperation.

"You think that because you haven't had it," Mrs. Archbald replied firmly. "All women who haven't had love overestimate its importance. The trouble with you, my dear, is that you're ingrown. I sometimes think," she whispered, with her usual sagacity, "that the whole trouble with the world is ingrown human nature."

"I can't help it." Aunt Etta's voice was hysterical. "I want love. I don't want any other interest. I want love."

"But I thought you were doing so well with your church work."

"I wasn't. I wasn't."

"Etta, you must hold on to your pride." There was a stern accent in Mrs. Archbald's remonstrance. "After all, no woman can afford not to save her pride."

"I don't care about pride. Oh, Cora, I don't care about pride any longer."

"Well, you ought to, and you will in the morning. Do you want everybody to think you've lost interest in the church just because the Rector fell in love with Annie Baylor?"

"I don't care what anybody says. I don't care."

"That's because you are hysterical, dear, but you will feel differently as soon as he is married."

A shrill scream, strangled before it escaped her lips, was Aunt Etta's only reply. But a moment afterwards she sobbed out defiantly, "What does appearance matter when you are dying of misery?"

"It matters," Mrs. Archbald answered emphatically, "more than anything in the world. Look at Isabella if you want to know how important it is to save your pride."

"I can't see what Isabella has to be miserable about. She can't step out of doors without having somebody pay attention to her."

"But not the right kind of attention. Surely you do not wish to attract the wrong kind of attention."

There was a sound as if Aunt Etta had moved from the bed. "I may as well go back to my room and let you get some sleep before daybreak," she said despairingly. "If only I can keep from feeling so frightened as soon as I put out the light."

"But I don't want you to go until you are feeling better," Mrs. Archbald replied, stifling a yawn.

"Oh, I'm feeling better. I suppose I'm feeling better."

"Well, stay in bed to-morrow and let Dolly bring your breakfast. It makes such a difference in your face when you are rested and take a cheerful view of life. I told you, didn't I, that old Mrs. Mason said she thought you had such a sweet expression?"

"Yes, you told me, but that was only old Mrs. Mason."

"She has eyes as well as anybody." Then, as Aunt Etta trailed wearily out of the room, Mrs. Archbald crossed the floor softly and looked into the nursery where her daughter slept. "Jenny Blair," she said in a sepulchral but commanding whisper.

"Yes, ma'am," Jenny Blair raised herself on her elbow and answered obediently. In the illuminated square of the doorway, she could see her mother's spreading figure, which was so much larger at night than in the daytime, attired in a starched cambric wrapper. A smell of lavender salts filled the room, as if a stopper had been removed from a bottle.

"Are you awake? You were asleep when I looked in."

"I was asleep, but I woke up."

"Did Aunt Etta wake you?"

"I s'pose so."

"Did you hear what she was talking about?"

"Yes, ma'am."

"Well, she had a bad dream, and she came to tell me. It was nothing on earth but a bad dream."

"Yes, ma'am. Oh, Mamma, I feel so sorry for her!"

"So do I, darling. But there was nothing really to frighten her. She made it all up in her mind."

"Did she make up about nobody loving her?"

"Of course she did. She has plenty of people to love her. Even if men don't admire her as much as they admire Isabella, she has devoted friends among women."

"But they don't last, Mamma, and that hurts her. It hurts

her dreadfully, because she cried all the time after Miss Margaret Wrenn broke off with her."

"How did you know, my child," Mrs. Archbald demanded sternly, "that Margaret had broken off with her?"

"Oh, I heard it all when it happened. She broke off because she didn't like to be pinched, and Aunt Etta would pinch her until she was black and blue."

For a long pause Mrs. Archbald allowed this revelation to sink in. Then, recovering her authority, she exclaimed in a single significant phrase, "Jenny Blair, she was only making-believe!"

"But you aren't making-believe when you cry. Crying is real, and poor Aunt Etta was crying as if her heart had been broken."

"Well, you can't help her, my child, and the best thing you can do is to forget all about it and go back to sleep." She leaned over, smelling more strongly of lavender, and kissed Jenny Blair's cheek. "Try to be good, darling. You are all that I have."

Throwing back the thin summer coverlet, the child clung to the starched sleeve of the wrapper. "If I'm all you have, Mamma, won't it be dreadful if I turn out to be like poor Aunt Etta? Do you think I can possibly grow up as plain as Aunt Etta?"

"It is too soon to worry about that. There are more important things than being pretty or plain. Never forget that if you take care of your character, your face will take care of itself."

"But it doesn't, Mamma. It doesn't really."

"It will if you stop thinking about it. Turn over now and try to go back to sleep. You will be a fortunate woman if you never have anything more than your face to worry you."

Though she turned over obediently, Jenny Blair found going back to sleep less easy than usual. When the door was almost shut, the darkness began to stream and ripple, and something hidden beneath the streams and ripples waited, alive and hungry, to pounce upon her as soon as the gleam of light through the crack vanished. Was it something that had happened yesterday? Or was it something that might happen to-morrow? Was it the endless pain of being sorry for people? Or was it loneliness like Aunt Etta's because nobody loved her? Blackness closed over her, and she felt, as the gleam of light faded, that she was drowning in the fear, without beginning and without end, which waited there to devour her. Thicker and thicker churned the grey waters; nearer and nearer her bed floated that invisible enemy, alive and throbbing in the room, in the house, in the street, in the sky. She was afraid to call out, afraid to put up her hand lest this presence should spring on her before her mother could reach her. "There is nothing here," she thought, drawing the sheet over her head. "There is nothing here but Aunt Etta's unhappiness." And then more earnestly, "Please God, oh, please, don't let Aunt Etta's unhappiness come too near me!"

Then suddenly, while she shivered like a mouse in a trap, a voice spoke within her mind, and the dark enemy dissolved and was banished. "We must stand by each other, little sweetheart. We must never, never give each other away." Joy as sharp as light pierced her nerves. Terror had flown. Where Aunt Etta's unhappiness had been there was the bright and comforting smile of Mr. Birdsong. Instantly, she was safe again; she was enfolded in the bliss of his presence. All the black bats had scattered and wheeled out of her thoughts. "There isn't anything to be afraid of," she said aloud, and very dreamily the refrain hummed in her mind, "I know a secret, I know a secret!" The eyes and smile of Mr. Birdsong shone down on her, just as the eyes and smile of her father had shone down on her when she was little and awoke crying from fear in her crib in the old nursery.

CHAPTER 9

✿ ✿ ✿ ✿ ✿ ✿ ✿HEN SHE had dressed Jenny Blair for the party,
Mrs. Archbald knotted the blue sash more
securely at the waist and said emphatically,
"Now, try to be a good girl, and don't make any
trouble."

"Do you think we may tiptoe downstairs and peep in while Mr. and Mrs. Birdsong are waltzing?"

"You must ask Mrs. Peyton. Run away now, and don't forget to tell Aunt Etta how sweet she is looking."

"Is she really looking sweet, Mamma, or am I just to pretend?"

"She is looking better than I ever saw her. That dress of mousseline de soie softens her features, and she has washed and crimped her hair beautifully. I hope and pray she will enjoy herself. Have you seen your Aunt Isabella?"

"Oh, Mamma, isn't she handsome? I met her going down into the garden in her pink satin."

"Down into the garden?" Mrs. Archbald's face was blank with astonishment. "Why, what in the world was she doing in the garden?"

"Joseph came back for his saw, and p'raps she wanted him to see her dressed up. I think Joseph is a great help to her—I mean a great help about Thomas."

"Listen to me, Jenny Blair." Mrs. Archbald was speaking in her sternest tone. "I have told you over and over that Aunt Isabella broke her engagement because she was not sure of the state of her feelings. Remember those words—the state of her feelings. If Bena Peyton ever says anything about it, that is what you are to tell her. Aunt Isabella broke her engagement because she was not sure of the state of her feelings. Do you understand what I say?"

"Yes, Mamma." Running eagerly to the door, the child glanced back too soon, and saw her mother, for one instant of blighting reality, with the artificial cheerfulness wiped away from her face. While Mrs. Archbald sank down into her easy chair, her released mind sprang back from the severe strain of keeping up an appearance. Not her duty alone, but love, life, the world, the universe. God,—all these had become suddenly too much for her. Stripped of her pleasant smile, stripped even of her sunny disposition, she was only a tired middle-aged woman, who rested, for one precious hour, from the wearing endeavour to look on the bright side of things and hope for the best.

"Mamma, dear, don't you wish you were going?"

"No, darling." Mrs. Archbald's voice was faint but encouraging. "All I ask is a good night's sleep and a soft bed to enjoy it in."

Stabbed by this new vision of her mother, Jenny Blair whirled round in her party dress, and darting across the room, flung herself sobbing upon Mrs. Archbald's knees. "Oh, Mamma! Oh, Mamma, I've never seen you before!"

"My dear child! My darling child, what is the matter?" Clasping her tenderly but carefully, lest she should rumple the flounces of Swiss muslin, Mrs. Archbald tried to look in her daughter's face. "Have you a pain anywhere? Is your sash tied too tight?"

"Oh, I don't know. I don't know. But I've never seen you before."

"Why, Jenny Blair, how absurd!"

"I've never seen you before, but I love you, Mamma. I love you more than anything in the world."

"My precious child!" Almost sobbing in her turn, for she was genuinely moved in spite of her sentimental evasion, Mrs. Archbald forgot the flounces and the blue sash while she gathered her child to her bosom. "There, there. Mamma knows you love her. There is nothing to cry about."

"I wish you were going, Mamma. I don't want to go and leave you at home."

"But I'd rather be at home, dear. I haven't the strength to stand anything more after helping you and your aunts to dress. Poor Aunt Etta had another bad dream last night, and I had to sit up. Are you perfectly sure you don't feel a pain inside? I hope," she added gravely, "you haven't eaten anything I told you not to."

"It isn't that, Mamma. Oh, it isn't that."

"Then what is it? Has anybody hurt your feelings? You must remember that Aunt Etta is very nervous and sometimes she speaks more sharply than she means to."

"No, it isn't that. Nobody has said anything."

"Well, if there is nothing really the matter, you'd better run on and not keep your grandfather waiting. Mrs. Peyton promised to send you home early in the morning, and then you can tell me about the party."

"Oh, yes, I'll tell you about it." Love and sadness melted together and vanished. Immediately, Jenny Blair began to live in the hope of coming back, primed with news, to describe the evening to her mother. "I'll remember everything that happens, Mamma, and I'll bring you some of the little cakes with pink roses in icing. Bena told me they were going to have hundreds of little cakes, all iced exactly like flowers."

"I know they are lovely, darling. That must be Aunt Isabella's escort ringing the door-bell. I'll come down to see you off as soon as I am able to stand."

As Jenny Blair ran toward the staircase, a door opened, and she caught a glimpse of Aunt Etta, in a cloud of mousseline de soie, touching her cheeks with an artificial red rose-leaf she had borrowed from an old hat. Vividly, the child saw her reflected there in the silver light of the mirror. She saw her flat, slightly stooping figure, puffed out with ruffles across the bosom, and the long sallow face, from which the hair was drawn back over a high, stiff roll, filled, Jenny Blair knew, with a substance that resembled the stuffing of sofas. Something, either the expression straining for sweetness or the dot of black court-plaster near the corner of one wide-open eye, lent to the reflected face an air of indignant astonishment, as if poor Aunt Etta, for all her twenty-five years and platonic friendships, had never really seen the world as it is.

When Jenny Blair entered with a spring, the rose-leaf fluttered into the drawer of the bureau, and Aunt Etta turned away and picked up a shawl of Spanish lace, one of her dearest treasures, from the foot of the bed. Beside the shawl, Mammy Rhoda had laid out a pair of long white gloves, a fan of ostrich plumes, and an embroidered slipper-bag.

"How do I look, Jenny Blair?" Aunt Etta inquired nervously, stopping to pull the gloves over her arms.

"You look sweet," the child replied, with her mother's admonition in mind. But which was really Aunt Etta, the face of startled surprise in the mirror, or the composed lady who picked up her train, flounced with blue silk on the wrong side, and moved with the still fashionable "Grecian bend" to the head of the staircase?

"Do I look too pale, Jenny Blair?"

"Oh, no, you have the loveliest pink in your cheeks, just like a carnation."

"Wait till you see Isabella," Aunt Etta murmured, with a tremulous sound in her voice.

"Well, she doesn't want to go. She is going to save her pride."

A queer little laugh broke from Aunt Etta. "You're a funny child. I sometimes wonder how much you make up and how much you really know."

"I know that much. She doesn't want to go with Aubrey Weare. He is downstairs now waiting for her, and he doesn't know that she is going just to save her pride."

"Who on earth told you that?"

"Nobody told me. At least nobody meant to tell me," Jenny Blair answered, and she added proudly, "but you can't help having eyes."

"And ears too. Well, I know where you got that. It sounds exactly like your mother. The trouble with you, my dear, is that you try to be too much like older people. You'd better enjoy your childhood while you have it."

In the drawing-room, her grandfather looked stiff and ceremonious, with his grey hair shining as if it were polished, and his thick dark eyebrows overhanging the sunken fire of his eyes. Aunt Isabella, moulded into a princess robe of pink satin spangled with sequins, was handsome and light-hearted, though there was a subdued note of hostility in her laugh. Her hair was as lustrous as the wing of a blackbird, with a sheen of bluish light in its darkness, and the glow in her rounded cheeks was richer and more becoming than the stain of Aunt Etta's rose-leaf. She was much too splendid, Jenny Blair decided, to have so unattractive an escort as Aubrey Weare, a plain but facetious young man, who thought it amusing to be waggish with children.

"I suppose it is time for us to start," Aunt Isabella remarked with sullen animation, arranging her bouquet of lilies-of-the-valley.

For an instant Jenny Blair held her breath, and then sighed audibly with relief; for Aunt Etta also wore lilies-of-the-valley, and her waist was smaller by two inches than the severely pinched waist of Aunt Isabella. Mrs. Archbald, who was nothing if not farsighted, had attended to the flowers on her way to market that morning; and while Jenny Blair looked at the bouquet, and recognized the expert touch of the best florist in Queenborough, she thought how wonderful it was that her mother never forgot to give pleasure even to members of her own family. Though Aunt Etta lacked an escort (for Grandfather wasn't quite that), she was provided with all the outward signs of masculine admiration. "But I hope, all the same, that I shan't have to depend on Mamma for bouquets," the child said to herself, as she watched Aunt Isabella drive away in a hired landau, driven, not by a spirited young man, but by a coloured coachman who resembled Napoleon.

"I wish," Aunt Etta said a little peevishly, "that we could go in a landau. Our own victoria seems less like a party." Her face had changed, and she looked wasted and hungry, as she did when she prowled downstairs to the pantry in the dead of the night.

"Don't worry, my dear," the General replied cheerfully. "In a few years we may be going to parties in a motor car."

"Not to parties, Father." Mrs. Archbald was amiable but incredulous. "It is natural that young people should like the excitement of touring cars, but I cannot imagine, even if they are made safe, that motors will ever be used for church or for social occasions." As she kissed her hand to Jenny Blair, who sat folded in between Grandfather's broadcloth and Aunt Etta's mousseline de soie, she cried, with all the enthusiasm her voice could bear without breaking, "Take good care of my little girl!"

The General waved his hand. "And I trust you to look after William."

When the victoria had rolled away briskly, and the door was shut against the exhausting pleasures of life, Mrs. Archbald looked down on William with a benevolent but puzzled expression. Though she respected dogs, she was incapable of understanding them. Essentially matter of fact, even her realm of phantasy was a small, enclosed province, peopled by skeletons of tradition and governed by a wooden theology. Her heart was generous; but the native element of her mind was a drought, and she lacked the vein of mysticism that enabled the General and William to establish a communion superior to speech. So she patted the dog's head, and remarked, "Good fellow. You may come and lie on my rug," in a friendly but distant tone, as if she were addressing a distinguished member of the Mongolian race.

William, who understood her perfectly, wagged his tail

politely but without enthusiasm before he turned away. He was a handsome English setter, black and white, with melancholy eyes and not a little of his master's noble bearing. His old distrust of human nature still lodged in his tail, which was black, lustrous, and well fringed, but deficient in spirit. Already, as soon as he had seen the General prepare for a party, William had made his plans for the evening, and these did not include a nap on the rug in a lady's chamber. Since he had to be alone, for Mrs. Archbald did not count as a companion, he preferred to be alone in the coolest spot in the house, which, he had discovered long ago, was the tiled floor of the big bathroom upstairs.

"Dogs are queer creatures," Mrs. Archbald said to herself a moment later when she heard the tap-tap of his nails ascending the polished staircase. "Anybody would have thought he'd rather lie out on the nice green grass," which was only another proof that she was incapable of understanding any species except her own.

"Anyhow," Jenny Blair said to herself, holding fast to her sash, which was in danger of crushing between her grandfather's natural shape and Aunt Etta's artificial one, "when I grow up, I shan't be going to parties with Aubrey Weare." For he had plucked at her hair-ribbon on his way to the landau, and, justly indignant, she had been obliged to tie one of the bows all over again.

Squeezing as far back as she could, she let the self she called her real self sink down, down, far down into the vagueness from which painted images, like the tropical fish in her geography, emerged and swam aimlessly on the surface. A party! Wasn't it wonderful to be going to a grown-up party at last? Only she wished her mother had let her have a new dress. She was sure Bena would be dressed very fine. But her mother said Bena was so short and pudgy that nobody ever saw what she wore. Well, no matter, she was going to see the Birdsongs waltz together. Perhaps, when she grew up, she might waltz as beautifully as Mrs. Birdsong! Oh, how she wished she might stay up all night!

Weren't parties too lovely? She was wearing her prettiest blue sash and blue hair-ribbons; she was going to a real party for the first time in her life; and she was keeping a secret that nobody suspected. Immediately, the bright fish dived far below, and the current of life rippled and broke into waves and scattered a sparkling spray through her thoughts. "I'm alive, alive, alive, and I'm Jenny Blair Archbald!"

And beside her, the General was thinking, while this current of life paled and darkened and flowed on more quietly, "I hope Etta won't insist on staying too late. Why should she, poor girl, when she'll probably sit against the wall the whole evening? But parties aren't so gay as they used to be, and women, with the exception of Eva Birdsong, are not what they were in my youth. Or perhaps it is because my arteries are not all that they used to be. God knows how I shall be able to keep awake until midnight, especially if Bob Peyton insists on my drinking a glass of port. Keeping awake after ten o'clock is the hardest thing. Even when I go to bed as sleepy as William, I wake up at an unconscionable hour before daybreak. Getting old! That is the worst of life, getting old. Especially when you grow old without having had what you wanted. But it requires courage to take what you want in this world, and most people lack courage." Yet courage alone, he saw presently, was not sufficient. For courage, as well as cowardice, may trust in false values—even in evasive idealism. Great-aunt Sabina had had the rashness of infidelity—though he had always suspected that she had defied her Creator only in the days of her youth, and had returned to Divine mercy when age fastened upon her. Then poor Rodney had had the courage of despair at the end; and Margaret (the old pang still throbbed at the thought of her) had summoned up whatever spirit was required for her desperate adventure. These were ghosts. These were unquiet ghosts—but Isabella. Would Isabella have the courage not only to will but to act? They thought he had perceived nothing, that his old eyes were too dull to observe what went on under his nose. But he was sharper than they imagined. Almost from the first he had seen the way things were tending, and he had felt, in spite of his disapproval, an obscure satisfaction. "I'd like to see her pay back Thomas in his own coin. I'd like to see her pay back that cad. But it wouldn't do. It wouldn't do, though, God knows, the Archbalds have lived down many worse disgraces than overalls in the family." He chuckled under his breath. "After witchcraft, adultery, and murder (for Uncle Percival had killed his man in a duel), it seems an anticlimax to make a fuss about overalls." No, it wouldn't do in a woman, not even to pay back Thomas, who was beginning again, Cora said, to cast sheep's eyes at Isabella in church. A man with red blood in his veins would commit any folly for a girl as handsome as Joseph—but it wouldn't do in a woman. "Not that I shouldn't stand by her," he told himself, "not that I shouldn't help her to put a bold face on the matter."

This was wild dreaming, he knew, the kind of dreaming one would never acknowledge when it was over; yet even while he admitted that it was wild, he continued to indulge in his dreams. After all, class consciousness, like his arteries, was not all that it used to be. Like every other superstition, he supposed, it was doomed to decay. Perhaps new blood, new passions, and new social taboos were the only salvation of a dying order. Make Joseph a master builder, he mused idly, put him in the right clothes, and—but, no, it wouldn't do in a woman. It wouldn't do for a girl like Isabella to marry out of her class. Especially, it wouldn't do for her to run away as poor Margaret had done. The husks of his mind closed on the thought that it would not do in a woman; but far down in the centre of his being some dark impulse was appeased by the imagined flight of his daughter. Some dark impulse, perpetually thwarted and denied, was appeased—— Yes, he was good for one more fight, though he must never let Isabella suspect that he sympathized with her folly. The family would disapprove, but he could rely on the clan loyalty. All the old families that were not rotten within would close round him, just as they would close round him if he had forged a cheque or murdered his uncle. Cora, of course, would fall in with them. Without admitting the difference in station, she would contrive ingeniously to explain it away. Plain people would become quiet people. His chuckle was slightly sardonic as her cheerful tones rang in his thoughts. "Yes, the Crockers have always been quiet people. Baptists are so devout. Not that Joseph has ever had much religion——" Which was a step at least in the right direction of the Episcopal Church—— Drowsiness slipped into his mind; and beneath the thin veil, while his eyelids shut and opened and shut more heavily, he felt the current of life flow on into the cloudless area of youth and delight.

"Oh, how lovely it is!" Jenny Blair was exclaiming. "Look at the lawn hung with lanterns! Look at the open door filled with coloured lights! Oh, how I wish life could be all parties!"

Then welling up, sinking, spilling, going suddenly flat, the current of life sighed faintly through the loosened texture of Etta's mind. "I wonder if the curl is out of my hair. How I hope somebody will ask me to dance! I wish I'd put a little more red on my cheeks. Under those coloured lanterns nobody would know. If Margaret is in the dressing-room, I will make her speak to me. She has never been near me since I bit her arm that evening until she cried. But it was only in play. I didn't know it would hurt her like that. Anyhow, I wish I were dead. What is the use of being alive when you have to go to parties with an old man and a little girl? Oh, they have Chinese lanterns down in the garden! Doesn't it look just like fairyland? Wouldn't it be too wonderful if somebody I'd never met were to fall in love with me to-night for the sake of my sweet expression? Men have done that before. It has happened to Isabella, only she hasn't a sweet expression now, and last spring it happened to Daisy Bellows—but—— Oh, I know nothing will ever happen to me, and I wish I were dead!"

I KNOW something! I know something!" Bena cried, whirling round on her plump legs in a frock of pink organdie. She had a fair, expressionless face, with skin like an egg-shell, and was called a pretty little girl by persons who had never looked at her closely. Her thin, silken hair was tied on the top of her head with a bow of pink ribbon, and her short arms, creased with fat, were encircled by tight coral bracelets. "I know something you don't!" she repeated hilariously, breaking into the Highland Fling, not because she must, but from pure rapture. Though Bena was a valuable friend, as Mrs. Archbald often reminded her daughter, Jenny Blair had never been able really to like her. "I don't care who her father is, or her mother either," she decided now, "I know Bena is not all that she ought to be."

They were alone in the big nursery at Curlew, and across the hall, in the best spare bedroom (which was presided over by two very light-coloured maids in fluted caps and aprons), ladies of the romantic age were straightening their trains, settling their lace berthas, and giving a few final touches to light or dark masses of hair worn very high on the head. All the figures reflected in the cheval-glasses were queenly and elegant, with proud bosoms, straight fronts, and prominent hips, though the foundations beneath might be, as Jenny Blair knew, no firmer than ruffles.

"Mamma says we mustn't go down until she tells us," Bena whispered, as she peeped through the doors. Then twirling again on her square toes of pink kid, she chanted spitefully, "I know something that you don't!"

"I don't care if you do." Jenny Blair was looking gravely at her face in the mirror and wondering if she would always, even when she grew up, remind herself of Alice in Wonderland? But Alice was in a book, anyway, so it would have been just as easy to make her with hair that curled naturally.

"Bena," she asked, turning abruptly, "do you know what a wood-nymph is? Do you s'pose anybody ever really saw one?"

"Of course nobody did. There aren't any such things."

"There are."

"There aren't. You're saying the word wrong."

"No, I'm not. I know there're wood-nymphs because I've got eyes and hair like one. Somebody said so."

"I don't care. There aren't any such things. She was just poking fun."

"It wasn't a she."

"Well, he was just poking fun. Men do poke fun, don't they? I bet you anything it was that old Aubrey Weare."

"It wasn't."

"I bet you it was. I despise him, and so does Aunt Camilla." Then rising on the tips of her toes, she exclaimed derisively, "I know something that you don't! I know something that you don't!"

Jenny Blair tossed her plaits. "Well, it's just about babies, and I don't care what you know about babies."

"I know where they come from. Bessie Harrison found out when her little brother came. It hurts dreadfully."

"It doesn't."

"It does."

"She just made that up. And it doesn't matter to me, because I'm never going to have any. I like puppies better."

"You have to if you get married."

"Then I'll never be married. Some ladies aren't."

"They're old maids. Nobody wants to be an old maid."

"What are you fussing about, children?" inquired a voice of faded sprightliness, and Bena's mother, in blue and lavender gauze, appeared on the threshold.

"Mamma, won't she have to be an old maid unless she is

married?" Bena asked in the impertinent tone Mrs. Archbald frequently urged her daughter never to imitate.

"How silly, Bena. What in the world have you to do with old maids?"

"But she will, Mamma, won't she?"

What was it about Mrs. Peyton, Jenny Blair asked herself, gazing at the ashen hair and the long, thin face, with its pale skin the texture of a withered rose, that made her remember a Confederate flag in the rain? She wasn't, of course, in the very least like a Confederate flag. No lady could be. Yet Jenny Blair never looked at her that she didn't think of a flag going by in the rain to the inspiring music of bands. Was it because she had, as Mrs. Archbald said flatteringly, "such an air"? In her youth she had been admired less for her features than for her little ways and artless vivacity; and when her freshness began to fade, her little ways seemed only to multiply and her artless vivacity to increase. Animation, so challenging in youth to the masculine appetite, had degenerated at middle age into a nervous habit which kept the muscles of her face constantly twitching.

"I've no time to answer foolish questions, Bena. If you are good and quiet, you may tiptoe downstairs to the porch and look in at the dancing. But, remember, you are to come straight upstairs to bed when Mammy sends for you."

"May we see the ladies fix themselves? Somebody tore the lace on a train, and Matty is sewing it up."

"That was Mrs. Birdsong. She slipped as she was coming upstairs. Yes, you may peep in there if you promise not to touch anything or get in the way."

She floated down the stairs, while the two children, feeling shy and awkward, stole across the hall and into the guest room. "Oh, I'm so glad there isn't anybody left but Mrs. Birdsong!" Jenny Blair exclaimed, with a rush of emotion, while she watched Matty, kneeling on the floor, mend a bit of torn lace on the edge of the primrose-coloured train.

Standing beneath the gilt chandelier, Mrs. Birdsong glanced

round with a laugh, "Oh, children, I'm so happy! Tell me if I look as happy as any one in the world."

Dumb with worship, the children gazed up at her. Never, oh, never, thought Jenny Blair, trembling with admiration, could there have been, even in fairyland, any one so lovely to look at. Her hair, gleaming like November leaves, broke into a mist on her forehead and escaped in curls from the soft, loose knot she wore, regardless of changing fashion, on the ivory nape of her neck. The long aquamarine earrings sparkled like a pale reflection of her radiant eyes. From beneath the full bertha of rosepoint lace, the high puffed sleeves lent a royal breadth and dignity to her too slender shoulders, and over the starched ruffles that completed every fashionable curve, the primrose-coloured satin rose and fell and flowed and rippled in the shining depths of the cheval-glass.

"Do I look happy?" she repeated. "George says I am at my best to-night." And her eyes, even more than her words, asked over and over again, "How can I help being happy? How can I help being beautiful? How can I help being in love with life?" Yet, while her eyes asked the question, something deeper and darker than her eyes, something fugitive, defiant, and passionately mocking, glimmered in the faint smile on her lips.

"You look—oh, you look——" Jenny Blair checked herself because she wanted to burst into tears.

"When I grow up, I'm going to wear earrings," Bena was saying. "Mother had my ears bored when I was a baby, but you don't have to have holes in your ears any longer."

Mrs. Birdsong laughed, while the edge of irony trembled again in her voice. "By that time they may be all the fashion. Thank you, Matty, you mended that very nicely." Picking up her fan and a bouquet of orchids from the bed, she kissed her hand to the children and passed out into the hall and down the circular staircase to the crowded drawing-rooms, where the chandeliers were wreathed in roses and smilax and white crash was spread over the floors. At the foot of the stairs, Mr. Birdsong had waited, and slipping her hand and the feather fan through his arm, she melted with him into the kaleidoscopic maze of the waltz.

"Mamma says we mustn't go inside," Bena warned regretfully, "but we can look in from the porch. The porch is decorated just like the parlours, only there isn't any crash on the floor."

Slipping out through the back door, they ran to one of the long windows on the porch, and looked, beneath swinging Chinese lanterns, into the drawing-rooms. All the dancers had stopped, and stood in rows, watching Mr. and Mrs. Birdsong glide and dip, and glide and dip again to the intoxicating measure of *The Blue Danube*. Whirling, reversing, gliding, dipping, swinging, flowing, dissolving into the music, they waltzed from the end of the back parlour, past the open doors of the hall, where musicians were hidden in palms, to the front windows, which were festooned in roses and smilax. Clasping Bena's plump arm, Jenny Blair prayed with passionate intensity, "Oh, God, let my hair grow darker, and make me as beautiful as Mrs. Birdsong. Don't let me, God, look like poor Aunt Etta, or even like Aunt Isabella!" For poor Aunt Etta was sitting against the wall, between Grandfather, who nodded as if he couldn't keep his eyes open, and Miss Abby Carter, who pursed her lips into an affected smile, so that she seemed to be saying over and over, "I am having a lovely time, I am having a lovely time. Oh, I must tell everybody what a lovely time I am having."

"I believe I could dance like that if I tried," Bena said, for that was one of her little ways.

"You couldn't. Nobody ever waltzed as beautifully as Mrs. Birdsong. Grandfather says so."

"Your grandfather doesn't know everything." This was Bena's usual retort when she was pushed into a corner.

"He knows more than anybody else. He has been to balls with the Prince of Wales and kings and queens.

"That doesn't make him know anything. Kings and queens don't matter any longer."

"Yes, they do."

"No, they don't. But, even if they do, your grandfather couldn't have a party like this. You haven't got a country place and a garden and—and both a landau and a victoria and two pair of carriage horses."

Jenny Blair wrinkled her forehead. Hadn't she always insisted to her mother that Bena Peyton had no manners? "Well, I don't care," she retorted mysteriously. "We've got a curiosity, and you haven't. We've got the funniest bad smell that just comes and goes of itself."

"That's just a smell. Nobody wants a bad smell."

"But it's a funny smell. It's a curiosity."

"I don't care if it is. I don't want it. And a smell can't be a curiosity. You made up that, just as you did wood-nymph."

"Yes, it can."

"No, it can't."

Again the music had broken, and the dancers were assembling for a figure in the middle of the white crash. Mrs. Birdsong, with that summer radiance in her face, was standing beside old Colonel Hooper, who had been the best dancer in Queenborough for two generations. Aunt Isabella was walking slowly and haughtily across the floor, followed, Jenny Blair observed, by the pleading sheep's eyes of Thomas Lunsford. But Aunt Isabella, with her hand on the arm of a strange young man, took not the faintest notice of Thomas, not even when he strolled casually to her side and asked for a dance. Was it possible that she had got over caring? Was it possible that Joseph had cured her? And wasn't it strange that the more completely she ignored him, the more actively Thomas pursued? Well, that was one of the deep mysteries of conduct. Men always wanted most the thing you least wanted to give them.

Oh, if only somebody, no matter how old and ugly, would ask poor Aunt Etta to dance! Perhaps this one will, at least he is ugly enough. Grizzled, yellow, wobbling, knock-kneed, he seemed to be bearing down, as if driven, in Aunt Etta's direction. It can't be true. Yes, it is. He is really seeking her out. To be a man! Oh, the power, the glory, of being awaited in fear, of being hopefully awaited, in spite of the most unattractive appearance! But poor Aunt Etta will dance at last. She will be seen on the floor. She will be saved from the fate of a wallflower, if only by the intervention of Providence and an undesirable partner. Then Jenny Blair's heart fluttered and sank, like a wounded bird, far below her thin little chest to the place where a flannel band protected the depths of her being. For he had not stopped. He had passed Aunt Etta by and was boldly pursuing the prettiest and youngest girl on the floor. He was actually taking her from the arms of a blond and adorable youth. It was unfair of God to let Delia Barron have six men around her (Jenny Blair had counted them), while Aunt Etta was left sitting, with her sweet expression growing more false every minute, between Grandfather and Miss Abby Carter. Delia Barron was the prettiest girl in the room, after Mrs. Birdsong, who wasn't, of course, a girl but a married woman, even though she had never had children, and had never, so Mrs. Archbald had confided to Aunt Etta in Jenny Blair's hearing, wanted a child. "That," Mrs. Archbald had added in a lower tone, "is part of the trouble."

What did she mean by trouble? Jenny Blair asked now, gazing in speechless ecstasy from Aunt Etta to Mrs. Birdsong. How could any one who was all light and bloom and softness have trouble? Trouble was a drab word. When Jenny Blair shut her eyes and repeated it slowly, she saw a dull object, shaped like a bundle, which puffed out presently into an old woman, in a gingham apron, knitting a sock. But she could never, no matter how slowly she said the word, imagine Mrs. Birdsong. She couldn't even think of her mother, who had had trials, or of Aunt Isabella, who had had blows, or of Aunt Etta, who had had, and indeed was still having, disappointments.

A thin veil dropped between her eyes and the dancers. She saw the brilliant colours woven and interwoven into a tremulous pattern, and she thought, "I am so sleepy that I am here and not here." The bright confusion was flowing within and without, and it was like a stream that reflects but does not hold the images of the sunset. Slipping her hand up her bare arms, she pinched herself sharply. "I must not drop off. I must not shut my eyes. . . ."

Hours afterwards, it seemed, a hand touched her shoulder, and there was Matty's fluted organdie cap bending over her. "I'd rather put myself to bed, wouldn't you, Jenny Blair?" asked Bena, rubbing sleep from her eyes. "You slept a long time," she added. "You slept so long you didn't see Mrs. Birdsong run out of the room while the music was playing."

"Did she run far?"

"There, I told you so. You did sleep a long time. Yes, she dropped her partner's arm, and ran straight away while everybody was dancing. But Mr. Birdsong went first. He went out with Miss Delia Barron on his arm. I saw them go down into the garden. They came out on the porch, and I heard him say, 'Have you seen the lanterns down by the lily-pond?' "

"I don't care," Jenny Blair retorted, and she didn't. Even the music and the brilliant colours had ceased to excite her. Her eyelids kept coming down, no matter how hard she tried to keep them up, exactly like the eyes of a wax-doll when the spring that makes them open and shut has been broken. And this broken spring seemed to work within her mind as well as over her eyes. "I don't care," she repeated. "People may run out of dances and go down to lily-ponds as much as they please. I don't believe they are real. One thing I know, I've sat up as long as I want to."

In the nursery the night-lamp was burning low under a dark shade, while the strains of a polka floated merrily from downstairs.

"Mamma says I must let you sleep on the outside of the bed because you are company," Bena explained. "Turn round, and I'll unbutton your dress. Mammy had to go to bed with a headache, and nobody wants Matty about."

Untying the wide blue streamers at her back, Jenny Blair began rolling them smoothly, as her mother had taught her to do. Even if it took a long, long time, every child, when she hasn't a nurse, must see that her sash and hair-ribbons are rolled smoothly, unless she is satisfied to appear a frump at her next party. All the pressing in the world, she insisted urgently, while she went over the blue streamers, could not make rumpled ribbons look as fresh as they did when they were new. "All the pressing in the world," she droned sleepily, when a figure darkened the lighted doorway, and Mrs. Birdsong's voice cried in desperate pain, "Where is Mary Peyton? Oh, children, can you find Mary Peyton?"

An instant afterwards, she crossed the floor and flung herself down on a couch by the bed, while throbs of anguish shuddered through her in a convulsion. Her hair had slipped from its knot and hung in waving masses on each side of her face, which looked wan and stricken, as if it were the ghost of the happy face Jenny Blair had watched, so short a time before, in the assembling figure of the lancers. Even her primrose-coloured draperies were crushed, and clung about her shape in a desolate pattern of grief. As she lay there, shaken by those long, quivering sobs, which shuddered up from the tormented depths of her heart, she reached up quickly and tore the fragile rose-point bertha away from her bosom.

Frightened, yet full of pity and curiosity, the children were shrinking together when the open door shut quickly, and Mrs. Peyton swept in with a dose of medicine in her hand. "Drink this, Eva. It is only ammonia. Nothing in the world has happened," she continued in a soothing tone. "Your imagination is running away with you." Turning hastily, she added, "You'd better undress in my room, children, and be sure to see that the door into the hall is shut tight."

"Oh, I don't mind the children." Mrs. Birdsong sat up and pushed the measuring glass from her lips. "I don't mind anything." Sobs shook her afresh, and she flung back the waves of her hair with a passionate gesture. "But I cannot bear it. I can never, never, never live through it again."

"You don't do any good by giving way, darling. No woman

does." Mrs. Peyton's thin lips wrinkled and tightened, as if they were pulled by a string, and she added in an intense whisper, "You gain nothing in the world by not saving your pride."

"But I saw them, Mary. I saw them with my own eyes——"

"Hush, Eva. It is much wiser to pretend that you didn't. Even if you know, it is safer not to suspect anything."

"I'm flesh and blood. I've sacrificed everything."

"It's for your own sake, dear. Don't think I'm lacking in sympathy. Here, swallow this down quickly, and let me pin up your hair. Your lovely lace is all torn."

"It makes no difference. Nothing makes any difference. Oh, oh, oh, why did I come?"

"But you looked so happy when you were waltzing together. I never saw you more brilliant."

"I was—I was. Where is he now? Can any one find him? I must go home. I feel as if—as if——"

"Then I'll send for him." Mrs. Peyton glanced round with her anxious look, "Children, do you think you can find Mr. Birdsong? No, don't put on your sashes again. Just run downstairs and tell him his wife has been taken ill, and must go home. You needn't wait for the Murrays, Eva," she added, "I'll send you home in my victoria. Bena, as you go down, tell Johnson to order the victoria."

"Oh, I can find Mr. Birdsong," Bena said proudly. "Jenny Blair was fast asleep, but I saw him go down into the garden. I saw him go down to the lily-pond with Miss Delia Barron."

With a choking cry, Mrs. Birdsong started up from the couch. Then flinging herself down again, she sobbed out hysterically, "Oh, run and find him, Jenny Blair. He will come if you tell him I am ill. That I am ill, and must go home."

"Run on, children," Mrs. Peyton commanded, and while they sped toward the staircase, her voice followed them. "The trouble is, Eva, that you expect too much of life. Every woman must learn that sooner or later——"

Tingling with excitement and the piquant suspicion that her unbuttoned dress was showing her underbody in the back, Jenny

Blair raced ahead of Bena to the staircase, where she saved time
by sliding down as much of the banisters as she dared. From below, as she descended bravely but cautiously, she heard music
and laughter and the gay popping of corks.

"It's supper-time," Bena whispered yearningly, as they flitted
by, "and they're all wondering what has become of Mamma."
After making signs to Johnson, the butler, she seized Jenny
Blair's hand and tripped down the porch steps to one of the
winding walks that led into the garden. Here the illuminated
fountain was still scattering its tinted spray, and the summer
night was saturated with cool sweetness. "It isn't real," Jenny
Blair thought, pausing a moment to drink in the beauty. "It
isn't a bit more real than make-believe." No, it wasn't real. It
wouldn't last till to-morrow; but, oh, it was lovely, it was satisfying, as long as you looked at it. Suddenly she said aloud, "The
shadows are alive, and you can hear time moving among them.
Bena, if you'll only stay still, you can hear time stealing by."
But Bena called back spitefully, "No, you can't. It's just the
breeze from the river, and our breeze hasn't a bad smell. Besides,
you didn't make up that about time. I heard Mrs. Birdsong tell
you to listen and hear time going by in her garden."

It was true Mrs. Birdsong had told her that. When she stopped
and thought about things, it seemed to her that it was always
Mrs. Birdsong who put the loveliest fancies into her mind. Because of this, she ought to love her best of all—but she could not.
Their secret had woven a magic tie between her and Mr. Birdsong, and this magic tie was stronger than affection, was stronger
than gratitude. A thrill was in it, a deep hidden blow, which made
everything start out of a drifting haze, just as the trees, and the
dark wings of pigeons, and the whitewashed wall, and Penitentiary Bottom started out, alive and quivering, while they sat,
hand-in-hand, on the pile of lumber and watched the last flare
of the sunset.

"They are down there. I see them," Bena whispered, as she
skipped on the grass walk.

Yes, Jenny Blair could see them now, a dark and a white shape blended together by the swinging light from the Chinese lanterns. When the children flitted nearer, the dark and the white shape appeared to break up and melt apart, as the shadows of the elm boughs broke up and melted apart in a sudden breeze. There was a sigh, a laugh, a gay protest, and a voice asked a trifle sharply, "What are you doing up so late, children?" That was Mr. Birdsong. Only Mr. Birdsong could speak in an impatient tone with an edge of roughness that was charming.

"They sent us to find you," Jenny Blair answered gravely. "Mrs. Birdsong has had a spell, and she says she must go home."

"A spell? Eva?" His tone was all roughened now, the roughness of anxiety, not of annoyance. As he passed under the Chinese lanterns, Jenny Blair saw that his face was flushed and slightly moist, with the puffiness beneath the eyes she had observed regretfully that afternoon in Canal Street. There was the same look of having run too far and too fast, though apparently he had been sitting in one spot, fanned by the river breeze, for nearly an hour. His voice, too, when he spoke again, had that panting sound, like a rapid heartbeat, which had worried her in Memoria's parlour. "Well, run ahead. I'm coming. I'm coming as quick as I can."

While he started back to the porch, Delia Barron slipped from the shadows and clung to his side; but she might have been an apparition for all the notice he took of her. Through the illuminated garden, threading his way in and out of the box-maze, he rushed on, without a glance at the loveliness or a thought of the fragrance. Only when they reached the porch and he was about to enter the house, he appeared to remember the girl at his side. "Good-night, Delia," he said, and there was a resentful, almost an angry note, in his voice, "Forgive me for letting you go in alone." Then following the children up the stairs, he exclaimed in nervous desperation, "Run on, run on, show me where they have taken her!"

When Bena pointed to the closed door, he flung it open and rushed to the couch on which his wife was lying with her hair still loose on her shoulders and a tragic yet triumphant look in

her face. Curious but embarrassed, the children shrank back
to the bed, and caught up the half-folded sashes from the coverlet. After all, as they tried to make plain by their behaviour, the
nursery belonged to them by rights, and even if they were in the
way, they could scarcely be dismissed as intruders. To their astonishment, however, no one, not even Bena's mother, who let
so little escape her, appeared, for the first few minutes at least,
to be aware of their presence. For Mrs. Peyton was absorbed in
ministering to her friend, in supporting her, in smoothing away
the tragic yet triumphant expression:

"It was a sudden faintness," she said. "I am always uneasy
about her heart when she has these attacks."

"A sudden faintness," Mr. Birdsong repeated, as he swept
down, with his anxious tenderness, his exuberant vitality, and
seized his wife in his arms. "Eva, why didn't you tell me? If
I'd known you were not well, I should never have let you come."

"Will you take me home? George, I must go home as soon as
I can. Mary is sending us in."

"That's nice of her. Has the carriage come round?" Mr. Birdsong glanced over his shoulder. "Jenny Blair, will you look out
of the window?"

Yes, the victoria was there. Jenny Blair hurried to the window, glanced down on the drive before the door, and came back
again. Then, watching the look in Mrs. Birdsong's face, the
child was seized by the feeling of moral nakedness that came to
her whenever the veil slipped away from life and even grown-up
people stopped pretending. Like a tingling flush, this sensation
swept over her, and she knew that she was scorched with shame,
not for herself, but for Mrs. Birdsong. More than anything in
the world, she hated to see her elders begin to crumble on the
surface and let glimpses through of feelings that ought never to
be exposed, not even in the direst extremity.

"If you'll let me put her to bed. It has all been too much for
her," Mrs. Peyton urged mildly.

"Thank you, Cousin Mary, but she'd better go home. Come,
Eva, I'll take you." There was something so alive, so helpless,

so suffering, in his voice that Jenny Blair trembled with fear lest his wife should resist him. But, no, she did not resist him. She gave herself to his arms as if she were yielding up more than her body. "Yes, take me home," she said. "Take me home." That was all, but the words were ringed round with a flame, with the burning sweetness, the pure radiance, which flickered for a heartbeat, and then shone steadily in her eyes, in her smile, in her flushed and transfigured face.

"Shall I carry you? Are you able to walk?" How he loved her, Jenny Blair thought, with a twinge of jealousy, though she adored Mrs. Birdsong.

"Oh, I'm able to walk. I'll be all right again as soon as we are at home." Rising from the couch, Mrs. Birdsong tucked up her hair in a careless knot, and reached out her arms for the filmy wrap Bena had brought from the guest room. "Isn't my hair a sight?" she asked, almost gaily. "Hadn't I better throw a scarf over my head?"

"No, your curls are lovely." Mrs. Peyton touched the bright head here and there. "Be careful with her, George. She is still feeling faint."

"Oh, I'll be careful!" Slipping his arm about his wife, he led her out of the room and down the wide circular staircase. Though she clung to his arm, rhythm flowed again in her step, and when she paused for an instant to glance back, her loveliness pierced Jenny Blair's heart.

"Go straight to bed, children," Mrs. Peyton commanded, "and remember, if any one asks you about Mrs. Birdsong, that she had a sudden faintness and was obliged to leave early."

"A sudden faintness," the children repeated, while they ran to the window, where, a few minutes afterwards, they were rewarded by the sight of the victoria turning out of the drive, with the moonlight and the deeper yellow of the Chinese lanterns blending over the lustrous folds of primrose-coloured satin.

"I don't believe it was a sudden faintness," Bena muttered, with one of the darts of wisdom that lent her pert childish features the look of malicious age.

"It was, it was," Jenny Blair returned defiantly. "It was a sudden faintness. Your mother said so."

"She just said that for us."

"No, she didn't."

"Yes, she did. Besides, it happened in my home, so I ought to know more about it than you do." That was Bena's way, no matter where you were or what you were pretending.

Slipping out of her clothes and into her nightgown, Jenny Blair rushed back to the window for a last glimpse of the glowing lawn, the pale sky, and the thin mist that fluttered like a dropped scarf over the river. "It *was* a sudden faintness," she repeated firmly; for even at her tender age she had not failed to perceive that you may believe almost anything if you say it over often enough.

Then, without cause, without warning, while she stood there in her cambric nightgown, with the river breeze blowing in a sharp spray over her skin, she was visited by one of those swift flashes of ecstasy. Wordless, vast, encompassing, this extraordinary joy broke over her like an invisible shower. Without and within, she felt the rain of delight sprinkling her body and soul, trickling over her bare flesh, seeping down through her skin into the secret depths of her heart. "The world is so lovely," she cried, dancing round and round on her bare feet. "I'm alive, alive, alive, and I'm Jenny Blair Archbald!"

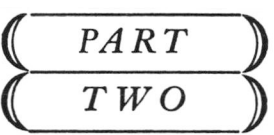

PART TWO

THE DEEP PAST

"Y<small>ES, IT IS TRUE,</small>" said old General Archbald, for he had passed his eighty-third birthday, and had found that phrases, like events, often repeat themselves, "you can't mend things by thinking."

Though thought may have created life in the beginning, though the whole visible world may hang suspended in an invisible web of mind, one could not by taking heed mend the smallest break, not the tiniest loosened thread in the pattern. All the thinking in the world, he mused, with a sense of unreality as vague as smoke, could not help Eva Birdsong. For months he had suspected that something was wrong. Not more than ten days ago, he had seen her stop suddenly in the midst of a sentence, while a shiver ran through her body, the smile twisted and died on her lips, and she looked at him with the eyes of a woman in torture. Then she had seemed, by sheer strength of will, to drive the spasm away, to keep the returning pain at a distance. "What is it, Eva?" he had asked, and she had answered with a laugh of protest, "Oh, nothing." That was all, "Oh, nothing." Yet he had not been satisfied; he had felt uneasy and agitated; he had known in his heart that something was wrong with her. And now he had just heard that they had taken her to the hospital.

"They have given her morphine," Mrs. Archbald was saying, "and George telephoned me that she will be operated on in the morning. If you'll go up late this afternoon, she thinks she will be able to talk to you. There is something she has on her mind." Arrested by the pain in his eyes, she added, "I sometimes think, Father, that Eva is more to you than any one in the world."

With his hands clasped on the ebony crook of his walking-stick, he stood on the front porch and blinked up at his daughter-in-law, while William (an old dog now, but carrying his years well) waited for him to go out into the April sunshine in Jefferson Park.

"Is there danger?" he asked, without answering her question. For it was true that Eva was more than a daughter, and nothing is so hard to speak aloud as the truth.

"There is, of course, always danger. For a year she has been really ill; but you know how long it took us to make her submit even to an examination."

"Yes, I know." The brooding eyes beneath the sardonic eyebrows did not waver.

"It does seem exaggerated to carry modesty to the point of endangering one's life. But with Eva, I think, it was less her own shrinking than the feeling that George might—well, might—— Oh, I don't know, of course, but she told me once he had a horror of what he called maimed women."

"Any man worth his salt would think first of her health."

"That is exactly what George said to me an hour ago. But women, especially romantic women like Eva," she added sagaciously, "make the mistake of measuring a man's love by his theories. She told me about it the day she was seized with that dreadful pain and I telephoned for Doctor Bridges." She broke off abruptly, with the feeling probably, the General reminded himself, that she was giving away some solemn league and covenant of woman.

If only she would tell him more! While the thought crossed his mind, he flinched and raised his eyes to the clement sky. If only she would tell him nothing! After all, there was wisdom in an era that smothered truth in words. For truth, in spite of the stern probings of science, is an ugly and a terrible thing.

"If women could begin to realize," he said, "how little what a man thinks has to do with what he feels."

"Had I ever doubted that, the way George has risen to this crisis would have convinced me. He seems to feel the pain more than Eva does. For three nights he has sat up with her, and he refused to go to bed even after he fell asleep in his chair. The night nurse made him lie down on a couch last night; but he looks dreadfully haggard this morning, and his nerves are on edge. No man," she concluded emphatically, "could have shown a greater devotion."

"I can well believe that."

"Then why—? Why——?"

"Those other things, my dear, have nothing to do with his marriage."

Mrs. Archbald looked puzzled. "But that is just what I mean. There have been so many things in his life that have had nothing to do with his marriage."

The General sighed with the usual male helplessness before the embarrassing logic of the feminine mind. "Well, George has the kindest heart in the world. But even the kindest heart in the world sometimes fails to get the better of nature. All that side of his life has no more to do with his devotion to Eva than if— than if it were malaria from the bite of a mosquito. That's what women, especially women like Eva, are never able to understand."

"No wonder. It seems so illogical."

"Men aren't logical creatures, my dear. Nor, for that matter, is life logical." Then he asked, "Have you seen Isabella to-day?"

"Yes, she stopped as she was taking little Erminia to the dentist. There's something wrong with her teeth. It's such a pity, for she is a beautiful child."

"All three of them are beautiful children. Nature seems to be on the side of Isabella. Well, so am I, if only because she let our family skeleton out of the closet. The only way to be rid of a skeleton is to drag it into the light and clothe it in flesh and blood."

Mrs. Archbald looked puzzled. "I don't understand, Father."

"I didn't mean you to, my dear, but Isabella would. She is like every other Archbald, only more so, and though she is happily unaware of it, the more so has been her salvation."

Seven years before, three days after the renewal of her engagement to Thomas Lunsford, Isabella had taken the morning train to Washington, and had returned the next afternoon as the wife of Joseph Crocker. "Life is too short," she had explained, with the dash of coarseness that embarrassed her sister and her sister-in-law, "not to have the right man for your first husband at least. As for what people say—well, if talk could kill, I should have been dead long ago." Etta had been prostrated; but Mrs. Archbald had been too busy readjusting the Crockers' station in life to give way to prejudice. When so few standards remained unimpaired, the distinction between plain people and quiet people was almost obliterated by the first important step from the Baptist Communion to the Episcopal Church. And everything, of course, was made easier because Joseph had so little religion. . . .

"You look tired, Father," Mrs. Archbald remarked, when she had studied him for a moment. "Hadn't you better lie down?"

"No, I like to feel the sun on me, and so does William. We'll sit in the park awhile and then walk up to the hospital."

"Jenny Blair will go with you. She can wait downstairs while you are in Eva's room. The child is so distressed. She has always adored Eva."

"Every one adores her."

"Well, try not to worry. Something tells me that she will come through. Doctor Bridges feels very hopeful."

"He would naturally—but maimed for life——" his voice trembled.

"We must try not to think of that. If only she comes through it well." Then after a moment's thought, she added cheerfully, "It isn't as if she were a younger woman and still hoped to have children. She is forty-two, and has been married almost twenty years. One would never suspect that to look at her."

After she finished, he lingered a moment, hoping and fearing that she might, if only by accident, become more explicit. Was she shielding Eva's modesty from him, an old man, who would have loved her had she been stripped bare not only of modesty but of every cardinal virtue? Or was such evasion merely an incurable habit of mind? Would George tell him the truth? Or was it conceivable that George did not know?

"Will Jenny Blair come in time?" he asked, pricked by sudden fear. "I should not like to be late."

"Why, you've at least two hours, Father, and if Jenny Blair isn't back in time, I'll go with you myself."

"But I don't need anybody. I am able to go alone." No man needed protection less; but because he had lived a solitary male among women, he could never escape it, and because these women depended upon him, he had remained at their mercy. It was impossible to wound the feelings of women who owed him the bread they ate and the roof over their heads, and so long as he did not hurt their feelings, they would be stronger than he was. Always, from his earliest childhood, he mused, with a curious resentment against life, he had been the victim of pity. Of his own pity, not another's. Of that double-edged nerve of sympathy, like the aching nerve in a tooth, which throbbed alive at the sight of injustice or cruelty. One woman after another had enslaved his sympathy more than his passion, and never had she seemed to be the woman his passion demanded.

Well, it is over, he thought, and knew that it would never be over. Again this secret hostility swept through his nerves, surprising him by its vehemence. Was it possible that he was beginning to break in mind before the infirmities of the flesh had attacked a single physical organ? Only yesterday, Bridges had told him that a man of sixty might be proud of his arteries. Only yesterday! And to-day he was annoyed by this queer tingling in his limbs, by this hollow drumming which advanced along his nerves and then receded into the distance. "Let us sit down a bit, William," he murmured, walking very erect, with a proper pride in his straight back and thighs and his well-set-up figure for a man of his years. "I suppose this bad news about Eva has disturbed me. I'd rather lose my right arm than have anything happen to her."

Dropping down on a green bench in the park, beneath a dis-

figured tulip tree, which was putting out into bud, he tried to
imagine her ill, suffering, and waiting calmly for that dreaded
hour under the knife. But no, she chose, as always capriciously,
her own hour and mood in which to return to him. Never had
he seen her cast aside her armour of gaiety. Never, among all
the women he had known, had she asked him for sympathy.
Never once had she tried to take care of him. For all her loveliness, she was, he found himself thinking aloud to William, curled
up on the grass by the bench, a strong soul in affliction. A strong
soul, still undefeated by life, she came to him now. She came
to him out of the pale green distance, out of the flying clouds,
out of the April bloom of the sky. Even to-day, he mused
proudly, there wasn't a girl in Queenborough who was worthy
to step into her shoes. Not one of them. Not Jenny Blair, a
vivid little thing, but lacking in queenliness.

Resting there, with his tired old hands clasped on the crook
of his stick, he told himself that Eva Birdsong in her prime,
before misfortune had sapped her ardent vitality, would have
put to shame all the professional beauties of Paris or London.
Why, he had seen Mrs. Langtry, and had considered her deficient in presence. "Eva would have had all London at her
feet," he meditated, without jealousy, since his devotion, at
eighty-three, was of the mind alone. Or was this deception? Did
one go down into the grave with the senses still alive in the
sterile flesh? Well, no matter. The thread had snapped, and the
question had floated out of his thoughts. Airy and fragile as
mist, he watched it blown away into the April world, into that
windy vastness which contained the end of all loving and all
living.

At least she had had, he pondered, sitting beside a triangular
flower-bed, beneath the pale buds on the tulip tree, what she
believed that she wanted. True, her life might have been easier
if they hadn't been poor. Yet being poor, which kept her from
parties where she once shone so brilliantly, had saved her also
from brooding, from that fatal introspection which is the curse
of women and poets. She had not had time to fall out of love.

She had not had time to discover that George was unworthy.

Or was it conceivable, as Cora suspected, that Eva knew the truth, and was merely preserving appearances? No, he could not believe this, he mused, poking the end of his stick into a tuft of young dandelions. Yet, while he rejected Cora's suspicion, he admitted that life would be more agreeable if women could realize that man is not a monogamous animal, and that even a man in love does not necessarily wish to love all the time. Certainly, there would be less unhappiness abroad in the world if good women could either accept or reject the moral nature of man. Over and over, he had seen the faithful lover lose to the rake in an affair of the heart. Over and over, he had seen a miracle of love that failed to make a conversion. Yet he knew, having much experience to build on, that even loose-living men are not all of one quality. It was not a simple question of merit. The diversity went deeper, far down through the nature of man into nature itself. George had lived according to life; his very faults were the too lavish defects of generosity. He was generous with himself always, and with his money whenever he was affluent. Not without a pang, the General remembered that long ago, when he was caught on the verge of financial ruin, George alone among his sympathetic friends had offered him help. The year before George had inherited his father's modest estate, and he would have sacrificed this fortune to save a friend from disaster. Later on, to be sure, he had speculated unwisely and lost his inheritance—but it was not of this that the General was thinking while he poked at the dandelions.

He saw George, with his thick wind-blown hair, his smiling eyes, his look of virile hardness, of inexhaustible energy. Well-favoured enough if you judged by appearances, and did women, or men either for that matter, ever judge by anything else? But it was more than George's fine features, ruddy skin, and friendly grey eyes that made one reluctant to blame him. Yes, there was something more, some full-bodied virtue, some compensating humanity. "But I am human too," thought old General Archbald, "and what good has it done me?" . . .

As a child, at Stillwater, they had called him a milksop, because he saw visions in the night and wanted to be a poet. The sight of blood sickened him; yet his grandfather assured him, with truth, that hunting had given greater pleasure to a greater number of human beings than all the poetry since Homer. Pity, said the men who had none, is a woman's virtue; but he had known better than this. A poet's virtue, it may be. He was not sure. So much virtue passed into a poet when he was dead; when his immortal part was bound in English calf and put into a library. Little girls, however, were not pitiful. Little girls were as savage as boys, only weaker. They had never failed to torment him. They had laughed when he was made sick; they had mocked at his visions; they had stolen his poems and used them for curl-papers. Strange, the images that were dragged up like bits of shell, in a net of the memory! All his life curl-papers had remained, for him, the untidy symbol of an aversion. No, little girls were not gentle. And even his tender-hearted mother, who nursed her servants in illness, and had never used the word "slave" except in the historical sense—even his mother was incapable of the pity that becomes a torment to the nerves. She accepted meekly, as an act of God's inscrutable wisdom, all the ancient wrongs and savage punishments of civilization. . . .

Again General Archbald sighed and prodded the dandelions. Again the thread snapped and a flock of unrelated images darted into his mind. . . .

"Where did the boy get his tomfool ideas?" his robust grandfather inquired sternly. "Was he born lacking?"

"Not lacking, Father," his mother protested, "but different. Some very nice people," she added, with an encouraging glance at her peculiar child, "are born different. He may even turn out to be a poet."

"Do you think," his father asked in a troubled tone, "that we had better try changing his tutor? Is it possible that Mr. Davis has infected him with newfangled ideas?"

His mother shook her head in perplexity, for it distressed her that one of her sons should be deficient in manliness. "But the other boys are all manly. Even if Mr. Davis has talked of abolition, after giving us his word that he would treat the—the institution with respect, I have never heard that New Englanders disliked bloodshed. I thought, indeed, it was exactly the opposite. Don't you remember I opposed your engaging Mr. Davis because I had always heard the Puritans were a hard and cruel people? Perhaps," she confessed bravely, "he may inherit his eccentric notions from me. Though I try to be broad-minded, I can't help having a sentiment against cock-fights."

"Pooh! Pooh!" his grandfather blustered, for he belonged to the Georgian school of a gentleman. "Would you deprive the lower classes of their favourite sport? As for this young nincompoop, I'll take him deer-hunting to-morrow. If he is too much of a mollycoddle to kill his buck, we'll try to scare up a fawn for him."

A famous hunter in his prime, the old gentleman still pursued with hounds any animal that was able to flee. Fortunately, game was plentiful and game laws unknown in the fields and forests of Stillwater. For nothing escaped his knife or his gun, not the mole in the earth, not the lark in the air. He could no more look at a wild creature without lusting to kill than he could look at a pretty girl without lusting to kiss. Well, it was a pity he had not lived to enjoy the war; for the killing nerve, as his grandson had once said of him, was the only nerve in his body. Yet he had fallen in love with a woman because of her fragile appearance; and when she had gone into a decline after the birth of her fifth child, and had lost her reason for a number of years, he had remained still devoted to her. Against the advice of his family and his physician, he had refused to send her away, and had kept her, behind barred windows, in the west wing of the house. To be sure, when she died, he had married again within seven months; but only his first wife, though he had buried two others, had given him children, and through her the strain of melancholy had passed into the Archbald blood. . . .

From his father, with filial patience, "For my part, I try not to kill a doe or a fawn."

"Fiddlesticks, sir! You talk like an abolitionist. Didn't the Lord provide negroes for our servants and animals for our sport? Haven't you been told this from the pulpit? I hope, sir, I shan't live to see the day when every sort of sport is no longer welcome at Stillwater." Even the field hands in the quarters, General Archbald remembered, had their "coon or possum dawgs," and went rabbit chasing on holidays when there were no cockfights. High or low, good or bad, manners at Stillwater were a perpetual celebration of being alive. No other way of living had ever seemed to him so deeply rooted in the spirit of place, in an established feeling for life. Not for happiness alone, not for life at its best only, but for the whole fresh or salty range of experience. There was, too, a quality, apart from physical zest, that he had found nowhere else in the world, a mellow flavour he had never forgotten.

Naturally, as a child, he did not hunt or shoot with his grandfather; but several weeks later, on a brilliant November morning, he watched a buck at bay pulled down by the hounds in a rocky stream. He could not remember how it had happened. By accident, probably, when he was out with his tutor. At first, watching the death, he had felt nothing. Then, in a spasm, the retch of physical nausea. For the eyes of the hunted had looked into his at the end; and that look was to return to him again and again, as a childish fear of the dark returns to the grown man when his nerves are unstrung. In how many faces of men, women, children, and animals, all over the world, had he seen that look of the hunted reflected? A look of bewilderment, of doubt, of agony, of wondering despair; but most of all a look that is seeking some God who might, but does not, show mercy. All over the world! North, South, East, West. On the heights, in the desert.

With blood on his hands and a savage joy inflaming his face, his grandfather strode over to smear stains on a milksop. "If you don't like the taste of blood better than milk, you'll have to be blooded. Hold still, sir, I say, and be blooded." Then, as the blood touched him, the boy retched with sickness, and vomited over the anointing hand and the outstretched arm. "Damn you, sir!" the old gentleman bellowed, while he wiped away the mess with his silk handkerchief. "Go back to the nursery where you belong!"

Still retching, furious and humiliated because he had been born a milksop, the boy rode home with his tutor. "I don't love people!" he sobbed passionately. "I don't love people!" Was it fair to blame him because he had been born different? Was anybody to blame for the way God had let him be born? . . .

How close that day seemed to him now, that day and others at Stillwater. The more distant a scene, the clearer it appeared in his vision. Things near at hand he could barely remember. Even yesterday was smothered in fog. But when he looked far back in the past, at the end of seventy years or more, the fog lifted, and persons and objects started out in the sunken glow on the horizon. Instead of diminishing with time, events in the deep past grew larger, and the faces of persons long dead became more vivid and lifelike than life itself. "It is old age," he thought wearily. "It is a sign of old age to lack proper control." Or was the cause deeper still? he mused, while the shadow of a bird flitted over the grass and was gone. Was this second self of his mind, as variable as wind, as nebulous as mist, merely the forgotten consciousness of the poet who might have been? Sitting here in the spring sunshine, was he living again, was he thinking again, with that long buried part of his nature? For his very words, he realized, were the words of that second self, of the self he had always been in dreams and never been in reality. Again the bird flitted by. He did not know. He could not tell. No matter how hard he tried, it was impossible to keep his thoughts from rambling back into the past. It was impossible to trace a connection between the past and present. Was he growing, in his old age, like poor Rodney, who had surrendered to shadows? Better let the past disappear, and hold firmly to the bare structure of living.

For an instant his look wandered from the trees in the park to the few carriages and many motor cars in Washington Street.

Yes, the world was changing rapidly, and he wondered what was waiting ahead. He could remember when Queenborough had the charm of a village; but now, wherever he looked, he found ugliness. Beauty, like every other variation from type, was treated more or less as a pathological symptom. Did Americans, especially Southerners, prefer ugliness? Did ugliness conform, he pondered fancifully, to some automatic æsthetic spring in the dynamo? But even if the scientific method destroyed beauty, there would be no more great wars, only little wars that no one remembered, said John Welch. What, indeed, would be left to fight about when people thought alike everywhere, and exact knowledge had spread in a vast cemetery for ideals all over the world?

So John Welch, being very advanced in opinion, would argue for hours; but when argument was ended, old General Archbald could not see that human nature was different from what it had been in his youth. To be sure, idealism, like patriotism, appeared to diminish with every material peace between conflicts; but he was near enough to the Spanish War, and indeed to the Civil War, to realize that the last battle has never been fought and the last empty word has never been spoken. Not that it mattered. All he knew now was that he was too old to bother about life. He was too old to bother about cruelty, which he had seen all over the world, in every system invented by man; which he had seen in a velvet mask, in rags, and naked except for its own skin. Yes, he was too old to suffer over the evils that could not be cured. Only, whenever he listened to John Welch assailing the present order, he was reminded of his own revolt against slavery in the eighteen fifties. The reformers of that age had believed that all the world needed was to have negro slavery abolished. Yet negro slavery was gone, and where it had been, John said, another system had ushered in the old evils with a clean, or at least a freshly wiped face. What the world needed now, cried the modern reformers, like John Welch, was the new realism of science. For one confirmed habit had not changed with the ages.

Mankind was still calling human nature a system and trying vainly to put something else in its place.

But a world made, or even made over, by science was only a stark and colourless spectacle to old David Archbald. A thin-lipped world of facts without faith, of bones without flesh. Better the red waistcoats and the soulful vapouring of early Romanticism. Better even the excessive sensibility of mid-Victorian æsthetics. Since he belonged to the past, if he belonged anywhere, his mental processes, it seemed, were obliged to be disorderly. When he said, "I am more than myself," when he said, "Life is more than living," when he blundered about "the nature of reality," he was still, or so John Welch declared, harping on a discredited idealism. "Transcendental!" John would snap when he meant "Nonsense!"

Glancing from the street to the sky, while the thread broke again, General Archbald reflected that it was easy to be an idealist in this pleasant spring of the year 1914, and to look with hope, if not with confidence, to the future. It was true that the familiar signs of uneasiness were abroad in the world. There was trouble not only in China and Mexico, where one naturally expected trouble to be, but among a part at least of the population of Europe. Power everywhere was growing more arrogant, and unrest more unrestful. Socialism was springing up and taking root in soil that appeared sterile. In Great Britain, Ulster and the suffragettes were disturbing a peace that turned in its broken sleep and dreamed of civil war. Nearer home, pirates had deserted the seas and embarked afresh as captains of industry.

But in the realm of ideas, where hope reigned, the prospect was brighter. There the crust of civilization, so thin and brittle over the world outside, was beginning to thicken. Religion and science, those hoary antagonists, were reconciled and clasped in a fraternal embrace. Together, in spite of nationalism, in spite even of nature, they would build, or invent, the New Jerusalem for mankind. In that favoured province, smooth, smiling, well-travelled, there would be neither sin nor disease, and without wars all the ancient wrongs would be righted. Nobody, not even the old sunning themselves on green benches, would be allowed to ramble in mind.

Well, perhaps. . . . No harm could come, he supposed, of a sanguine outlook. Only—only, did not that outlook approach a little too close to a formula? Were material ends all the world needed to build on? Was passion, even in the old, a simple problem of lowering your blood pressure and abandoning salt? Could a man discard his thinking self as lightly as he discarded the doctrine of an ultimate truth? When John said, "A green bench is only a green bench," was he wiser than old David Archbald, who replied, "A green bench is not the green bench I touch"? True, men no longer wrangled in public halls over the nature of reality. But he could not see that exact knowledge and precision of language had improved the quality of mankind. Well, the wonder in every age, he supposed, was not that most men were savage, but that a few men were civilized. Only a few in every age, and these few were the clowns in the parade. . . .

Suddenly, while he meditated, it seemed to him that the shape of the external world, this world of brick and asphalt, of men and women and machines moving, broke apart and dissolved from blown dust into thought. Until this moment he had remembered with the skin of his mind, not with the arteries; but now, when the concrete world disappeared, he plunged downward through a dim vista of time, where scattered scenes from the past flickered and died and flickered again. At eighty-three, the past was always like this. Never the whole of it. Fragments, and then more fragments. No single part, not even an episode, complete as it had happened.

In each hour, when he had lived it, life had seemed important to him; but now he saw that it was composed of things that were all little things in themselves, of mere fractions of time, of activities so insignificant that they had passed away with the moment in which they had quivered and vanished. How could any one, he asked, resting there alone at the end, find a meaning, a pattern? Yet, though his mind rambled now, he had walked in beaten tracks in his maturity. His soul, it is true, had been a rebel; but he had given lip-homage, like other men all over the world, to creeds that were husks. Like other men all over the world, he had sacrificed to gods as fragile as the bloom of light on the tulip tree. And what was time itself but the bloom, the sheath enfolding experience? Within time, and within time alone, there was life—the gleam, the quiver, the heart-beat, the immeasurable joy and anguish of being. . . .

The trail plunged straight and deep into the November forest. There was the tang of woodsmoke far off in a clearing. Frost was spun over the ground. The trees were brilliant with the yellow of hickory, the scarlet of sweet gum, the wine-red of oaks.

Why was he here? How had he come? Was he awake or asleep? Ah, he knew the place now. A forest trail at Stillwater. But they had left Stillwater fifty years ago. Well, no matter. No matter that he was a boy and an old man together, or that the boy wanted to be a poet. It was all the same life. A solitary fragment, but the same fragment of time. Time was stranger than memory. Stranger than his roaming again through this old forest, with his snack and a thin volume of Byron tucked away in his pocket. Here was the place he had stopped to eat his snack, while his pointer puppies, Pat and Tom, started game in the underbrush.

Then, as he stood with his head up and his eyes on the westering sun through the trees, he knew that he was watched. He knew that there were eyes somewhere among the leaves, and that these eyes, the eyes of the hunted, were watching him. It was the look in the eyes of the dying buck, but now it was everywhere. In the trees, in the sky, in the leaf-strewn pool, in the underbrush, in the very rocks by the trail. All these things reflected and magnified to his quivering nerves the look of the hunted. Because of the fear in his nerves, he cried out, expecting no answer. But before his call ended, there was a stir in the woods; the leaves scattered; and through the thick branches, he met the eyes of a runaway slave. Ragged, starved, shuddering, a slave crouched on the forest mould, and stared at the bread and meat in the boy's hand. When the food was given to him, he gulped it down and sat watching. Haggard with terror and pain, a dirty rag wrapping his swollen jaw, his clothes as tattered as the shirt of a scarecrow, he had been driven by hunger and cold up from the swamps. His breath came with a wheezing sound, and his flesh shed the sour smell of a wild animal. (A sour smell and a filthy rag after nearly seventy years!)

For weeks—for months, even, he may have lain hidden; but the deep swamps were far away, and he was the first fugitive slave to come within the boundaries of Stillwater. Beyond speech, beyond prayer, nothing remained in his eyes but bewilderment. "Nobody will hurt you," the boy said, emptying his pockets of the cornbread he had brought for the puppies. "Nobody will hurt you," he repeated, as if the creature were deaf or inarticulate. While he gave the promise, a wave of courage, of daring, of high adventure, rushed over him. For the second time in his young life he was defying the established order, he was in conflict with the moral notions of men. Is it true, he asked himself now, that man's pity and man's morality are for ever in conflict? Is it true that pity is by nature an outlaw? Well, he liked to think that he had not hesitated; no, not for an instant.

Again that day he had returned to the hidden place in the forest. He had brought clothes taken from the old garments in his father's and his grandfather's closets, food that he had found put away in the pantry, and a little wine that had been left over in the glasses at lunch. From his own bed he had stolen a blanket, and from his grandfather's "body servant" he had borrowed, as if in jest, the "ticket" that permitted Abram Jonas to visit his wife in another county. "When it is over, they will have to know," the boy thought, as he trudged back into the forest with the help he had come to fetch. "When it is over."

And then what had happened? His memory faded, died down to ashes, and shot up more brightly. Two mornings later, he had set out in an old buggy, with a decently clothed servant on the seat at his side. Miles away, screened from the turnpike, he had put a knapsack of food and the money he was saving to buy a colt into the hands of the runaway. "Your name is Abram Jonas. This is a paper that says so. You belong to Gideon Archbald, and you are going to visit your wife in Spottsylvania. Do you remember that? What is your name? Say it once more." "Abram Jonas, marster." "You'd better repeat it as you go along. I am Abram Jonas. Here is the paper that says so." "I'se Abram Jonas, marster. Dis heah is de paper." The fugitive looked up at him, first with the fear of the hunted, then with a dawning intelligence. "Thanky, marster," and turning, he had limped away from the turnpike into a forest trail. What had become of him? Had he escaped? Was he caught? Did he drop down like an animal and die of the shuddering misery of life?

After all these years General Archbald was still curious. But no word had come. Only silence. Only silence, and the feeling that he had taken his stand against the forces men about him called civilization. He had defied not only the moral notions of his age and his place, but the law and the Constitution and the highest court in the land. The truth came out at last when the real Abram Jonas asked for the return of his "ticket"; and, as a measure of discipline, David's father sent his youngest son abroad to be educated. He was sixteen then; and years afterwards, when he left Oxford, he had lived in Paris and London. Ironically, he had begun to think of himself as a stranger in his world and his age. Yet when the war came, he was drawn back to his own. He was drawn back to fight for old loyalties. After the war he had endured poverty and self-denial and, worst of all, darned clothes for a number of years. Then, while he was still burdened by defeat, he had compromised Erminia and proposed to her the next morning. Well, the past was woven of contradictions. For eighty-three years he had lived two lives, and between these two different lives, which corresponded only in time, he could trace no connection. What he had wanted, he had never had; what he had wished to do, he had never done. . . .

A fog clouded his mind, and he heard a voice like his own remark testily, "Rambling is a sign of age, but I can't keep hold of the present." He couldn't keep hold of yesterday, of last month, of last year, of the faces he knew best, of the features even of his wife, which had grown vague since her death. Now, at the end, all faces of women, even the faces of women he had slept with, looked alike to him. All faces of women, except, perhaps—he wasn't sure—the face of Eva Birdsong. "No, I can't remember," he repeated, while this suppressed irritation clotted his thoughts. "I'm too old to remember that anything, especially any woman, made a difference in life."

Then, softly, while he was thinking this, the fog in his mind dispersed, and the crowd of women's faces melted to air, and reassembled in a solitary face he had not forgotten. Fifty years— nearer sixty years now—since he had lost her. What was the use, he pondered resentfully, in dragging back that old memory, that old passion? Why couldn't the dead stay dead when one had put them away? Half a century of dust! Yet she came to him, unspoiled by time, out of the drifting haze of the present. Was it because he had loved her alone? Or did she shine there, lost, solitary, unforgotten, merely because she was farther away than the others? Not that it mattered. The cause was unimportant beside the vast significance of that remembrance.

But why, after all, had he loved her? Even when he had fallen in love with her that April in England, he could not point to a single perfection and say, "I love her because she is beautiful, or brilliant, or gifted." There was nothing unusual about her, his friends had remarked wonderingly. Dozens of women he knew in London were handsomer, or wittier, or more conspicuously good. Small, shy, pale, she was utterly lacking in the presence so much admired by English society in the eighteen fifties.

When he first met her, she was married to the wrong man, and was the mother of two delicate children. Had he fallen in love with a veiled emptiness, a shadow without substance? Yet her blue eyes, as soft as hyacinths, had promised joy that was infinite. Or had he loved her because he had seen in her face the old fear and bewilderment of the hunted? Had her memory endured because it was rooted not in desire but in pity? Happier loves, lighter women, he had forgotten. No matter what people say, he thought moodily, it takes more than going to bed with a woman to fix her face in one's mind. For this woman alone he had loved and lost without wholly possessing. Yet she was there when he turned back, clear, soft, vivid, with some secret in her look that thrilled, beckoned, and for ever eluded him. Her eyes were still eloquent with light; the promised joy was still infinite; the merest glimmer of a smile had outlasted the monuments of experience.

Yet like everything else in life, important or unimportant, his passion seemed, when it occurred, to come at the wrong moment. He had intended to leave London; his ticket to Paris was in his pocket; his bags were packed. Then a tooth had begun to ache—a tooth he had lost only last year—and he had decided to stay over a day or two and consult an English dentist who had once treated him for an abscess. Not an act of God, he told himself (unless a twinge of pain were an act of God), but a toothache had decided his destiny. Had the pain come a day later, just one sunrise and one sunset afterwards, he might have escaped. But falling as it did in that infinitesimal pin point of time, his fate had been imprisoned in a single luminous drop of experience.

Looking back, he had often wondered why there had been no suspicion of danger, no visible or invisible warning that he was approaching the crossroads. Even the voice of his old friend was not ruffled when she met him on his way to the dentist and asked him to dinner. Some one had dropped out at the last moment. Tony Bracken (he had not forgotten that it was Tony Bracken) had been summoned to the deathbed of his great-uncle, and since Tony was the heir, he was obliged, naturally, to go when he was summoned. So, in spite of an occasional twinge, young David had braced himself with whiskey, applied laudanum to his tooth, and set out on an adventure beside which all the other occasions of his life were as flat as balloons that are pricked.

Even then, if she had not stood alone in that particular spot, between a lamp and a window, he might never have noticed her. "I wonder who she is," he thought, observing her loneliness; and then, as she raised her lowered lashes and he met her gaze, "She looks frightened." Was he called or driven when he went straight to her through the crowded room? Was it pity or the compulsion of sex that awakened while he watched her hesitate, bite her lip with a nervous tremor, and try in vain to think of something to say? "What can have frightened her?" he thought, as his hand closed over hers. Her eyes held him, and he asked, "Are you alone?" She shook her head. "No, my husband is with me." Her husband! Well, most women had husbands, especially most women one met at dinner in London. It was too late after that first look to think of a husband. It was too late to think even of children. In the end her marriage had won, as dead sounds inevitably win over living voices; but while he stood there and looked into her upturned face, that sulky, well-set-up sportsman and his two vague children had no part in the moment. Nothing mattered to him but the swift, tumultuous, utterly blissful sense of recognition—of now, here, this is my hour. Not the indefinite perhaps, to-morrow, some day in the future. The world, so colourless an instant before, had become alive to the touch. People and objects, sights, sounds, scents even, were vibrating with light.

And now, after sixty years, he could see that moment as clearly and coldly as if it were embedded in crystal. What is memory, a voice asked on the surface of thought, that it should outlast emotion? For he remembered, but he could feel nothing. Nothing of the old rapture, the wildness, the illusion of love's immortality. He still mused with remorseful sympathy of Erminia, whom he had never loved, whose death had brought him release; but the burning ecstasy of desire had left only emptiness. Only emptiness, and the gradual chill of decay. Why had it happened? What was the meaning of it all? he demanded, caught within the twisting vision of age. Why had passion strong enough to ruin his life forsaken him while he lived? Why had it left only two diminished shapes, performing conventional gestures in a medium that was not time—that was not eternity? Did they still exist, those diminished shapes, in a timeless reality? Were they blown off from time into some transparent substance superior to duration? Did he survive there and here also? Which was the real David Archbald, the lover in memory, or the old man warming his inelastic arteries in the April sunshine? Or were they both merely spirals of cosmic dust, used and discarded in some experimental design? . . .

For an hour, a single hour, of her love he would have given his life when he was young. Her death had left a jagged rent in the universe. Yet if she returned to him now, he knew that it would mean only an effort—only the embarrassment that comes to persons who have loved and separated when they were young, and then meet again, unexpectedly, after they have grown old apart. Strangely enough, if any woman were to return from the dead, he preferred that she should be Erminia. Were the dead like that to the old? Were the intenser desires obliterated by the duller sensations? Joy, longing, disappointment, personalities that impinged upon one another, and then, separating, left only a faint outline of dust. Life was not worth the trouble, he thought. Life was not worth the pang of being, if only that faint outline remained. For the passion of his youth had ended as swiftly as it had begun, and at first he had not even suspected that the vehement craving was love. Helpless, bewildered, he had struggled blindly in the grasp of a power he could not resist and could not understand. All he knew was that her presence brought the world into beauty, that his whole being was a palpitating ache for her when she was absent. Inarticulate, passive, without the compelling ardour of sex, she had exercised that ruthless tyranny over desire. Or was it true, as he had sometimes imagined, that he himself was a rare, or perhaps a solitary, variation from sex? Were his deeper instincts awakened only by pity? As the generations went on, would there be others and still others of his breed born into an aging world? Was he more civilized than the average race of males, or simply more white-livered, as his virile grandfather believed? Well, he was too old, he repeated stubbornly, and life was too long over, to bother about what couldn't be helped. All he asked now was to sit in the April sunshine and wait for death with William beside him.

But was it really long over? What if it were true that some fragment of his lost ecstasy still survived there, burning with its own radiance, beyond that dim vista of time? What if it were true that such bliss, such agony, such unavailing passion, could never end? All that spring and a part of the summer they had met secretly and joyously; and their secret joy had overflowed into the visible world. The landscape in which they moved borrowed the intense, quivering brightness of a place seen beneath the first or the last sunbeams. Spring was as fair as it looks to a man about to be hanged. Never again were the fields so starry with flowers, the green so luminous on the trees, the blue of the April sky so unearthly.

Years afterwards (sometimes as a young man in a strange bed, or again in the long fidelity to a wife he had never desired) a flitting dream of that English spring would flood his heart with an extraordinary delight. For a moment, no longer, since he invariably awoke while the joy flickered and died. Always, except in dreams, the past had escaped him. The anguish alone had stayed by him in the beginning, closer than the flesh to his bones or the nerves to his brain. And even in sleep, his bliss, when it returned, was only the tremor of light before a dawn that never approached.

Would it have been different if she had lived? For she had not lived, and he could never know what his life might have been without that ugly twist in the centre. They had planned to go away together, he devoured by love and longing, she fearful, passive, yielding mutely to that implacable power. In July, they would go to Venice and begin life over in Italy. The tickets were bought; her few boxes were at the station; the compartment was reserved; and then the merest accident had detained them. In the middle of that last night, while she was destroying her letters, one of the children had awakened with a sore throat. The nurse had come for her; she had sat till dawn beside the crib in the nursery; and when morning came she had lost the courage for flight. Fear, the old fear of life, of the unknown, had triumphed over them both.

For an eternity, it seemed to him, he walked the station platform. The guard shut the doors fast; the train drew out slowly. Still he watched with an intolerable ache of desolation while the engine was sliding over the straight track to the gradual curve in the distance. Then, turning away, he wandered, distraught with misery, out into the street. Why? why? why? he demanded of a heaven that seemed as unstable as water. Overhead, low, flying clouds scudded like foam driven by wind. In the country, he walked for hours through rain vague as suspense, soft, fine, slow as mist falling. Afterwards, she wrote that the struggle was over; she could not give up her children—and in the early autumn he heard from a stranger that she had drowned herself in a lake. Lost, vanished, destroyed by the fear for which he had loved her in the beginning!

When he knew that she was dead, he went alone into the country, to the secret places where they had met and loved in the spring. In his memory, these places shone out suddenly, one after another, as scattered lights come out in a landscape at dusk. The woods, the fields, the stream where cowslips bloomed, the grey bench with its blurred marking, the flowers, the bright grass. Now it was spring, but in this flickering scene, he walked there in autumn. Everything returned to him; the falling leaves, the trail of autumn scents in the air, everything but the vital warmth in his agony. Yet he knew, while this light flashed out and moved on again, through the encompassing darkness, that the form, if not the essence, of his passion had lain hidden somewhere beneath the surface of life.

In his anguish, he had flung himself beyond time, beyond space, beyond the boundaries of ultimate pain. A panic stillness was in the air; the whole external world, the blue sky, the half-bared trees, the slow fall of the leaves, the grass sprinkled with bloom,—all this was as hollow as a bubble blown from a pipe. Nothing remained alive, nothing but his despair in a universe that was dead to the touch. Again and again, he had cried her name in this panic stillness. He had cried her name; but she was gone; she could never return. Not though he waited for ever in the place she had left, could she return to him. In the end, she had escaped the terror of life. She had escaped his love and his pity. She had escaped into hollowness. But while the light shone in that vacant place, every twig on the trees, every blade of grass stood out illuminated.

Then this also had passed, anguish, he discovered, was scarcely less brief than joy. The light went out and moved on again. Days, weeks, months, years passed, and a thick deposit of time hardened into a crust of despair over his wound. "I do not wish to forget," he said, and in forming the thought had already begun to forget and to recover. Yet, though he enjoyed life again, he never lost entirely the feeling that he was crippled in spirit, that there was a twisted root, an ugly scar, at the source of his being. The poet had died in him, and with the poet had died the old living torment of pity. When he sailed home to fight with his people, he found that the hunted buck, the driven slave, the killing of men in battle, left him more annoyed than distressed. Nothing, not even death, not even dying, seemed important; yet it was amazing to discover how much pleasure could come after one had ceased to expect happiness. Little things began to matter supremely. A smile, a kiss, a drink, a chance encounter in love or war. Appetite, he told himself, with gay cynicism, had taken the place of desire; and it was well that it should be so. There was much to be said in favour of living if only one were careful not to probe deeply, not to touch life on the nerve. If only one were careful, too, not to shatter the hardened crust of despair.

Even so, there were moments, there were hours when he was visited by the old sensation of something missing, as if he were part of a circle that was bent and distorted and broken in pieces. Life, as well as himself, seemed to be crippled, to have lost irrevocably a part of the whole. Still, in the solitude of the night, he would awake from his dream of a bliss that hovered near but never approached, and think, with a start of surprise, "If I awoke and found her beside me, would all the broken pieces come together again? Should I find that life was simple and right and natural and whole once more?" Then the dream, the surprise, the pang of expectancy, would fade and mingle and dissolve into emptiness. Like a man hopelessly ill who realizes that his malady is incurable, he would distract his mind with those blessed little things of life that bear thinking about. Well, he was used to it now, he would repeat again and again; he was used to the ache, the blankness, even to the stab of delight which pierced him in sleep. He had accepted the sense of something missing as a man accepts bodily disfigurement. After the first years of his loss, he was prepared, he felt, for all the malicious pranks grief can play on the memory. He was prepared even for those mocking resemblances that beckoned him in the street, for those arrowy glimpses of her in the faces of strange women, for that sudden wonder, poignant as a flame, "What if the past were a delusion! What if she were within reach of my arms!" No, it had been many years, thirty, almost forty years, since life had so mocked him.

He had fought through the war. Strange, how insignificant, how futile, any war appeared to him now! He could never, not even when he took an active part in one, understand the fascination war exercised over the human mind. Then, when it was over, he had let life have its way with him. Though the poet in him was lost, he became in later years a prosperous attorney, and a member in good standing, so long as one did not inquire too closely, of the Episcopal Church. . . .

Sitting there in the pale sunshine, so carefully brushed and dressed by his man Robert, he told himself that, in spite of the ugly twist in the centre, he had had a fair life. Nothing that he wanted, but everything that was good for him. Few men at eighty-three were able to look back upon so firm and rich a past, upon so smooth and variegated a surface. A surface! Yes, that, he realized now, was the flaw in the structure. Except for that one defeated passion in his youth, he had lived entirely upon the shifting surface of facts. He had been a good citizen, a successful lawyer, a faithful husband, an indulgent father; he had been, indeed, everything but himself. Always he had fallen into the right pattern; but the centre of the pattern was missing. Once again, the old heartbreaking question returned. Why and what is human personality? An immortal essence? A light that is never blown out? Or a breath, a murmur, the rhythm of molecular changes, scarcely more than the roving whisper of wind in the tree-tops?

A multitude of women people the earth: fair women, dark women; tall women, short women; kind women, cruel women; warm women, cold women; tender women, sullen women—a multitude of women, and only one among them all had been able to appease the deep unrest in his nature. Only one unit of being, one cluster of living cells, one vital ray from the sun's warmth, only one ripple in the endless cycle of time or eternity, could restore the splintered roots of his life, could bring back to him the sense of fulfilment, completeness, perfection. A single personality out of the immense profusion, the infinite numbers! A reality that eluded analysis! And yet he had been happy as men use the word happiness. Rarely, since his youth, had he remembered that something was missing, that he had lost irrevocably a part from the whole, lost that sense of fulfilment not only in himself but in what men call Divine goodness. Irrevocably—but suppose, after all, the loss were not irrevocable!

Suddenly, without warning, a wave of joy rose from the unconscious depths. Suppose that somewhere beyond, in some central radiance of being, he should find again that ecstasy he had lost without ever possessing. For one heart-beat, while the wave broke and the dazzling spray flooded his thoughts, he told himself that he was immortal, that here on this green bench in the sun, he had found the confirmation of love, faith, truth, right, Divine goodness. Then, as swiftly as it had broken, the wave of joy spent itself. The glow, the surprise, the startled wonder, faded into the apathetic weariness of the end. He was only an old man warming his withered flesh in the April sunshine. "My life is nearly over," he thought, "but who knows what life is in the end?"

A cloud passed overhead; the changeable blue of the sky darkened and paled; a sudden wind rocked the buds on the tulip tree; and in the street, where life hurried by, a pillar of dust wavered into the air, held together an instant, and then sank down and whirled in broken eddies over the pavement.

PART THREE

THE ILLUSION

ENNY BLAIR was coming to him through sunlight netted with shadows. With an effort, General Archbald detached himself from the past, from the twisted fibres of buried hopes and fears and disappointments. For an instant, as he reached the surface of living, it seemed to him that he was suffocated by the thicker air of the actuality. Then, collecting his thoughts, he rose unsteadily and leaned on his stick. "An old mind is a wandering mind," he said aloud to William, who rose also and stood at attention. "The important thing is to hold the thread, to keep the connection." After that dim vista, the light of the present dazzled his eyes, and he blinked as he watched his grand-daughter come to him along the gravelled walk between plots of grass sprinkled with buttercups.

He saw her first as a small bright shape in living blue. Then, while she came nearer, he asked himself where was the fascination of youth, and why age had surrendered so completely to its arrogant power. Jenny Blair was lovely, as most budding things are lovely to old eyes; but she would never have been called a beauty, he told himself, by King Edward VII. Nor, indeed, by Prince Albert, who also admired queenliness. She lacked height; she lacked repose; she was entirely wanting in presence. Yet she walked well (happily the sheath skirt, so cramping to Isabella's voluptuous style, had gone out), and she was a pretty little thing in her way, fresh, sparkling, dewy with innocence. Women were wearing wide collars of white lawn, and her small ivory throat arched delicately from the sheer fabric. There was a wreath of cornflowers on her hat, and under the dipping brim of black straw her hair shone with the pale lustre of honey. A shallow face, vague and heart-shaped in contour, but with flashes of pure loveliness. Beneath the golden curve of her eyebrows, her yellow-hazel eyes, set wide apart, held the startled and expectant gaze of a child. More than any trait in her character or disposition, he recognized this look, curious, watchful, amazed, as an inheritance from his own youth. Nothing else in her features or expression belonged to his past. Even her colouring, with its honey-softness and transparent rose, had come from her mother's family (all the Wellfleets except Cora had that pale golden hair), and bore no kinship to the rich dusk of the Archbalds. But this startled wonder in her eyes, as if some winged thought were crying, "Let me out! Let me out!" never failed to appeal to his tenderness. That captive impulse, he assured himself, was not inherited from her mother.

"Have you waited long, Grandfather? I am so sorry." Through the web of sun and shadow, she flitted in her long blue dress over the tender grass in the park. Her face was flushed with the bloom of spring; her eyes were shining with sunlight; her moist red lips, which had a sullen droop when she frowned, were parted in a smile of contrition.

He drew out his watch. "No, it is early yet. You came just at the right moment. I must have been dozing."

Looking down on her, he felt suddenly bowed, he felt flattened out beneath the pressure of age. Before she came he had been tranquil, detached, confirmed in disappointment; but now he was aware, with an aching regret, of his withered flesh, of his brittle bones, of his corded throat, of the pouched skin and bluish hollows under his eyes, of the furrows between his jutting eyebrows, and the congested veins in his nose. "I am too old," he thought, "but an hour ago, on that green bench, I was young. I was beyond time, and I was young. Is this impression more real than that one? Is the fact more living than the idea?" Then holding tight to his stout ebony walking-stick, he threw up his head with the bridling movement of an old race horse. The chief thing was to govern one's faculties, to keep control of one's thoughts. At eighty-three, it did no good to have a buried poet pop up from the depths and caper gallantly on the frozen surface of pretense. After all, nothing mattered very much, not even the rambling mind of the old. In another decade he would know more, or perhaps less, of the nature of reality.

"Hadn't you better take my arm, Grandfather?"

"No, thank you, my dear. I'm still able to walk alone."

"Of course you are. But the pavement is so rough. Anybody may stumble on this pavement," Jenny Blair added in the tactful tone of her mother.

"Well, it's true my legs aren't what they used to be. If you could give me a new pair of legs, I'd be as sound as I ever was."

Yes, she was a dear little thing. Even her wildness, which he deplored, was the natural craving of youth for delight. In a few years she would probably fold her wings and settle down as her mother had done before her. Next winter, when she was eighteen, she would be presented to established society in Queenborough; and Mrs. Archbald had already decided that, after a reception in the afternoon to mature ladies of consequence, a fancy ball, which provided unlimited opportunities for dressing up, would be more amusing than the conventional coming-out party.

But, with that ancient perversity which is called modern by the elderly in every generation, Jenny Blair rejected both Queenborough society and the fancy ball. Instead of conforming to habit, she declared vaguely but passionately that she wished to go away to New York, or even to Paris, and be something different. A great many girls, she insisted, were being something different even in Queenborough, and she had determined to share in their efforts. She was not quite sure what she wished to be; but she was inclined to think that she might become an actress. Bena Peyton, who was trying to write for magazines, would go with her, and they could perfectly well take a little apartment and live comfortably, with one coloured maid, on the money their mothers saved from presentations to Queenborough society. Naturally, Mrs. Archbald, who had hoped for a second blooming from her daughter's formal introduction to parents and aunts and cousins of boys and girls she had played with all her life, was annoyed and displeased; but her father-in-law showed an astonishing sympathy with the revolt of youth. True, his prejudices were on the side of society; but he had been always, he was fond of saying, "a believer in not doing the things one did not wish to do."

Walking now by Jenny Blair's side, he remembered the time when he, too, had longed to go away and be different. But much experience, and especially long waiting, had taught him that there is no place in the world where one can be different from one's self. Places, like persons, he observed to William, who had paused to examine the smells about the roots of a tree, vary chiefly in the matter of climate. Warm or cool, an altitude or a plain; but no spot on earth contains the natural resources of happiness. Take Washington Street, for example. In Washington Street, where elegance had once flourished and fallen, only the disfigured elms still struggled to preserve the delusion of grandeur.

But it was useless to regret. It was useless to sigh for the plumed hearse of one's ancestors. And even the old families that were driven away by a taint in the wind were sufficiently near to rally on occasions of sorrow or threatened disgrace. Tides of soberly dressed persons still ebbed and flowed wherever white flowers and purple ribbon muffled a door-bell; and less than a decade ago the entire connection of Goddards, supported by the friends of the family, had contrived to outflank suspicion in the famous murder of Breverton Goddard. Everybody, even his relatives, believed that the nephew (General Archbald couldn't think of his name now) had shot Breverton in a quarrel over the uncle's wife, who was thirty years or more too young for her husband. Gossip had buzzed on as loud as a deafened ear; but the Goddards, who were connected with all the best people in Queenborough, had united in the heroic pretense that plain murder was pure accident. By force of superior importance, they had ignored facts, defended family honour, shielded a murderer for the sake of saving a name, turned public execration into sympathy, and politely but firmly looked the law out of countenance.

Less than a decade ago; yet could any family connection, the old man asked himself, win so complete a conquest to-day? Or, indeed, any conquest at all? People, even the best people, were more selfish now, and fought only when their material interests were menaced. Though the present was softer than the past, he couldn't see that it was an improvement—except in the way one could turn on a bath or a light, or warm one's self through and through instead of merely toasting one's front or back by a fire. Certainly, it seemed to him, the young were more insolent and the old more exacting. Wildness there had been always, and would be always, he supposed, only the vague wildness of Jenny Blair lacked, he felt, both dignity and direction. To be sure, as Jenny Blair was too apt to retort, we were living in the twentieth century, and ideas were modern. Modern, yes, but there had been modern ideas in every age, not excepting the long ages that were probably arboreal.

"Grandfather," Jenny Blair said in a low voice, "I met Mr. Birdsong, and he looked so dreadfully tired. He hasn't had any sleep for three nights. Is that because Mrs. Birdsong is in danger?"

The General sighed. "Yes, she is in danger, my child, but we must hope for the best."

"Don't you believe she will get well?"

"I hope so, my dear."

"Wasn't she the most beautiful woman in Virginia, Grandfather?"

"She is, my child, the most beautiful woman in Virginia—or anywhere else."

Jenny Blair sighed. "It must be lovely to be so beautiful."

"You, my dear, are pretty enough."

"Is anybody, I wonder, ever pretty enough?"

"For me, you are. I shouldn't sigh if I were you. Great beauty is not always a blessing. Sometimes it seems only to invite tragic circumstances."

"I wonder?" Jenny Blair repeated softly, raising her wistful glance to the sky.

While he slackened his pace and leaned a bit more heavily on his walking-stick, he asked himself if she would hold her own after the freshness of youth had passed, as well as her mother, who had much character but little temperament, had been able to do. Her complexion was lovely now, with its faint rose and honey-pallor, but that flowerlike skin of the Wellfleets was disposed, he knew, to wither early. Would her soft flaxen hair fade and darken to a dingy fawn-colour? Who knows, he thought, flinching from a thread of pain in his hip. Who knows anything? The present was hers; the past and the future belong only to life. "Now, she is the freshest thing in the world," he thought, "and there are men who find freshness more intoxicating than beauty."

"She was very much in love, wasn't she, Grandfather?" Jenny Blair asked after a long silence in which her dewy mouth drooped and grew sad.

"She *is* very much in love, Jenny Blair." Why, he wondered, did the child persist in using the wrong tense? For no one, not even Jenny Blair, with her childish perversity and her moist geranium mouth, seemed to him so indestructible in charm as Eva Birdsong. Youthful, too, not in appearance alone, though she was, in his eyes, as clear and brilliant as she had ever been, but in mind, in heart, in some effervescent fountain of life. Yet Jenny Blair, he suspected, and the suspicion pricked like a thorn, was already assuming the faintly arrogant manner, the air of secret wisdom, with which inexperience surveys the mistakes of experience.

Glancing down on the wreath of cornflowers and the sheer crown of Jenny Blair's hat, he told himself, in exasperation, that he really knew nothing about her. Nothing. Only that she was young and pretty (people had not thought highly of mere prettiness a generation ago) and sufficiently attractive, no doubt, to hold her own in a Queenborough that had forgotten the famous beauties of the nineteenth century. But these qualities or defects were on the surface, and he knew as little of her inner life as a man could know of a granddaughter who had grown up in his house. True, he loved her devotedly, more devotedly than he loved Isabella or Etta, though not so deeply as he had loved his only son, Jenny Blair's father. Yet his preference for her may have sprung only from the sentimental appeal which made him, and all other civilized men, tender to the small, the young, the helpless, the immature. Was this fondness akin to his aging solicitude for babies too young to walk and birds just out of the nest?

No, there was, he felt, a stronger bond than mere sentimentality. For he realized that the difference which separated him from his daughters was an actual diversity. Ages were scarcely involved in it, nor were alterations in manners. In many ways, indeed, he felt himself more advanced than a modern. But both Etta and Isabella appeared to him to be little deeper than air-plants by nature; they lived so entirely in feeling that they were devoid of conviction, and their inconsequential beliefs were as variable as moods. "They always want; they never think," he reflected.

Though Jenny Blair wanted, too, she wanted, he mused sadly, not with her emotions alone, but with what passed for her mind also. She craved more than satisfied desire, for she craved the freedom to seek. If he searched far enough into his past, he might find some blighted intimation of his granddaughter's perversity. Something within himself, some impulse of wildness, had always longed, he realized, to be free, to be selfish, to live its own life untrammelled by consideration for others. But even this much, he told himself, was conjecture. He knew as little of Jenny Blair's hidden self as he knew of the intimate nature of the universe.

His gaze roved from the girl at his side to the long straight street, where drab asphalt was replacing the fine old red of the brick pavement. Neutral, he thought indignantly. That was the way modern life compared to the variegated hues of the past, as neutral as asphalt. Here and there a dignified Georgian house retreated, like an aristocrat of architecture, from inferior associates. It was pathetic, he told himself, to see Washington Street sink down to the level of boarding-houses and shops, as the relict of a Confederate general might fall into honourable but neglected adversity. A black-and-white cat strolled across the pavement in front of William, looked round in angry astonishment, and sprang, spitting, to the top of a fence—the sort of cat that mouses along the steep decline of gentility. A woman in a motor coat and one of the small motor hats all old men dislike came out of a gate and bowed to him as she crossed the pavement to her touring car. A poor exchange, he thought, for the graceful victoria in which every beauty of the eighteen nineties had discreetly flaunted her charms.

Through the buzz and purr of approaching motor cars, he heard the lifted notes of Jenny Blair's voice, as clear as a flute and as deficient in suavity. Even the sounds of the present, and certainly the smells, were less romantic than they used to be.

"What did you say, my dear? I wonder how we live in the midst of this noise and dust. It's positively stifling. Now that summer is coming, we'll probably have that stale odour back again."

"You can smell it sometimes in winter, Grandfather, if the windows are open. Aunt Etta says it makes her hay fever worse."

"No doubt, no doubt, poor child. But what were you saying?"

The buzz and purr had subsided, but Jenny Blair's voice was still high and fluting. Talking against noise. So much of modern life was merely talking against noise. "I was only wondering about Mrs. Birdsong. If she was so beautiful, with that lovely voice, how could she be content to live all her life in a small place like Queenborough?"

"She fell in love, my dear. You will understand when you're older."

"But why did she fall in love? I don't see why she fell in love, do you?"

"I'm not a fair judge. No man I've ever met seemed to me worth losing one's heart to, much less one's head also."

The girl's high tones dropped to a quiver of intensity, "I don't like fair men. I could never fall in love with any man who hasn't dark eyes."

"There are plenty of dark men in Queenborough. There are all sorts of heads here, too, including red ones. Have you ever looked at young Welch, by the way? He's a fine boy and will make a good doctor."

"I don't care. I wouldn't look at him. I have always," the girl added crisply, "despised the name John."

"Well, I'm afraid you're a fastidious young woman. But red heads are everywhere, and so are Johns. I've met them in the desert calling themselves Mohammed."

"I don't care," the girl repeated, pressing his hand. "I don't care about men. All I want to do is to live my own life."

She had spoken coyly, but she had spoken. While he listened to this familiar declaration of principles, General Archbald reminded himself that it was futile to expect originality in the ideas of youth. From his earliest years in the obscure thirties, he had heard the immature utter this exact wish in these exact words. Only one other motive appeared as inevitable as the desire of youth to live its own life, and this was the determined effort of age to nip that desire in the bud. Yet, since he was unpolemical by nature, he remarked gently, "It is not easy to lead one's own life, my child. Many have tried, and very few have succeeded. Circumstances have a habit of making impediments."

"If they're only circumstances, I don't mind so much. But I do wish people wouldn't try to interfere with me."

"What people? Surely you must know that your mother and I wish only the best for you."

"I know that, Grandfather. I love you and Mamma better than anything in the world, but I must live my own life."

"Don't forget that your mother has given up her life to you. She has had only you since your father died."

"Yes, I know she has been splendid. Only now she has forgotten how she felt when she was my age, before she had Father and me to fill her mind."

"If she has forgotten, I haven't, my dear. She wished, like every other inexperienced creature, male or female, man, animal, bird, or fish, to live her own life in her own way. Only circumstances, or nature, if you please, took a hand in the situation, and settled matters by making you and your father her life."

Jenny Blair listened respectfully until he had finished. Then she repeated all that she had said before he began, and continued with energy, "There is no use in Mamma's making me come out next winter in Queenborough. I want to go to New York and study to be an actress. That is the only thing in the world I want to do. You know yourself that you wouldn't like to give up your career and be a wallflower at dances. Especially if you didn't like boys and were not a girl who made the right sort of appeal."

"Nonsense!" the General exclaimed. "Stuff and nonsense! You'll make the right sort of appeal quick enough if you start going. But you cannot imagine, my dear little girl," he added, with a sense that he was reciting the part of a creed in which he had ceased to believe, "how many temptations there are in the world to-day." Well, that was the way parents had always talked, no matter what they believed; and though he had long ago discovered that temptation may wriggle like moths into the tightest family cupboards, he reminded himself that, in training the young idea, moral precept is less inflammable than historic example.

"But don't they get into the home too, Grandfather?" Jenny Blair asked in a tone of wistful sincerity which robbed the question of pertness.

"I suppose they do, my child. However, your mother will never consent to your going away and living alone."

"But so many girls are doing it now. It isn't as it used to be when Mamma was young. Things are different now. Nobody objected to Sally Burden's going to New York to study."

That was true on the surface. Conventions were less exacting, no doubt, than they used to be. But Sally Burden, he reflected, was plain, and there were three other Burden girls who were handsome—or at least handsome enough. Plain daughters had been a problem even in the ages of chivalry, and a very little talent had often covered a multitude of physical defects. His grand-daughter, however, was not plain. Though her unfinished appearance might not satisfy an Edwardian taste, she measured up, he felt, to the less elevated standards of our democracy. Many modern faces, he reminded himself the next instant, had this unfinished look, especially the faces of very young women, before years or experience refined the edges and deepened the plastic impressions. Modelled too hastily, he thought, so hastily that neither joy nor sorrow has had time to sink through the flesh into the spirit.

"Well, there's time enough to think it over," he heard himself saying. "Here is the hospital, and I suppose I'd better go up alone. Will you keep William out in the yard? No doubt you'll be able to find a bench somewhere." They had reached a long drab building, the exact colour, he thought whimsically, of convalescence, flanked by a sickly row of evergreens. Down the steps a young nurse was hurrying on eager though aching feet in white canvas shoes.

"There's a yard for patients to walk in. I'll wait for you there," the girl answered, slipping her fingers through William's collar as they entered the hospital. "If it's about her will," she added, "I'm afraid I'll have to wait a very long time. People are always so slow about wills."

"No, this has nothing to do with her will. But if you get tired waiting, you'd better go home without me."

"Oh, I'll wait, darling Grandfather. Only I hope those poor evergreens haven't anything catching."

Glancing down on her, a moment later, as he was borne upward, he thought wistfully, "How much in a man's feeling for women depends on whether they are coming toward him or going away? When a man is young, every woman seems to be moving in his direction. When he is old, he realizes that they are all moving away. That is why, I suppose, they appear, like everything else in life, to diminish with time."

CHAPTER 2

THROUGH the window he saw a mist of green and the dying flare of the sun.

The white iron bed had been rolled into the middle of the room, and Mrs. Birdsong raised herself on the pillows, as he entered, and held out her hands. Fragile hands they were, a little too thin, a little too worn. Strange how much sooner hands aged than faces, especially delicate hands that have been roughened by work. She was wearing, over her white nightgown, a wrapper of lace and blue silk the colour of her eyes when she smiled. Her hair had slipped from the ribbon that held it back from her shoulders, and a single loose curl hung over a bosom which was still queenly even when unconfined. As pure as alabaster, he thought, gazing down on her. Yes, it was true even now. There was no woman to compare with her in the formless immaturity of the rising generation.

"I have been waiting for you," she said eagerly. "Oh, I am so glad you have come."

For an instant, while he watched her, it seemed to him that the lost radiance of youth shone in her face. Never had she been more lovely, more flamelike, than she looked since suffering had burned its way through her flesh. Then, with her clinging hand in his grasp, he found himself wondering if this animation were really so natural as it appeared. Had they given her drugs? Or was it fever that glowed beneath her transparent skin? But his eyes were old eyes, not to be trusted. They still looked at life through the iridescent film of a more romantic age. The young laughed at him now, as the young always laugh at their elders. As he himself had laughed at the light morality and the ponderous etiquette of the eighteen fifties.

"I should have come at any hour, day or night, if I had known you wanted me." His voice quivered, and something within his breast fluttered and sank down like a tired bird. He could see now, as the glow left her face, all the faint lines traced by sorrow or anxiety about her eyes, and the deeper impression between her finely arched nose (the nose of a goddess, they had said in the 'nineties) and the rich curve of her mouth. Yes, she was yielding, however gallantly, to the slow deposit of time.

"I know you would," she answered, smiling again.

Suddenly it was borne in upon him that she smiled so brightly because it was easier to smile than to weep. While his heart seemed to pause, he told himself that it was wrong to think youth died until age was dead also. A moment before he had thought that love, with its torment of pity and despair, was over. He had thought of it as a light that is blown out. He had thought of it, except in moments of rhapsody, as utterly ended in time. But he felt now, without knowing why, that this was a mistake. Nothing was over. Nothing was ended. No, it is not true that love dies, he mused, borne upward on the winged curve of Victorian faith—of that morning belief in the rightness of life, the essential goodness of God. "No, it isn't true," he repeated. "After all, I am a Victorian at heart, and even when the Victorians doubted the existence of God, they still believed in His goodness."

The trembling had passed now. A little rest was all that he needed. Old arteries were as inelastic as old habits. But the sinking back on belief, on some confident affirmation of life, rippled in flashes of energy through his mind. If only the smile would not twist in pain on her lips. When her smile faded, the lines between nose and chin tightened austerely, and her mouth, like ripe fruit in moments of happiness, looked suddenly pinched and straight. He remembered that some persons (his daughter-in-law was one of these) insisted that Eva Birdsong was close. But how could she have lived at all, he demanded, if she had spent herself lavishly? It was true that she was more saving, more sparing, than Cora. Yet he, for one, could not blame her.

If ever a woman had an excuse for saving, for nagging—— If ever a woman had an excuse——

"It will soon be over now," he said cheerfully. "What's his name—the doctor——" His voice wavered angrily, while he felt himself floundering in the desolation of age. "I know his name as well as I know my own. But I can't think of it now when I want it. I'm getting too old, Eva. I'm getting too old, and I'm not reconciled to forgetting. Not to forgetting names I know as well as my own."

"Bridges," she said softly, stroking his hand.

"Bridges. Yes, I've known him all his life. I went to school with his father, and yet his name went out of my mind like that when I wanted it." For an instant, no longer, it seemed to him that every misfortune was dwarfed, was blotted out, by the tragedy of the old. By growing infirm, by fumbling for things, by forgetting names that you know as well as your own. "In a few months, he says, you'll feel better than ever."

"Yes, he says so, but it isn't that. I'm not worrying about that."

"Then what is it, my dear? What is it?"

She turned toward the sunset, and he saw that she was still beautiful. The thin cheeks, the pinched nostrils, the silver lustre on her bronze hair made no difference. Nothing on the surface could alter the serene integrity of her loveliness. While the glow from the sky transfigured her, he told himself that her head had the quality of light, the pure outline of legend. "Even when she is dead," he thought, "her skeleton will have beauty."

Aloud he repeated tenderly, "What is it, my dear?"

"I'm not afraid of dying," she said slowly, and her words were as empty as the April breeze that stirred the lace on her bosom.

"Thank God, there isn't any danger of that," he maintained stoutly. The chair felt very small, and he shifted his weight.

"But nobody knows what may happen. I want you to stay with George until it is over. I want you to come in the morning and stay with George."

"I'll be here. You know I'd be here even if you hadn't asked me." Her arm, with the blue sleeve falling away, lay on the coverlet, and he reached out his trembling hand and stroked it softly from elbow to wrist. How delicate her skin looked beneath his swollen and mottled fingers! The bark of a tree, he thought in disgust; his skin beside hers was as harsh and rough as the bark of a tree. "I promise to stay with him. I'll be here with him the whole time. But it won't be long. They tell me it will all be over within an hour."

"They don't know. They don't know anything."

"Well, you'll have that boy, John Welch, with you. He will help Bridges, and he worships you, Eva."

"Yes, he's a good boy, and George——" She broke off and began again, "George has been wonderful."

"I never doubted that. You've been the apple of his eye since you were as young as Jenny Blair."

"He hasn't had any sleep since I was taken ill. Every night he has sat up with me. It has been terrible for him. I sometimes think it has been harder for him than for me. He has never thought of himself for a minute. He has been wonderful."

"He would be, my child. I used to tell him that he must have been born in a crisis. Do you remember the time I was caught in that panic, and George was the first man to stand by me? If I'd let him, he would have turned over every penny he had." Drawing out his white silk handkerchief, on which Mrs. Archbald had embroidered his monogram, he blew his nose and furtively wiped the moisture from his eye. Strange that age should be so much more sentimental than youth! "That is the kind of thing," he added, "that stays by a man till the end."

Her face brightened. "I remember. That was before we lost our money."

"Well, as long as I have a penny left, my dear, it is yours. You won't deny me that privilege?"

She smiled at his courtliness. "You are always generous. I sometimes think men are more generous than women."

"You can't have all the virtues. That wouldn't be fair."

Her smile changed to a laugh. "Have you ever expected us to be fair? Have you ever expected life to be fair?"

"I am not sure." He was trying desperately to preserve the gaiety, though he knew it was only the false gaiety that thrives in hospitals. "Anyhow, women are life, aren't they, for most of us?"

"I think," she answered, and the thought, he could see, spun in her mind like a slowly revolving wheel to which she was bound, "that I have really made George's life."

"You couldn't have helped it. He loves you too much."

"Yes, he loves me. He has always loved me." Her voice was so quiet and detached that she seemed to be listening for an echo. "If I hadn't believed that he loved me, I couldn't have borne it."

"You couldn't have borne being poor."

"I couldn't have borne—everything."

"It has been hard for you, I know. You were not made to pinch and scrape.

"If I hadn't known that he loved me," she repeated, as if he had not spoken, "I couldn't have borne everything."

"But you never doubted. You had no reason to doubt."

"So you feel that? You understand? Nobody else does."

"You oughtn't to say that. All your friends understand."

"As long as there is love," she continued, thinking aloud, and excited (the suspicion crossed his mind) by the drugs they had given her, "a woman can forgive anything. A man can be amused in strange ways, I understand that, though some women cannot. But if it were real—if it were not just amusement—if it were real——" She broke off with a shiver, and threw him a frightened glance. Then, after a short silence, she murmured in a voice that ran like a thread of pain through his nerves, "So often, too, it is kindness. It is nothing more than trying to help people. You and I know that George has the kindest heart in the world."

"He would strip himself of his coat for a friend—or even

for a stranger who was colder than he was. I have often said that he is generous to extravagance." After all, that was true, that was just, and he delighted to praise George when he could.

"To extravagance! You are right. Over and over again designing persons have taken advantage of him, and he has been too proud to explain to anybody but me. Do you remember the night he was taken so ill in that—that dreadful place, and they sent for us because they thought he was dying?"

"Don't think of that. It isn't worth thinking of." For he remembered the night only too well. Hastily summoned, he had gone with Eva and Doctor Bridges to bring George home or to be near him at the end.

Afterwards there had been a great deal of gossip. They had found George unconscious (ptomaine poisoning, Bridges had said). Well, even in memory, it was an ugly picture. A kaleidoscopic blur assailed him—paper roses, plush furniture, pink shades, and straw-coloured hair. The woman had managed to dress George before she summoned a doctor, and Bridges had picked up a pair of socks and stuffed them into his pocket. It was the last place on earth George would ever wish to see Eva; but after she heard he was in danger, there was nothing anybody could do with her. Self-willed, beneath all her softness. Why, he had seen her become unmanageable when her primitive emotions rushed to the surface. That night, she had been frantic at first, going suddenly quiet, as still as marble, as soon as they ceased to oppose her. But it was an occasion of horror for them all, indecent, repulsive, grotesque. Yet in some strange way known only to religion and lust, the shadow of death or the substance of scandal worked, temporarily at least, a miracle of reform. For several years after that George had appeared to reform, or at least to refrain. Then, when his health was restored, nature again had its way with him. His exuberant vitality overflowed afresh into the old channels. Yes, Eva was right. It was George's impulse to spend himself, somehow, anyhow, just as it might be another's impulse to spare himself and to save. But John Welch, who had the straight outlook of science, showed little patience with George. "No man has a right to make a muddle of life," he had said, and then bitterly, "God! how I hate a muddle!"

And Eva? What had she really thought under her long patience? Though her bearing may not have been natural, it was, the old man admitted, heroic. The code of perfect behaviour supported her as firmly as if it had been a cross. Never by word or gesture, never by so much as a look, had she betrayed herself. All that had happened ten years before, and this was the first allusion, so far as the General knew, she had ever made to the old scandal.

Now, while he watched her, a thin, faint rose drifted into her cheeks, as if they were stained by the sunset. She had raised herself on her arm, and the blue silk fell away from the curve of her elbow. Though she was looking beyond him to the broken clouds in the west, he could see that her eyes were dark with pain above that still smile on her lips. Then the last edge of the sun vanished in a red rim below the horizon, and at the same instant her smile wavered and died.

"I have always wanted to tell you that he was not to blame that night," she said very slowly. "He was there trying to help her. It was about a will. Some relative had defrauded her. I want you to know this. I want you to believe this." She stopped, choked a moment, and asked in a breathless whisper, "You do believe what I tell you?"

"Yes, I believe you."

"I felt that I wanted you to know," she continued, after a long pause in which he heard the spasmodic rise and fall of her breath. "One can never tell what may happen. If I should die before George, I want you to know how—how splendid he has been. I want you to be his friend always."

"Of course I am his friend, and, most of all, I am your friend. Nothing can change that."

"No, nothing can change that." She had fallen back on the pillows, and lay looking out at the shadowy branches of elms against the vivid light of the afterglow. "You are like George in some ways," she added presently, "and in others so different."

"I suppose human nature is much the same in all of us, my dear."

"It isn't just human nature. There's something more. John Welch has human nature, too, but there's nothing of you in him, and there's nothing of George."

"Well, that doesn't keep him from being a fine lad. As I've told you before, I sometimes wish my little girl could take a fancy to him. It would not be a brilliant marriage, but he would make a good husband, if character counts."

Eva sighed vaguely, listening to the soft April wind in the trees. "Yes, he's a fine boy. I'm very fond of John; but he isn't the kind a young girl falls in love with. Somehow, he is too—too honest—and perhaps too unselfish. It takes more than character to awaken love—especially first love." Suddenly, without a sound, her tears brimmed over, and failing to find the handkerchief under her pillow, she wiped her eyes on the lace of her sleeve.

"Don't cry. Don't cry," pleaded the old man. "There is nothing in the world for you to cry about, Eva."

"I know there isn't. Nothing in the world," she responded, while her tears flowed all the faster. "It's just nerves. Doctor Bridges and John tell me so. It is just nerves." When he drew out his silk handkerchief and put it on the coverlet, she caught it up and hid her face for an instant.

Turning away from her, he looked over the small neglected garden to the scattered spires of Queenborough. Everywhere it is the same, he thought. Everywhere people are loving, suffering, hating, hoping, going into hospitals, coming out of hospitals, laughing, weeping, trying fruitlessly to make life what it is not. All the striving for an impossible happiness, for an ecstasy that endures. All the long waiting, the vain prayers, the hope that is agony! And who knows what the end of it is? Who knows that the end ever comes? But what we see and touch cannot be the whole of it. There must be a plan, there must be a meaning, he insisted, still faithful to a creed he had forsaken.

All life isn't lived in a hospital. For the young there is joy some-where, and for the old there is the end of expectancy and a green bench in the sunshine.

Presently, while he still gazed out of the window, he felt her hand close on his, and turning quickly, he saw that not only her lips but her eyes were smiling up at him. A moment before she had seemed to lose courage, and his heart had sunk down in despair; but now, with the change in her look, he felt that he was able to face life again.

"I ought to know all about first love," she said brightly, "be-cause I fell in love with George when I was eight years old."

Heartened by her tone, he replied as cheerfully as he could, "Well, I'm glad they don't all begin so soon, my dear." Almost, but not quite, he had touched the inside curve of her elbow. Then, with his eyes on the wine-purple veins and swollen joints of his hand, he drew back and grasped the crook of his walking-stick. No, the hands of youth and age could not clasp without flinching. Yet Jenny Blair, God bless her, thought of forty-two as the downward turn. Well, no matter. If one had to be eighty-three, it was better to be eighty-three alone with the past.

"Oh, that was long before he thought of me." She was laugh-ing with her old archness, and he told himself that the music of chimes was in the sound of her voice. "It began when he plunged into that burning shanty down near Penitentiary Bottom and brought out Memoria. George was only a small boy then, but I fell in love with him, and I never got over it. Acts like that al-ways made a tremendous appeal to me, even when I was a child. Somehow, I saw him after that always rushing into flame and smoke and rushing out again with a bundle in his arms. You re-member Memoria, who does our washing? Of course the fire-men could have saved her as well; but George wouldn't wait for the fire engine. That was exactly like him, wasn't it? He can never bear to wait when an impulse seizes him."

"Yes, yes, I know, but you oughtn't to have been there. You were too small."

"That's what Mother said; but Mammy was Memoria's

grandmother. We were playing out in the street, and when Mammy heard the fire-bells, she ran down as fast as she could, and all the children followed her. I wouldn't have missed it for anything in the world. It was the first time I ever saw Memoria. She couldn't have been more than three years old, and she was exactly the colour of brown sugar."

"I remember, but aren't you talking too much?" He flinched and shifted his heavy body, which had once been hard as nails, he told himself, but was now soft and flabby.

"Are you in pain?" she asked, laying her hand on his arm.

"A twinge in my joint. All my age seems to have got down at last to my legs. I was telling Jenny Blair on the way up here that I'd be as sound as I ever was if I had a new pair of legs."

She was silent so long that he began to wonder if she had forgotten him or had fallen asleep from fatigue. Nothing, he decided, while he waited, but the false excitement of drugs could have broken down her reserve so completely. When, at last, she spoke again, it was in the low wandering tone in which one muses aloud. "No, I wouldn't have missed it for anything. Mammy lost her head when she heard of the fire. You couldn't blame her. Memoria was her grandchild. All the children on the block ran down as fast as they could. The alarm was ringing over the city, and presently the fire engine came dashing down the hill, with all the splendid white horses. There was a crowd of negroes praying and shouting in front of the house, and Memoria's mother was shrieking that she had forgotten her baby. She had saved her spring hat, her best set of plates, her sewing-machine, and even a bushel of black-eyed peas; but she had forgotten that Memoria was asleep in a trundle bed. Afterwards, she said she thought Memoria was with the other children out in the yard; but I believe she had simply forgotten her in the excitement."

"You were too little," he said. "You ought not to have been there."

"Oh, but nothing so exciting as that ever happened to me again. Only, like Memoria's mother, the things I recall most vividly are trifles. My mind is like that. Trifles always stick to the sides of it. I remember I was wearing a sprigged cambric, white and pink, and ribbed white socks, with a pair of shiny black slippers, tied with a bow of grosgrain ribbon over the instep. These are the things I remember best, and the way George ran down from a vacant lot, with a ball in his hand. He had been playing baseball, and there was a long jagged tear in his breeches where he had climbed over a fence. I have never forgotten the look of that tear and the bows on my new slippers. Is there any meaning in memory, I wonder."

"Who knows? The things I recollect best happened forty years and more ago. But you mustn't let yourself talk too long. If you get excited, you won't sleep."

"He came running down with the other boys," she resumed, as if there had been no interruption, "and Memoria's mother shrieked at him, 'I'se done lef' my baby. Gawd in heaven, I'se done lef' my baby!' George shook her hand off his arm and called out over the praying and shouting, 'Well, I'll get her, Cindy. Just hold my ball for me.' Would you believe it?" Eva asked suddenly, with a laugh of pure happiness. "Cindy stood there rocking the baseball as if it were a baby the whole time George was bringing out Memoria. She stood there swinging the ball back and forth in her arms, and screaming at the top of her voice, 'Oh, Lawd, I'se a sinner! Oh, Lawd, I'se a sinner, but I ain' gwine sin no mo'!' Then George came out of the smoke and threw a flannel bundle (he had rolled up Memoria in a blanket) into Cindy's arms. 'Give me my ball,' he said, just like that. 'Give me my ball.' He ran back to the vacant lot at the very instant the fire engines came rushing down the steep street. No," she continued pensively, "nothing so exciting ever happened to me again. But I fell in love with George then, and I never got over it. I think the thing I really loved him for was his courage. Courage has a lasting quality," she added, and for the first time her voice trembled with feeling. "Sometimes I think it is the only virtue that has a lasting quality."

"Perhaps you're right," he answered, and wondered if it were true. "Anyhow, it is well to love people for the sake of virtues that stay by one."

"That is what I mean. That is what I am trying to tell you." She spoke eagerly, grasping his tired old hand as it lay on the coverlet. "I don't know how to put it into words, but this something that stays by you makes last love more important than first love to a woman. And it is even stronger when it is all one love, first and last, like mine for George. First love is simply between two persons, you and your lover, and it changes as everything must that exists merely between two human beings. But last love has courage in it also; it has courage and finality, and facing the end and all the emptiness that is life. Finality is the only thing, isn't it, that really survives? Everything else, even love, passes." Her face was pale in the thickening dusk, and her eyes shone like blue fires as she looked up at him. What was she trying to tell him? How much did she suspect? How much did she know? How much had she always known?

"Don't ask me, my child. I cannot answer." He sighed under his breath, realizing that he looked on a last gallant endeavour to defend an illusion. Yes, he was right when he said that hers had been, and no doubt was still, a great passion. And was he right, too, when he thought that women had passion, but men (all men, he corrected himself, who were not poets) had only passions?

"That is what I had in my mind to tell you," she repeated, though she had told him nothing. "If anything should happen to me, I want you to feel that George has been—has been splendid. You do feel that now, don't you?"

"Yes, my dear, I feel that now."

"I made an excuse to John about my will, though, after all, I have only a few trinkets to leave. Most of my jewels I sold without telling George, and I even sold every piece of Mother's silver that we weren't obliged to use on the table. After the coffee service went, I used to take the goblets and forks and spoons down, one at a time, to old Mr. Mapleson. He never gave me away. Even George has never suspected, because I saved those six Georgian goblets Grandfather always used for mint juleps. And I didn't tell even you. I don't know why I am telling you now. Perhaps it is all the morphine I've taken, but something seems to have broken down in me. All the walls have been swept away, and I can't divide my mind into compartments. But I want Jenny Blair to have my aquamarine necklace and earrings. They aren't valuable; but she has always liked them, and the setting is good."

Though her eyes were dry and shining, he felt the tears brim over his withered eyelids and roll unchecked down the furrowed skin of his cheek. Yes, there are cracks even in stone, he thought. "You told me your silver was in the bank," he said, and wondered, in spite of his pity, if her confession were as natural, as impulsive, as he had believed.

"I couldn't bear you to know. That was false pride, I suppose, but it has always been stronger in me than anything else."

"Well, you ought to have come to me. There is nothing the old like so much as to be needed." The desire to talk of himself, to pour out his interminable disappointments, shuddered through his nerves in a spasm of longing. He had much to tell, and it seemed to him that from any point of view what he had to tell would be interesting. He had suffered deeply; he had had wide experience; he had lived through dramatic epochs in the world's history; he had observed; he had reflected; he had gathered, little by little, the long wisdom of eighty-three years. If only once he might open his closed soul and let the past gush out in a torrent of memory! But she wasn't thinking of him. Nobody was thinking of him except as a prop in weakness, a pillar to lean against. No matter how he had suffered, no matter how much talking might help him, there wasn't anybody who cared to sit down and listen.

"I don't know what we should have done without you, George and I," she said, but her voice was listless, the blue flames had died down in her eyes, and her clinging hand felt cold and limp in his grasp.

"You've talked too much," he answered. "I'd better be going."

The door opened, and a nurse bearing a tray came in briskly. She was tall, thin, active, and moved as if she were strung on wires beneath her starched uniform.

"It is time for your nourishment now," she said, with the artificial cheerfulness of a hospital or a nursery. "I hope you feel that you are going to have a good night." With an expert touch, she beat the pillows, arranged them at Mrs. Birdsong's back, and placed the tray on a little bed-table over her knees. "If you sip the milk very slowly, it will do you more good."

Eva glanced from the nurse to the old man, who had risen and was waiting to leave. "This is Miss Summers, General. She is very good to me."

Was the nurse really so sanguine as she looked? General Archbald wondered, trembling a little from the twinge of pain that shot through his right leg at the knee. Or was her cheerfulness also strung on wires underneath? As she bent over to stretch the coverlet under the bed-table, he saw that her reddish-black hair was grey at the roots. Trying to keep up an appearance, he supposed, moved by some stern compulsion to pretend that life was something she knew it was not.

"She's going to be all right, Miss Summers, isn't she?" he asked.

"Oh, perfectly all right!" The nurse's accents were more than cheerful, they were almost jubilant, as if she were singing in chorus. "It isn't really so bad, you know. The whole thing will be over soon, and in a few months she will feel as well as she ever felt in her life. I have a friend Doctor Bridges operated on for this same trouble, and she told me she felt like a girl afterwards. It isn't serious. Not really. Nothing is so serious as people think," added the nurse, who knew, because she had a mother dying of cancer and a father serving a life sentence in prison.

"You hear that, my dear?" the General said, but he was unable to sustain the pitch of Miss Summers' sprightliness.

"Yes, I hear," Eva replied indifferently. The light had ebbed from her face, and she looked wan and tired and almost old. "I hear, but there are times when I am worn out with hoping. I've hoped too much in my life."

"There, now, you're letting yourself droop again," Miss Summers remonstrated. "You must try to fix your thoughts on pleasant things. Nothing is so bad for you as depression."

"I'd better go," the General repeated. "I've let her talk too much. Old men are like that." Patting her shoulder, he added, "Try to sleep well, my dear, and remember I'll be here the first thing in the morning."

She looked up over the glass of milk. "Nine o'clock is the hour, isn't it, Miss Summers?"

"Yes, nine o'clock. I always like my patients to be first. Then it's over before you begin to expect it." She had a gold eyetooth which flashed when she smiled.

"And you'll stay with George? You won't leave him?" Eva was clinging to the hand he held out.

He stooped to kiss her cheek. "Not for a minute. John Welch will see you through. Where is John?"

"He was here just before you came. Nobody knows how good he has been." As he was turning away, she caught his sleeve and asked in a tone that was faintly hysterical, "You won't forget?"

"I shan't forget. Take the rest of your milk, and try to settle down for the night."

He walked hurriedly to the door, and without looking back, shut it after him when he went out into the long and narrow hall. Through the window at the end he could see the paling afterglow, and from this afterglow a thick shadow approached him. Then the electric light flashed on, and he saw that the shadow was John Welch.

"I couldn't see you against the light, John." Grasping his arm, he drew him farther away from Eva's door into the sunroom, where a few friends of patients were waiting. As he entered, they glanced at him curiously over old magazines, every eye rolling automatically in his direction, and he noticed that all the faces wore the same look of vacant expectancy. Turning hastily from the room, he walked to the farther end of the hall. "I am anxious, John," he said in a shaken voice. "I can't help feeling anxious. But I suppose the nurse is right when she says the operation is simple."

"Did she say that? Oh, of course she would." His face was drawn and sallow, as if he had not slept, and there was a frown beneath his still flaming crest. While he looked at him General Archbald remembered that John had once called the romantic mind "disorderly." But that was his favourite criticism. All emotion, even a love of beauty, seemed disorderly to him, and his ideal world had all the clean bareness of a laboratory or a tiled bathroom. A fine character, no doubt. Yes, certainly a fine character if it is possible to make character according to formula. "I don't know how simple," John continued, lowering his voice until his words were almost inaudible. "She has a fifty-fifty chance, I should say. Her heart isn't quite as strong as it ought to be, but her kidneys are sound."

The General stared back mutely, while he moistened his lips which felt suddenly blistered. It was distressing, it was indelicate, to hear Mrs. Birdsong's vital organs spoken of as plainly as if they were blocks of wood. Young people were more direct than they used to be, and he knew that John, after the habit of all realists in every age, disliked sentimentality. Well, perhaps he was right. There was no doubt that he loved Mrs. Birdsong devotedly, though he was able to stand by and watch a surgeon cut into her body. He was clean, competent, and as hard as nails even in his affection. "I'm not sure," the old man thought, "that it isn't the better way. Wherever there is softness, life is certain to leave its scar." Glancing over his shoulder at the vases of flowers which had been placed outside the doors for the night, he asked in a muffled tone, "Everything, then, is in her favour?"

John nodded. He had pleasant, sharply cut features, with lips that were too thin and tight beneath the reddish shade of a moustache. When he smiled, his light eyes behind rimless glasses appeared to change colour, and his face was not, the General thought, unattractive. If only he would smile frequently, any girl might be forgiven for falling in love with him. But he smiled very seldom, only when he meant it, and he was not smiling now.

"Everything," he replied, "except that worry. There's something on her mind. You know how secretive she is."

The other's assent was scarcely more than a sigh. "I think you'll find her easier. She talked to me very frankly."

"I am glad of that. For weeks, for years, I suppose, she has been worrying. She has gone round and round in her mind, like a squirrel in a cage, but not a word has escaped. All the conditions of her life are unnatural. I honestly believe," he burst out harshly, "that she has never drawn a natural breath since she was married. If she dies," he added, dropping his voice again, "it will be the long pretense of her life that has killed her."

The old man glanced nervously down the deserted hall. "I understand that better than you can. We were brought up that way. It was part of the code."

John's thin lips curled, and the General expected a laugh. But none came. Instead, the young man merely muttered under his breath, "And no doubt the code takes care of George too?"

"Not entirely; but George has his points, you know."

"I admit that. God knows, I'm no moralist, but I dislike a muddle. I dislike a—a disorderly world."

"It's easy to blame George," the old man rejoined sadly. "All of us are ready to do that, but we must remember that the wrong side of his life has had nothing whatever to do with—with his marriage."

John glared at him. "The devil it hasn't!" he exclaimed, and bit back his unuttered laugh. "Well, I'm no moralist. I'll look in on Cousin Eva again before she goes to sleep."

There was an abrupt, angry note in his voice; but, then, as the General reflected, John was always a little abrupt. That was why he could never really talk to him. It would be easier to talk of himself to George, who was unstable and sympathetic, than to John, who was hard and sincere. Again he was convulsed by the longing to speak of himself, to let the past gush out in a torrent of memory. But what could he tell? What was left of his joy, his anguish, and his despair? No, there was nothing he could put into words. Nothing had ever happened to him. Nothing but life; and life had happened to all persons everywhere under the sun. He felt dazed and tremulous, and it seemed to him that his will to live was spinning down, like a top that revolves more and more slowly before it comes to rest.

"After all," he said to himself, in a futile effort to restore his equilibrium, "I suppose fortitude will be the last thing to go."

s Jenny Blair went out into the yard, spring rushed to meet her, and she thought, with wistful vagueness, "I wish I knew what I wanted!" The breeze on her cheek and the scent of pale spring flowers made her restless. Though the ground near the house was bare, an uneven border of jonquils trailed beside the new asphalt walk, and the cool afternoon shadows spread like pleated silk under the magnolia trees by the gate. Between the walk and the gate, the unmown grass was sprinkled with small white heads of clover, and all the clover blossoms and the fringed grasses seemed to be running before the wind. Suddenly, the whole world, even the magnolias and the shadows, joined in the race. The April afternoon was running somewhere—but where? A flushed light was blown into her mind. "Spring is so lovely. Everything is so lovely. Oh, I feel as if I were melting!" A little ahead of her, William looked back, sniffed the air, and bounded over the jonquils in pursuit of an unattainable scent.

Slackening her steps, the girl remembered, with a stab of reproach, that Mrs. Birdsong was very ill and might die. "It is too dreadful," she added in a whisper. "It would be too dreadful to die in the spring."

But the thought was as empty as her voice. No matter how hard she tried, she could not make herself feel that illness and death really touched her. She could not believe that anything in the world mattered, except to be alive and to know what she wanted from life. She adored Mrs. Birdsong. She adored her so passionately that it was impossible to associate her with illness or death. "God wouldn't let it happen to her," she said, putting the fear out of her mind. "God wouldn't let her suffer like that." The next instant her thoughts sprang back to herself and to the promise of joy that glittered in the vagueness ahead. At one moment she longed to go away from Queenborough—to go anywhere. But immediately afterwards, she would think of her grandfather, too old and feeble to do more than sit in the sun and think about nothing. What could he have to think about since he had given up law? And her mother would miss her, too, she reminded herself. Her poor mother had had, as everybody said, a sad life, though her sad life had failed, apparently, to make her unhappy.

"If only I knew what I wanted," Jenny Blair sighed again; for it had occurred to her that what she really wanted most was something beyond her reach—something as far away as the moon. "Perhaps, if they were to say I could go, I shouldn't wish ever to leave them."

At the end of the yard, she came upon a roofless summerhouse smothered in ivy, and when the smoke of a cigar drifted to her, she thought, "Yes, he is there. I knew all the time he was waiting." Without surprise, she felt that she had been coming all her life down this walk to the summer-house where she expected to find him.

"Thank God, it's you, Jenny Blair!" George Birdsong exclaimed, as he caught sight of her. "I was afraid to turn when I heard you coming. Since I stole out for a smoke, I've had to ward off the advances of two nurses and four patients."

He looked harassed and miserable, and there was an anxious question in his usually smiling eyes. Even his skin, which she had thought so fresh and clear, was darkened by smudges of pain and fatigue. Everything about him, from his light chestnut hair, so thick and upspringing that it seemed blown back on his head, to the short curve of his upper lip under the faint moustache, looked dejected and listless. Even his hard, strong body appeared to have given way and softened within from an invisible break. A throb of sympathy pulsed through her, not in her heart alone, but deeper, far deeper. She longed to put her head down on the railing of the summer-house and burst into tears. About what? She did not know. Only she could have wept because something too brilliant to be true was blurred and tarnished by suffering. Yet she couldn't tell why she suffered like this. It was all as vague as the rest of her discontent.

"Do you mind me?" she asked. "I am so sorry. I am waiting for Grandfather."

"No, I'm glad you came." He was still standing beside the bench from which he had risen. "It will do me good to talk to you. I am smoking because I have to. I've lost my nerve, and I have to hold on to something, if it's no bigger than a cigar."

"Yes, I know. I feel that way too." She sat down stiffly on the end of the bench, and he dropped back in his place. The smell of his cigar made everything more alive, and she remembered that Grandfather had said a man could always smoke himself into submission to fate. That was when Doctor Bridges had taken away his pipe because of a cough. She couldn't say it aloud to anybody oider than John Welch, but she wished women in Queenborough would begin smoking in public and not just up the chimney, as Aunt Etta had always done.

"I haven't had a wink of sleep for two nights and scarcely any for a week," Mr. Birdsong said, and his tone sounded hurt and astonished, as if he were protesting against an injustice. "How can I sleep when Eva is going through hell? I was afraid to drop off lest she should wake up and want me. And now my nerves are all shot to pieces. Don't get the idea I've been drinking. I haven't. I haven't touched a drop, and I'm not going to touch a drop until all this is over."

Sinking back in the corner of the rustic bench, Jenny Blair stared at him with eyes that she felt were expressionless. Though she was aching with sympathy, she could think of nothing to say that seemed right in her mind. Never before had she seen him stripped of his charm, his gaiety, his effervescent good-humour. Yet, in some strange way she couldn't explain, she found that she liked him better when he appeared merely human and suffering.

"You're sure you don't mind my talking?" he asked abruptly.

"It makes it easier for me if I can talk to somebody. I have to get away from things. I'm not like a woman."

"Women want to get away too."

"No, you're wrong about that." She could see that he was not interested in the point. "You don't know anything about women. Not yet. Women like to sit down with trouble as if it were knitting. But men are different. Men must get away or take a drink, one or the other. Is your grandfather in the hospital?"

"Yes, she wanted to see him alone. That's why I'm keeping William. Where's William?" She glanced round the garden, and at the sound of his name, William came, with his tongue lolling out, and stretched himself on a bed of grasses and clover. "I hope," she added in a tone softened to affliction, "that it isn't really serious."

He had finished one cigar and was immediately beginning another. "You don't know what you are talking about," he replied, and she noticed that the fingers with which he struck a match were shaking. "Everything like that is serious. And it's Eva!" He almost cried the words in his agony. "It's Eva! I know I oughtn't to talk to you like this. Don't listen to me. You're only a child."

"I'm seventeen and a half."

"That's only a child. But you understand. You always understood things."

She looked at him gravely, still speaking in the firm and soothing tone she had learned from her mother. "I don't think you bear trouble as well as she does."

"As Eva? Of course I don't. If I could go away or take a drink, I shouldn't keep on smoking one cigar after another."

"Then why don't you go away or take a drink?"

He answered with a gesture of irritation. "I told her I'd stay by her and not touch a drop, and I'm going to keep my word. I'm going to keep my word to her once. If I were to go home, even for a minute, the temptation might be too strong for me.

The best thing I can do is to sit here until your grandfather goes and they send for me."

"I wish I could help."

"You're helping just by letting me talk. If I talked like this to other people, they would think I was out of my head. But you don't."

"No, I don't," she responded proudly. In spite of her effort to sound firm and soothing, she was unable to banish a note of triumph. She tried to feel sad and hopeless because Mrs. Birdsong, whom she had always adored, was ill and unhappy and a surgeon would be obliged to disfigure her lovely body; but the regret slipped like quicksilver out of her mind, and the place it had occupied was overflowing the next instant with a sensation of surprise and delight. Life was adorable. How she wished everybody in the world could be happy! "Poor Mrs. Birdsong," she repeated vacantly to herself. "Poor Mrs. Birdsong;" and immediately afterwards, she began to wonder if she really wanted to go away. It might be more fun to stay in Queenborough and go to balls and cotillions, and have all the lovely dresses her mother would order from New York and Paris. Through the mesh of ivy, as rusty as old iron, she could see the tall, pale grasses and the white heads of clover racing faster and faster in the April wind, which was scented with Mr. Birdsong's cigar. And it seemed a part of the spring frolic that the smoke of his cigar should be strangely exciting and mysterious as it drifted about her.

Beyond the magnolias, the drab walls of the hospital blotted out the horizon. On the porch, she could see an old lady in a crepe veil walking slowly up and down with a man who moved as if his legs did not belong to him. Above, at one of the uncurtained windows, a nurse was reading aloud, and directly over her head, at a higher window, a young woman in a purple kimono was looking out at the sunset. Suddenly, from the dark boughs of a magnolia, a bird sang the same note over twice and was silent. At the bird's call, it seemed to Jenny Blair that the flying grasses and clover and her own thoughts stopped an instant together, and then raced on again in an ecstasy. But she ought to be sad; she ought not to share in all the quivering and flying of April. Mrs. Birdsong was ill. Mrs. Birdsong would be given ether in the morning; she would be put on a table; she would lie unconscious while they cut into her body. "I'd do anything in the world for her," thought Jenny Blair, "I know it is terrible." Yet knowing it was terrible could not keep her from feeling this ecstasy. "I'd do anything in the world for her," she repeated aloud.

"So would I. I'd do more than anything. If there were anything to be done, do you think I'd sit here chewing this cigar like—like an idiot?"

She wondered what reply he expected. Or, since he was talking to relieve his mind, perhaps he did not wish her to speak. "I might be anybody," she thought. "I might be one of the nurses, if one of the nurses had time to listen. It's strange that men have nerves too. I never knew it before. But I don't care. He is more attractive, even if he isn't dark, than any boy I know. Yes, I do like older men best."

"There was never a woman to compare with her," George was saying almost roughly, as if he were contradicting somebody or something. "I've seen plenty of women, but I've never known one that could compare with her."

"That's what Grandfather says. He thinks she would have been as famous as Mrs. Langtry if she had lived out in the world."

"Well, but for me, she might have been famous." He smoked in short puffs, with a frown that was half whimsical, half savage, as if he enjoyed hurting himself. "I'm not worth her little finger. I don't need anybody to tell me I'm not worth her little finger. The trouble with me," he added fiercely, "is that I have no endurance. I can summon up as much courage as any man; but I can't stand things."

She nodded. "I know. I believe I'm like that myself."

A laugh broke from him, and his face cleared. "What can

you know about it at your age? You are scarcely more than a child. But," his features darkened again, "I don't need anybody to tell me I'm not worthy of her."

"You will never make her believe that."

His features twitched with that odd expression of helpless injury. "I don't know. Nobody will ever find out what she believes. I'd give my right arm to spare her this; but the truth is I'm not good enough. I've never been good enough to lace her shoes. You will always remember this, won't you? No matter what anybody says, remember I told you I wasn't worthy to lace her shoes."

"Yes, I'll remember." Her small, flushed face, with its shallow profile, was as sweet and empty as a wild rose; but she was thinking without softness, "I wonder if he is misunderstood too? Perhaps she has never really understood him."

"It must be wonderful to be as beautiful as she was." Not until the words had crossed her lips did she realize that she had spoken in the past tense. Well, maybe he hadn't noticed it. He seemed to be occupied with his own thoughts. "Grandfather says that nature has lost the art of making queenly women."

"Yes, they seem smaller now, whether they are or not. You're a mere wisp." For the first time he looked at her searchingly, and a blush stained her face while his glance, so sad and indifferent a moment before, swept from the scalloped waves of soft, pale hair under the brim of her hat to her slender ankles arching trimly from the silver buckles on her suède slippers. "Yes, you're a wisp, and you look soft; but you're not. All that softness of youth is only a glaze. Touch it, and you'll find that it is as hard as—as glass underneath."

"I'm not," she replied angrily. "I'm not hard." But when his voice roughened to harshness, a quiver of pleasure shot through her nerves. Why, she wondered, should she like the roughness of his tone better than gentleness? "But I'm not," she repeated, hoping that he would contradict her imperatively and make the sudden change, the quiver of pleasure, begin all over again.

"You are. I can tell by looking at you. All that dewiness is just a film. You are like every other girl in the world. No matter what happens so long as it doesn't happen to you." Suffering had faded from his expression, and his features were charged with vitality. Even the dark smudges of pain had vanished.

Reaching up, she broke off some rusty leaves from the ivy and tossed them into his face. How surprising life was, how thrilling! Yes, she was positive now that she liked older men best. She liked them when they were not shy and awkward like boys, but imperative and tender and rough altogether.

"I'm not hard," she tossed at him with the leaves of ivy. "You don't know. You don't know everything."

"I know you."

"You don't."

"I do." The old gay challenge to life shone in his eyes, as if he had found a brief escape from the anxiety that consumed him.

"I don't see how you know so much. I never told you." What did his look mean? Did it mean everything? Did it mean nothing?

"There are things you know without being told. I know something else about you. I know John Welch likes you too much."

She shook her head. "Well, I don't like him. I could never, never," she insisted audaciously, "fall in love with a fair man."

He threw back his head with a laugh, and the amusement sounded so natural that she glanced nervously at the hospital. Had he forgotten, she wondered, where they were? No, of course not, he could scarcely have forgotten his troubles so soon.

"I'll bet you anything you like—I'll wager a box of marsh-mallows that you fall in love first of all with a fair man."

"I don't like marshmallows," she rejoined, with dignity.

"Well, chocolates, then. I wager a box of chocolates against— against——"

"Against what?"

"I'm trying to think. Whatever you please, because I'm sure

to win. Suppose we say a kiss. That won't cost you anything. I shouldn't like to make you sacrifice a pair of silk stockings."

Though she laughed disdainfully, she felt a tremor of expectation, of imaginary adventure, and the thought darted through her mind, "Oh, I'm so happy! I have never been so happy before!"

"That's the easiest thing for little girls, isn't it?" he asked in the teasing tone with which her elders used to annoy her when she was a child.

"But I don't like kissing," she replied severely. "It is silly." Through the ivy, she still watched the light on the blown grasses and clover, and it seemed to her that this light was both without and within, that it was as living as music.

"You don't, eh? Well, you used to when you were small." His voice sounded rough again, almost as if he were angry, and he was staring hard straight away from her at the walls of the hospital.

"I used to like marshmallows too." Provoked because he would not look at her, she rose to her feet and flicked at his hand with the fringe of her small beaded bag. "It isn't polite not to look at the person you're talking to."

"You don't like it, eh?" he repeated in that queer brusque tone, while he slipped his arm about her and drew her to his side. For an instant he was so close that she felt his hardness and strength, as if he had turned to a figure of bone and muscle. Even his lips were hard and rough as they pressed into hers, and not only her resistance but her very flesh seemed to dissolve. After a single shuddering beat, her heart quivered into a stillness that was more terrifying than violence. "Everything has stopped," she thought desperately. "I can't see. I can't even see." Then, as she reached out and caught hold of the bench for support, she heard an inner voice saying triumphantly over the dark waves in her mind, "I never knew kissing was like this. I never knew anything was like this."

Drawing away, he said carelessly, in a voice that trembled slightly, "It's time we were going in. You're a nice little girl;

but you must remember you're only a little girl. This isn't the first time I've kissed you."

Yes, it was true, he had kissed her before, but never like this. Oh, never, never, like this. If only she might stay here, within the safe shelter of the ivy, and sink down on the bench until the vehemence had subsided. She felt suddenly limp, boneless; her will had oozed out of her.

"We'd better go back. Your grandfather may be waiting," he added hurriedly, and she saw that he was impatient to return to the hospital. Perhaps it was only the fading light that made him appear different. Could he have forgotten so soon? How soon did men forget after they kissed you?

He seemed so eager now that she could barely keep up with him. As they started back, she saw his cigar still smoking on the ground where he had thrown it, and she thought, in a flight of irrelevance, "Oh, isn't everything wonderful! Isn't it lovely to be alive!" The glow in her senses still lingered, as if it were a part of the flushed evening air; but with every step away from the summer-house, this quivering harmony, without and within her mind, melted into the twilight.

"I'm sorry to hurry you," he said when they reached the porch. Where, she wondered, had this happened before? "But they expect me to go up as soon as your grandfather comes down. I'm afraid he's waiting."

"No, there he is now. William has found him," she replied in a tone she tried in vain to make as casual as his. Indignantly, she thought, "I hate him. Never, never could I really like a fair man, and one who is old too." Yet, while these words were still in her mind, she felt a throbbing soreness far beneath the surface of thought. Something stirred there, helpless as a bird just out of the shell, and she felt that this something—anger, jealousy, desire, disappointment—would outlast any effort of will, any fiercely uttered resolve. "After all, it wasn't my fault," she told herself passionately. "I didn't mean anything. I didn't mean anything in the world."

"Yes, there he is," George said quickly, and his voice, she

realized, was suave with relief. "Have you just come down, General? We were watching for you."

Stroking William's head, General Archbald blinked in a dazed way, as if he had heard only half of the question. Never, his eyes said, as he held out his hand, had he known before what it felt to be old, to be finished, with life still unappeased in his heart.

"I stayed longer than I expected to," he replied wearily, "but I did not know. She seemed to like having me. I hope I haven't tired her."

"She had been looking forward to your visit. There were things she wished to talk over with you."

"Yes, I thought talking might do her good. John Welch came as I was leaving."

"I said I'd meet him. How are you going home? Is your car there?" Youth had dropped from George as quickly as it had revived in the summer-house. Lines of fatigue and that strange look of injured resentment hardened his features.

"No, Isabella said she would stop for me. She is probably waiting."

"Let me go out and look for her. If she isn't there, I'll drive you home before I go up to Eva. It won't take but a minute."

The General shook his head a trifle impatiently. It was kind of George to be solicitous; but solicitude in younger men was one of the favours he preferred to reserve for the last. "Don't worry, George," he said, knowing that the walk back was indeed too much for him. "Though William and I are not so spry as we once were, we are not yet decrepit."

"Of course you're not," George agreed; and for the first time since they had entered the hospital, he glanced at Jenny Blair with a smile. "Well, then, since there's nothing I can do for you, I'll go up to Eva. This is a nice little girl, General," he added, patting her shoulder. "It's hard to realize she's grown up, isn't it?" Without waiting for an answer, he turned away, while Jenny Blair stared through the front door at the row of empty cars by the pavement.

"I hope I didn't keep you too long, my child."

"No, I didn't mind. There was a lovely sunset."

"I know. Mrs. Birdsong's room faced that way. It is hard to watch her suffer. The hardest thing in life is to watch suffering and feel helpless."

"Is she suffering now, Grandfather?" Jenny Blair asked in a despondent tone. Mrs. Birdsong, who had been as vague as light in the summer-house, had suddenly become as vital as pain within the walls of the hospital.

"They have quieted her nerves, and she is so gallant—so gallant. . . . But I mustn't depress you, my dear. If your mother and I had our way, we would keep all knowledge of suffering out of your life. There is time enough to be sad. Time enough, Heaven knows, when one is old."

Jenny Blair sighed. "I am not sure, Grandfather, that I wish to go away. I mean to go away and study for the stage."

"Bless your heart, my darling, I knew you'd feel that way. I knew you didn't really wish to leave us." As he enfolded her with his protecting arm, which trembled a little, his voice quivered with the unavailing tenderness he felt for another woman.

CHAPTER 4

✿ ✿ ✿ ✿ ✿ ✿ ✿T THE corner they found Isabella and the two
✿ older children in the big open car which Joseph
✿ Crocker was driving.
A ✿ Handsome, robust, warm-hearted, Isabella
✿ was happily married to a man who combined the
✿ ✿ ✿ ✿ ✿ ✿ ✿ evangelical virtues with the untroubled face of
a pagan. After a restless youth, she had settled into marriage as
comfortably, Mrs. Archbald had once remarked, as a blanc-
mange rabbit settles in a bowl of jelly. Though a trifle heavy
in figure, she was nimble in mind and vivacious in conversation,
a little too wide for the sheath skirt which was just going out,
and not quite broad enough for the modern ideas which were
just coming in.

"Sit by me, Father," she said, making way for him. "I won't
let the children bother you, and there's plenty of room for
William between us. Be quiet, Erminia, I can't hear what your
grandfather is saying." Joseph, at the wheel, was silent, expert,
and amiable. Fortunately (and this was one of the very nicest
things about Joseph) his conversation was almost as limited as
his religion.

While she nestled as far down as she could beside the children,
Jenny Blair felt rather than heard the monotonous ripple of
words punctuated with laughter. In the west, as she looked back,
there was a shadowy green afterglow, like the thin branches of
trees. The wind blew the scent of buds in her face; and it seemed
to her that the twilight was whispering in her ears and playing
slowly over her flesh. Gradually, while the car sped down the
street, the soreness in her heart melted away, and she recovered
the sensation of surprise and delight she had lost in the hospital.
The farther she passed from experience, the more real her happi-

167

ness was in her thoughts. "It is all my own," she said over and over, with the feeling that she was swept onward by some dark current of life. "I have something precious to think of that belongs only to me." It was strange; it was new; it was different from anything she had ever imagined; yet, in some secret way, she felt that she had always expected it, that all the years she had lived began and ended with that kiss in the summer-house. Not with her mind. She had never really known with her mind that a lover could kiss like that; but her heart had been prepared, though her mind had never suspected. "It is all my own, and it won't hurt anybody," she thought. "This is enough. I don't ask anything else. Nobody need ever know. Even he need never know that I think of him. If only I may see him for a single minute every day, I shall be perfectly happy." And it seemed to her, lying back in the car, with the April wind in her face and shivers of delight playing over her body, that a hopeless passion was far more romantic than the happy end of all the fiction she was permitted to read. With a wave of exultation, she remembered that she might stand at her window and look across two intervening roofs to the Birdsongs' house. She might stand at her window, with nobody suspecting why she was there, and watch him cross the pavement and open the front gate, or even, if she went to the back window and leaned very far out, she might catch a glimpse of him in the garden where Old Mortality used to live in the lily-pond. Suddenly, as if by a miracle, the world was glistening with joy.

Was the car stopping already? Why, they had started only a minute ago. In a dream, she followed her grandfather and William out on the pavement; in a dream, she called "Goodnight!" to Joseph and Aunt Isabella; and in a dream, she clung fast to her grandfather's arm while they went up the steps and into the house. From the library, she heard her mother's anxious voice, "I hope Eva is not worse. You were so late, I was getting uneasy."

A wood fire had driven the chill from the air, and the ruby leather and English calf borrowed a fine glow from the flames.

Under their feet, the immense floral designs in the Brussels carpet blossomed out like a garden; and William flung himself down, with a happy sigh, on a field of roses and pheasants. For forty years, General Archbald had tried in vain to keep the library for his own use; but there had always been the dread that a closed door might hurt somebody's feelings. Now, Mrs. Archbald's work-bag of flowered silk lay on his desk, with the contents of bright scraps and spools scattered over his blotting-pad. The evening paper, read but neatly folded again, was waiting under the lamp on a table beside his favourite chair.

"No, she's as well as I expected," the old man answered. "But it was a shock to me to see her. It was a shock, Cora."

"Come and lie down on your sofa, Father. I'll cover you up, and you may take a little nap before dinner. You'd better let me bring you a sip of brandy," she added, while he lay down obediently on the soft old sofa, and she drew the blanket of ruby wool over him. "I never saw you look as if you needed it more."

"Yes, I need something," the General assented, watching her as she moved about in the cheerful glow, patting the cushions, arranging the chairs, putting out a lamp or two, and finally placing a fresh log on the andirons. "I am a very old man, Cora, but I only found it out this afternoon."

"Nonsense, Father. The idea of your talking like that. After all, you're only eighty-three. Why, to look at you, any one would think that you were still in the prime of life."

Usually her flattery succeeded; but to-night, after that trying excursion into the past and the still more trying visit to the hospital, he felt that he required a tonic more inspiriting than evasive idealism. So he asked with a slight frown (strange how everything seemed to exasperate him!), "Is William there? I did not see him come in."

"Yes, he is here by the fire. He came in with you."

"He is old too, Cora."

"You may keep him a good while yet. Rufus lived to be sixteen." With a last comforting pat, Mrs. Archbald murmured,

"Shut your eyes tight," in the soothing tone she used to Isabella's baby, and tripped through the hall and out into the garden. Returning a moment later with a few fresh and very young sprigs of mint, she found Jenny Blair looking for her in the pantry.

"Mamma, I want to ask you something."

"Well, you must wait, dear, until I make your grandfather a mint julep. The strain has been too much for him. He ought not to have stayed so long. Clayton, bring me the brandy, and crush some ice as soon as you can."

"I only want to ask you if I may give away the kimono you gave me at Easter. I feel so sorry for Mrs. Birdsong. All the afternoon I've been wondering what I could do for her. My light blue kimono with purple wistaria would be so becoming to her, and I've never worn it."

"That's very sweet of you, but don't you need it yourself? I gave it to you because your old one looks faded from so much cleaning. Wait now, while I pour out this brandy. Your grandfather likes just a thimbleful." With tightly pursed lips and the utmost precision, Mrs. Archbald measured the brandy into the silver goblet. Then relaxing slightly, she reached for the ice, and after filling the goblet to the brim, decorated the top with her sprigs of young mint. Immediately, a pattern of frost was woven at the touch of air on the silver.

"Then you won't mind, Mamma? I should love to take it to her. And, of course, you can always give me another."

Mrs. Archbald laughed happily. "Why, I shan't mind in the least, darling. I think it is sweet of you, and the blue and purple will look lovely on Eva. Now, don't stop me. Your grandfather is waiting."

The General was dozing when she entered; but he started up at her touch, and held out his trembling hand for the goblet. "I hope it is just right, Father," she said in her sprightliest tone. "You looked so tired that I made it a little stronger. It won't do you a bit of harm. I don't care what anybody tells you."

"Yes, it is just right, my dear. I felt a sudden weakness in the hospital. If only my legs wouldn't give way."

Picking up her work, Mrs. Archbald sat down between the lamp and the sofa, and waited patiently for the invigorating effect of the julep. Though she neither drank nor smoked, she derived genuine pleasure from the drinking and smoking of others, especially if they were men; and she was fond of saying that the whiff of mint always made her feel better. The nearest she had come, however, to the flavour of brandy was when she played occasionally with the crushed ice that was left in the goblet. "I was so touched by Jenny Blair, Father," she said presently. "The child has been trying to think of something she could do for Eva; and she asked me just now in the pantry if I'd mind her parting with the blue and purple kimono I gave her Easter. She wishes to take it to Eva."

"I'm glad of that. I was beginning to think she was less sympathetic than I liked her to be."

"Oh, it isn't that. She has a great deal of feeling. Only in some ways she takes after me, and the deeper her feeling, the less able she is to express it."

"Well, I'm glad," the old man repeated, and indeed he was. Even in his weakness, he had been visited by a vague apprehension while he waited those few minutes for Jenny Blair to come to him from the yard of the hospital. An impression, nothing more, he told himself now with relief, and in that queer faintness, that giving way of his legs, impressions were apt to be less accurate than usual. "I am glad, too, that she has given up her wild idea about going to New York and studying for the stage."

"Why, I didn't know that." Mrs. Archbald glanced round in astonishment. "She told me only last night that she was more than ever determined to go."

"I suppose she has changed her mind. They are always changing their minds at her age."

His voice had grown stronger, Mrs. Archbald noticed with satisfaction, while she put down her work and reached out her hand for the goblet. When he had given it to her, she picked up a spoon and put a scrap of ice flavoured with sugar and brandy into her mouth. "I thought Isabella was coming in with you," she said presently, sucking the ice with enjoyment. "This is her cook's afternoon off."

"She said something about the baby. I didn't pay much attention."

Mrs. Archbald edged her chair nearer the sofa. "Don't you remember my telling you, Father, that I believed the Crockers were more quiet than plain? I always thought there must be good blood somewhere."

"I remember, my dear. You thought there was good blood in Joseph's nose."

"Well, I was right. There is." Mrs. Archbald was sprightly, for she could see a joke, but firm also, for she was defying a precedent. "I've had several genealogists look up Joseph's family. Those experts charge a great deal, but it is wonderful what they are able to find out from old records."

"What have they found out this time?"

"For one thing," her tone was impressive, "the first Joseph Crocker came over in 1635 and settled in James City County. He must have been Joseph's earliest American ancestor. It isn't likely there should have been two Crockers of that name, and it is more than probable that Joseph's family was a branch of the real Crockers."

"As real as any, I imagine, but what did the first Joseph do after he came?"

"We've nothing yet but the name. That is most important, and it seems better to go slowly about everything else. Of course the family must have had many reverses, and I imagine they were always quiet people, and very devout. More like Puritans than Cavaliers. Not that it really matters. It does seem funny," she added brightly, "that the less religion people have, the more they seem to desire it in their ancestors. It is so distinguished, I suppose, to lose it. That is what everybody understands about Joseph. But even allowing for the gap where the county records were lost or burned in the war, the descent is all perfectly clear. Then an English genealogist wrote me that he had traced Joseph's descent, through the distaff side, from one of the barons of Runnemede. It is all very interesting; but I am not sure that the information is worth as much as he asks. We never bothered about our family tree, did we?"

"Only to lop off decayed branches. It might, however, be worth more if Joseph is able to convince Isabella that she married above her."

"Oh, I haven't told Isabella! She would only make fun of it and ask me to spend the money on little Erminia's teeth. But I'm doing it all for Erminia. Isabella is so lacking in class feeling that Erminia is sure to have too much of it. When she grows up she may want to join the 'Daughters of the Barons of Runnemede' through her father's line. The world moves that way."

"Yes, I've noticed it in other matters, particularly in the profession of law."

"It is strange, though, about families," Mrs. Archbald observed, as she rose and swept up the spools and scraps from the desk. "I mean the way they go down and come up again. Every one thinks the Crockers' family history has been most extraordinary." Small, bright-eyed, very erect, she stood with her work-bag in her arms waiting to help him to his feet.

"After all, we're stronger than I thought, Cora. I feared that *noblesse oblige* had been exhausted by Breverton Goddard. It is still true, however, that the only real test of importance is to fly in the face of it."

"I know you think it ridiculous, Father, but there is little Erminia——"

The old man smiled at her perplexity. He knew her mind as well as she knew it herself, perhaps better, and he had often wondered how so good a woman could have so little regard for truth. There wasn't a kinder person on earth; but if she ever spoke the truth, it was by accident, or on one of those rare occasions when truth is more pleasant than fiction. Not that he distrusted her now. Her documents were in order, no doubt, and the deception in this particular instance resided, he suspected, in record or even in genealogy. No, it was the way her higher nature lent itself to deceit that amused his intelligence while it exasperated his conscience. Had it been her lower nature, he thought whimsically, one might become more easily reconciled. But because she was charitable and benign, her dissembling became, in some incredible fashion, the servant of goodness. How much innocent pleasure had she conferred, how much painful embarrassment had she relieved! Even when she had stood between him and happiness, he had never doubted that she was ruining his old age from the noblest motives. Yet what is goodness, he asked himself, with a flash of penetration, and how do we recognize it when it appears? If it exists at all, pure goodness must be superior to truth, superior even to chastity. It must be not a cardinal but an ultimate virtue.

Rising very slowly, as if his joints were brittle, he balanced his weight without taking the hand Mrs. Archbald stretched toward him. From the centre of the floral design, William looked up and thumped his tail three times on the carpet. He also had grown stiff in the joints, and he realized that, since the dinner hour was approaching, the separation would be only a brief one.

"Shall I call Robert?" Mrs. Archbald asked, and her tone was full of solicitude.

"No, I can manage the stairs by myself. He is probably waiting for me. All I need to make me young again, my dear, as I've told you so often before, is a new pair of legs." He crossed the room, and holding firmly to the back of a Queen Anne chair, looked round at her. Was there something he had forgotten? Or did his slowness mean that he was too tired to walk upstairs by himself?

"Father," her voice was cheerful but pleading, "won't you let me call Robert?"

"No, my dear, there is nothing the matter. Only," his brow wrinkled in annoyance, "I remembered that I'd forgotten to ask after Etta."

"She had a bad morning, poor thing, but the doctor gave her

codeine, and that relieved the pain in her head. I told Clayton to take her dinner up a little early. She so often feels better after she eats something. Doctor Pembroke thinks her headaches come from sinus trouble, and he is treating her every day."

"I'll stop to speak to her as I go by."

"Wouldn't you rather wait till after dinner? You will feel stronger then."

"Well, I'll see. I'll see." Yes, she was right—she was usually right—he needed the unfailing solace of food. After dinner, he would feel braced, he would feel replenished in courage.

As he reached the head of the stairs, Jenny Blair, in a new dress of rose-coloured chiffon, ran out of her room. "Aren't you coming down, Grandfather? I thought I was late."

"In a minute, my dear. Run ahead."

"I wish our house had a place downstairs where you could wash your hands and brush your hair. The Peytons have one."

"Well, I don't envy them. I like where I've lived and the ways I'm used to. I don't mind the stairs, but I miss the feeling of my old velvet jacket." And he thought, as he watched her flitting down the stairs, "The child grows prettier every day. That rose-coloured frock gives her the glow she needs." Soft, starry-eyed, with a centre of inscrutable mystery, she slipped away from him, while he said to himself, "The poets are right. Nothing in life is so precious as innocence."

Glancing through Etta's half-open door, he saw that she had pushed aside her dinner-tray, and was reading a book with a yellow cover by the light on the candlestand.

"Don't you find that reading makes your head worse, my child?" he asked, pausing a moment.

Etta, who had been lost to the world in the French language, thrust her book under the bedclothes and turned a dejected face on her father. Dangerous reading had been her only vice ever since the days when she had hidden under the bed to enjoy in secret a borrowed copy of *Moths*; but even Ouida had begun to seem stale—or was it immature?—in the twentieth century.

While he gazed down on his invalid daughter, the old man

wished, and reproached himself for the wish, that Etta had been
born with a little—a very little would suffice—of Isabella's attraction. If only sympathy were softened by the faintest shadow of
luxury! There was nothing, he told himself, that he would not
do, no sacrifice that he would not make, for her comfort. In one
way, at least, she was closer to him, she was dearer than Isabella,
or even than Jenny Blair; but it was a way that made him long
to look somewhere else, that depressed him unbearably. Just as
Isabella's defiance appeased some secret revolt, some thwarted
and twisted instinct for happiness, so Etta revived in the flesh
another and a defeated side of his nature. She embodied all those
harsh and thorny realities from which he had tried in vain to
escape. He had closed the door on ineffectual pity, and she had
opened it wide. He had hardened himself against desire that is
impotent, and she wore the living shape of it whenever he looked
at her. Now, as he bent over and stroked her head, he felt for
a moment that she gazed up at him with the incredible eyes of
his own disappointment.

"Isn't it bad for you to read so steadily, my child?" he asked
again, because he could think of nothing to add to the question.

"I have to do something, Father. I can't just lie here and
think." Her long sallow face, with its opaque expression and im-
perfect teeth, was like a waxen mask which concealed every
change of thought, every wandering gleam of intelligence. The
jagged streaks from a menthol pencil had left a yellow stain on
her forehead, and she had pushed back her pale brown hair until
it hung in a straight veil to her shoulders. Some women, he reflected, appear to advantage in bed; but poor Etta was not one
of these fortunate creatures. In all her clothes, after the tem-
porary repairs achieved by Mrs. Archbald, she was sufficiently
attractive for a woman who put no strain upon the fragile emotions of men. But prostrate from a severe headache, and too ill to
submit to the simplest improvements, she was scarcely more ap-
pealing than some heartless caricature of feminine charms. Poor
girl, poor girl, if only one were not so helpless against illness!
For she was the victim of life itself, not of human or social in-

justice, not even of any system invented by man. No system could help her, not all the rights of suffrage piled on one another could improve a mortal lot that had been defeated before it came into the world. It might be possible—it was always possible, of course, to blame heredity; but Isabella, with the same inheritance, he reminded himself, was strong, handsome, magnetic, with a hearty relish for life. Had there been some secret flaw in his own nature, or in Erminia's open and innocent soul? We know so little of inheritance, he thought, we know so little of anything. Perhaps when we learn more . . . Perhaps, poor girl, he sighed, and turned away from the old spectre of impotent pity. . . .

Before Jenny Blair undressed that night, after she had put her lessons away, she took out the Japanese kimono and unfolded it on the bed. How exactly like a spring afternoon, she thought, with the blue sky shining through trailing clusters of purple wistaria! While she wrapped it delicately in white tissue paper and tied the package with blue ribbon, she thought with a rush of pleasure, "It is the prettiest thing I have, but I wish it were more beautiful still. I'd give her anything in the world I have if it could do her the least bit of good. If Mamma would let me, I'd give her my pearl and diamond pin." She longed to sacrifice herself for Mrs. Birdsong; she pitied her from the depths of her heart. "I couldn't bear to hurt her," she thought, "but how can it hurt her for me to feel this way in secret? Even he will never, never suspect that I care." Vaguely, she repeated, "I don't mean anything. I don't ask anything for myself. If only I may see him from a distance, even if we never speak a word, I shall be perfectly happy." This was all that she asked. And yet, though she had parted from him only a few hours before, she was already tormented by the longing to be with him again—to be with him again just for a moment! But the torment was less of pain than of a joy too intense for the memory to hold.

After she had opened the window, she tried to see beyond the intervening houses into the Birdsongs' garden; but there was nothing more than a pattern of darkness and moonlight under the moving branches of the old mulberry tree. Slipping out of her clothes at last, she tossed them in a heap on a chair and stretched her body, in its batiste nightgown, between the cool linen sheets, which were scented with lavender. Mamma had promised to let her wear nightgowns of pink crêpe de chine when she had her coming-out party; but cambric or batiste was considered more suitable for children and very young girls.

"Now I have something to think of," she whispered, as she clasped her hands on her bosom and gazed straight over the foot of the bed at the glimmer of moonlight and darkness beyond the window. "Now I can let myself really remember." Immediately, as if the phrase were some magic formula, she discovered that all she had to do was to let herself sink back into the luminous tide which ebbed and flowed through her mind. Not by thinking but by feeling, by lying very straight and still and feeling with all her heart and flesh, she was able to live over again the startled wonder and the burning rapture of love. "I never knew it was like this," she said under her breath. "I never dreamed life was so wonderful." And with the flowing tide of sensation, her pulses sang again in her ears, and the grasses and clover raced ahead of her into the future. Was happiness outside, at the end of the race? Was happiness roaming beyond the room and the house and the garden, through the darkness of the world and the universe?

All night, in a pause between waking and sleeping, she fled in circles through a dark forest, from a pursuer she could not see, though she heard the breaking of boughs and the crackling of dead leaves as he followed her. All night she ran on and on; yet no matter how far and how fast she sped, always she came again to the place from which she had started. Round and round in circles, and never escaping.

W H E N General Archbald came out of the house the next morning, he found his daughter-in-law waiting for him in the car.

"I couldn't let you go by yourself, Father. It will be a great strain on you, and besides," she added, with the anxious sweetness that never failed, he reflected, to stroke him against the grain, "I want to be there in case Eva should need me. George is so helpless."

"If you feel like that, my dear, you must not let me keep you from going."

"I shan't be in your way. While George is talking with you alone, I'll wait outside in the visitors' room."

As the old man stepped into the car, he glanced up uncertainly at the promise of rain in the sky. "There is no reason he should talk to me alone. I can imagine nothing that hasn't already been said. If we drive fast, we may get there ahead of the shower."

"Yes, I told Baxter. But one never knows about George. He has so little command over himself when he is really moved. I never saw any one give way so completely, though he tries hard to keep up when he is with Eva."

The General frowned. "That means, I suppose, that he will unburden himself to me. I don't want it," he said testily, "I won't have it. You'd better stay with him, Cora. You have more patience with people than I have."

"But didn't you promise Eva? That was one of the things she wanted to ask you."

Yes, he had promised. He had promised, and he had no idea of breaking his word. But the very thought of George put him into an ill humour. Ever since last evening, ever since he had

had those abrupt words with John Welch in the hospital, he had preferred not to see George. He liked him; he did justice to his good intentions; but he wanted to keep out of his way, at least until the morning was over. Of course it couldn't be done. He had given his promise to Eva. George was probably waiting for him at this minute. "I suppose," he said aloud, and Mrs. Archbald jumped at the grim sound of his voice, "fortitude will be the last thing to go."

"You are so wonderful, Father," she replied, and he realized, with an inward chuckle, that her artificial resources had failed.

An admirable woman, he mused, looking at her profile in the oblique light from the window, admirable and unscrupulous. Even the sanguine brightness of her smile, which seemed to him as transparent as glass, was the mirror, he told himself, of persevering hypocrisy. A living triumph of self-discipline, of inward poise, of the confirmed habit of not wanting to be herself, she had found her reward in that quiet command over circumstances. From her first amiable word, he had known that the excuse on her lips was merely another benign falsehood. Ever since he had complained of the tingling in his limbs, she had determined, he realized, not to let him go out alone. Sitting rigidly beside this small, compact, irresistible force, he felt the hot flush of temper spread in a stinging wave over his features. He was easily nettled nowadays, sometimes by trifles, sometimes by nothing at all; and whenever his temper was ruffled, that hollow drumming began all over again in his ears, as if the universe buzzed with a question he could not hear clearly.

All night (and it had been a bad night) he had dreaded the return to the hospital; but as they went down the long hall upstairs, Eva's door opened, and he heard her voice speaking in natural tones. A minute later, when they entered the room, he saw that she had been placed on a stretcher which the nurses had wheeled away from the bed. They had put on her one of the hospital nightgowns; he could see the neck of it rising above the grey blanket, which covered her smoothly and was folded back almost under her chin. Her hair was combed away from her forehead, and the two thick braids, tied at the waving ends with blue ribbon, fell over her shoulders and bosom. So she had worn her hair as a child, he remembered, and so had the shining mist escaped from the parting. Her face was very pale; even the full, soft lips had lost their clear red and were faintly pink as they had been when she was little. It seemed to him, too, that her eyes were the eyes of a child, not of a woman, large, wistful, as changeable as the April sky, and encircled by violet shadows which made them appear sunken.

So seldom had he, or any other man, he imagined, surprised her with the animation drained from her face, that he had thought of her spirit as effortless. Not until the last few months had he suspected that the sudden radiance of her smile was less natural than the upward flight of her eyebrows. But, as he looked at her now, a quiver ran through his heart, and he felt, with agitated senses, that he was seeing her stripped naked, that he was helplessly watching a violation. For they were looking at her through the ruin of her pride, and her pride, he understood, with a stab of insight, was closer to her than happiness, was closer to her even than love.

"I've had a good night," she said cheerfully, "and I am just going up. You must stay with George and try to keep him from worrying. There isn't anything really to worry about. It will all come right. Whatever happens," she added, in a whisper, "it will be right." For an instant, when he bent over her, she gazed up into his eyes, and he knew, even without the note of weariness in her voice, that she did not wish to come back alive, that she did not wish to go on. What she feared most was not death, but life with its endless fatigue, its exacting pretense. As George turned to the door, she seemed to give way, to snap somewhere within, and the old man saw that John Welch, whose eyes never left her, leaned down quickly and put his hand on the grey blanket. Then George glanced round again, and an inner miracle happened. A long breath shuddered through her; her slender body straightened itself on the stretcher, and her look, her voice, her gestures, were charged with a fresh infusion of energy.

Radiance streamed from her anew. Her face was glowing but not with colour; her eyes were shining but not with warmth.

"I am feeling so well," she began again in a voice that sounded excited yet remote. "Ever since John gave me that last hypodermic, I've felt as if nothing were the matter. George is suffering more than I am this minute. He ought to be out in the air with a cigar."

Yes, it was true. George was really suffering more than she was at the moment. His handsome florid face had changed utterly since the beginning of her illness. The rounded contour, so youthful a few weeks before, had sagged and hardened, and there were lines of anxiety between nose and mouth and beneath the still boyish grey eyes.

"I shan't smoke so much as a cigarette or touch a drop to drink till you've come through it, Eva," he said with obstinate misery. "I told you I wouldn't, and this time I'm going to keep my word."

The scene was so painful to General Archbald that he glanced from the stretcher to the bare little room, which was stripped also. Surely there was nothing worse in a crisis than the way it tore away all pretenses. Nothing, he reflected, not even external objects could withstand tragedy. Even if she doesn't die, he thought, we shall never be the same, for we have gone through the expectation of death. He stared at the sickly green of the walls, at the white iron bed, as hideous, he told himself, as a rack; at the painted bureau, with drawers that stuck when the nurse tried to open them. The vases of flowers were still outside the door; but there were violets in a cream-coloured bowl on the window-sill, and their fragrance seemed to him faded and sad. Then, while he still looked away, the stretcher was rolled out into the hall, and turning at last, he found that he was alone with George in the room.

"Did Cora go up with her?"

George nodded. "Only to the door. Eva wouldn't let me go even that far."

"Well, she has John. John will stay with her until it is over.

That's a fine boy," the General added, for the sake of hearing himself speak. "He will make a good doctor."

"Yes, he will make a good doctor."

"It was a fortunate day when you took him to live with you. Let me see, he is Eva's cousin's child, isn't he?"

"Betty Bolingbroke's. His father was a rolling-stone, and the poor little chap was knocked about from pillar to post. He always bore a grudge, even as a child. I was sorry when Eva took him in, but I'm glad now that she did."

"It was a good thing. Yes, it was a very good thing." Walking back to the window, the old man looked out with dazed eyes on the yard. Rain was falling. The jonquils were beaten down and spattered with earth. At the end of the asphalt walk, he could see drenched ivy on a summer-house. Well, he had nothing to say to George. He had no time to listen to him. "We need rain," he said aloud. "This country needs rain." He turned to George and their eyes met. Nobody ought to look like that. There was such a thing as proper pride, even in misery. Nobody ought to look stripped to the soul.

"Try to brace up," he said. Somewhere he had heard that phrase before, and it was the only one he could think of that sounded as unnatural as the moment, as unnatural as life.

"There are some things I can't stand up against," George replied, smoothing the hair back from his damp forehead. Walking slowly across the room, he dropped into a wicker rocking-chair by the window. "Why," he asked despairingly the next instant, "should it have to be Eva?"

"Nobody knows. Nobody knows anything." But silence, the old man felt, was what he wanted. Not complaints, not self-accusations, not the kind of confession that is wrung by torture from brittle emotions. Not words; above all, not words.

"I've got to talk," George said defiantly, as if he had read the other's thoughts. "If I have to stay bottled up, I'll go out of my mind." Haggard, limp, lost to all sense of proper reserve, he was not, even in his naked misery, entirely without charm. Something large, simple, primitive, and unashamed, looked out of his

pain-streaked face and his wide grey eyes, which were darkened
by the shadow of injury and defeat. He was not only unhappy,
the General realized, but indignant because he was compelled
to submit; and his indignation, even more than his unhappiness,
made him appear simple and human.

"Are you sure," General Archbald inquired, "that you
wouldn't be better in the visitors' room?"

"God, no! What do you imagine I'd be doing out there?"

"It is sometimes better to be in the midst of people."

"Not for me. I like people as long as things are easy; but I
take to cover when I begin to break."

"Well, after all, don't you think you are taking it too hard?
Bridges thinks she has a fine chance——"

"He says that, but he doesn't mean it. He talked to me. It's the
worst they can do, the very worst. Even if she comes through,
she'll be an invalid. She'll never come up again. I know Eva."
His voice flinched and quivered as if it were a living nerve. Yes,
it was impossible to doubt that he loved her. Deception was
nothing; infidelity was nothing; only that authentic passion endured.

"Many women have gone through this, my dear boy, and
lived happily. John assured Cora most positively that there is
no sign of—that there is not the slightest sign of an incurable
malady."

"Bridges says that, too, but there must be a test. He can't be
absolutely sure until afterwards." He raised his head with a jerk
and stared out into the rain. "Why, in God's name, should it
have to be Eva?" A groan burst from him, and he exclaimed in
a smothered voice, "I could bear it better if I had measured up!"

The General sighed. He wished Cora would come back. Cora
knew the right tone to take, even with grief. "You have measured up," he answered, after a pause. "You have made her
happy."

"No, I haven't made her happy."

"Well, even if you haven't, she isn't aware of it. She has never
known that you failed."

"You can't tell what she has known. That's the worst of it now. I could never tell what she was thinking all those months—all those years."

"She thinks the best of you. She believes in you."

"You don't know," he repeated obstinately. "Nobody knows. If only she hadn't smiled all the time. I could bear it better if she would stop smiling."

"That is the habit of a lifetime. Nothing can change it."

"It isn't natural. I am always thinking she will smile like that when she is dead."

"Morbid thoughts. You should try to govern your mind."

"I sometimes wish," George said desperately, "that she didn't believe in me. If she saw me as I am, I might be able to measure up better. But she would idealize me. She expected too much. I always knew it was hopeless."

"It wasn't hopeless." The old man altered the tense quickly. "It isn't hopeless. So long as she feels that you've made her happy."

"I tell you she isn't happy," George rejoined, almost angrily. "She has never been happy. It was all too big for me, that was the trouble, what she is, what she feels, what she thinks, what she expects—everything. I am not worth her little finger. Nobody need tell me that. But, after all, you can't make a man bigger than he really is. I know I'm not a big man, and when I come up against anything that is too much for me, beauty, goodness, unhappiness, I give way inside. I can't stand but so much of a thing, and then I break up, and that's all there is of me. When that happens, I am obliged to get out of it. Anywhere. No matter which way. Sport, women, drink. No matter."

It was incredible; it was distressing; it was uncivilized. How much better to have smoked a cigar on the porch, or to have taken a brisk walk in the rain. "There is some brandy on the table," General Archbald said, observing the bottle. "A stiff drink might steady your nerves."

George shook his head again in stubborn despair. He was determined, the old man realized, to bear his martyrdom to the end, to inflict as many stabs as his tormented mind could endure. "No, I said I wouldn't drink or smoke, and I won't. I'd give anything—my soul almost—for a cigarette, but I won't even look at one."

How utterly lacking in logic, General Archbald sighed, with annoyance, are human emotions. Night after night, Eva must have waited for George in disappointment, when by staying at home, by sacrificing some trivial inclination, he might have made her perfectly happy. Yet now, when she was beyond his power to help or hurt, when she was indifferent to his remorse, he insisted upon making this savage display of grief. The truth is, however much we disguise it, that a Red Indian lurks in every man we call civilized. There is cruelty in the last one of us, even if it has turned inward. "He doesn't give me a thought," the old man pondered. "Well, I'm used to that. Nobody gives me a thought unless he wants something, except, of course, Cora, who thinks of me entirely too much. After all, there is freedom in not being loved too deeply, in not being thought of too often. Possessive love makes most of the complications and nearly all the unhappiness in the world."

Yes, it was a relief to drift alone into old age and beyond. Life ceased to be complex as soon as one escaped from the tangle of personalities. Rising from the small, hard chair on which he had dropped a few moments before, he crossed the room and looked out of the window. Rain was still falling. A slow, sad, very straight rain, like splinters of desolation. Had he felt cheerful, he reflected, no doubt the rain would have reminded him of splinters of joy. And the fading sweetness of the violets would have seemed, not the odour of melancholy, but the fragrance of happiness. For his spirit created the mood and perhaps painted the living hues of the scene. A lifetime before, he had walked in the rain under an English heaven, and had asked himself why he could not escape, why he submitted to life. In another lifetime that was. Yet that English rain was still falling, slow, silent, eternal, somewhere within a lost hollow of memory. For years, for a generation, he had forgotten—or at least forgotten sufficiently.

Then yesterday, without warning, he had stumbled again into that lost hollow.

"This shower won't wet the ground," he said, turning. "What the country needs is a hard rain."

A coloured maid, holding a brush and a dustpan, looked in and retreated abruptly at sight of them. The door had no sooner shut behind her than it opened again, and a pupil nurse, with folded sheets and pillow-cases in the crook of her arm, entered and murmured apologetically that the maid wished to come in and clean. "If you will go over to the sun-room for a few minutes." Then, just as they started away nervously, driven out among strangers, they saw Mrs. Archbald coming toward them down the long hall. Though her face looked puffy in contour and faintly greenish in colour, as if she were fighting off sickness, her expression was still bright and hopeful.

"I never saw any one so brave," her voice was low but firm. "She sent you word that there is nothing to worry about. Before the door shut, she smiled and waved her hand to me."

"Good God!" George exclaimed, frowning at vacancy.

"I may go now," the old man thought. "I may leave him with Cora. She will know how to manage him." It was true that George had his good points; but there were occasions when he seemed to wear too thin a veneer of civilization. "Sincere and selfish. His emotion will probably blow over before Eva is well." Walking slowly down the hall, beyond the sound of Mrs. Archbald's comforting voice, the old man came to the sun-room at the back of the hospital. Here the same visitors, or others like them, lounged dejectedly in wicker chairs and turned over the pages of magazines, while they stared now and then through the blurred window-panes. Sinking on one end of a sofa, he gazed steadily at nothing, until it seemed to him that the anxious expectancy brimmed over from the faces around him and flowed into his own. A woman in a green hat; a woman in a black hat; a woman in a red hat; a woman wearing no hat at all. In a far corner, a man, young, thin, and poorly clad, was bowed over a florist's box on his knees, and in his face also there was this look of anxious expectancy. What were they thinking, those human beings, within touch but beyond reach, under that thin wash of reserve? Each spinning its separate cocoon. Each an ephemeral cluster of cells. Each, perhaps, an eternal centre of consciousness. Each as brittle and fugitive as life itself.

The young man in the corner glanced up suddenly, pushed the white pasteboard box to one side, and then pushed it back again where it had been. Turning his head, he looked with fixed, opaque eyes through the window; and immediately, as if moved by a spring, every head in the room turned toward the window and looked out into the rain. "It must be over," General Archbald thought. "It must be over by now." Taking out his watch, he glanced at the face of it, pondering, while all the eyes in the room turned slowly and followed his movements. Two hours since they had taken her away. Time to go back. Nothing like that could possibly take two whole hours.

Rising from the sofa, he crossed the room slowly and carefully and went to the door. Before he had taken a step into the hall, a needle of burning pain stabbed into his joints, and he thought, with tightened lips, "Why is it always like this? Why is pain so much sharper, so much more living than joy?" As he steadied himself with his stick, Mrs. Archbald hurried out of Eva's room, and slipped to his side. "It is over, Father, and she stood it splendidly. John has just told us, and he says Doctor Bridges was wonderful. I am so thankful."

He tried to follow her words, to take in all she was telling him. But the pain in his joints was too intense. "Yes, I'm thankful, I'm thankful," he repeated. "If it is over, may we go home now?"

"Yes, we'd better go home. George is coming with us. I have persuaded him not to stay with her when she comes from under the ether. She asked me not to leave him."

"Then we'd better go, we'd better go." For he had borne all he could bear. This pain was growing worse every minute. "Do we have to wait long?"

"Just a minute. He is to join us in the car as soon as she is brought down. He isn't satisfied to go until he has had a glimpse of her, but after she comes to, she will be too sick to see any one, even George—especially George." To the old man's astonishment, he found that Cora, who so seldom cried naturally, was crying now as if she enjoyed it. "I can't help it," she said, taking a handkerchief out of her bag and wiping her eyes. "I can't help it," her voice was a sob, "because I have a feeling that she would rather not—would rather not——"

Yes, he had felt that too. In his heart he was convinced that Eva did not wish to come back. "One has no choice," he murmured, more to himself than to Cora. "Unfortunately, in such matters, one has no choice."

"I don't know what they told her; but she seemed to know that she might, even if she lived through it, be an invalid for a long time—for a very long time."

"Shall we go down now?"

"I told George to come out to the car. George," she continued, as if she were thinking of something else, "can be very trying." Then, still thinking of something else, she began to weep afresh, and he realized, with a dull recoil from emotion, that she was putting herself in Eva's place, and responding with Eva's temperament, not with her own.

"Let's go, let's go," he said urgently. "It will be easier outside in the air." Clinging to her arm, he hurried her downstairs, into the hall, and through the door of the hospital. As they crossed the pavement, he noticed that the rain had stopped and the heavy clouds in the west were scattered by a spear of sunlight. While they waited for George, the old man huddled down in one corner of the car and counted the red-hot twinges of pain in his joints. One, two, three; then over again, one, two, three. Eva an invalid, he thought, without feeling the sharp edge of the blow. No matter how long the world lasted, there would never be another woman like her. Nature had ceased to make queenly women. There was the fiery dart coming back. One, two, three.

Would George keep them waiting much longer? One, two, three.

Mrs. Archbald leaned over and patted his hand. "As soon as I am at home, I shall go down on my knees and thank God that she came through it so well."

EORGE left the hospital as if he were running. The skin about his mouth was drawn and sallow, and there were swollen and inflamed puffs under his eyes.

"She looks well," he said. "I had a glimpse as they were taking her into the room, and she looked like a girl asleep." Then jerking off his hat and running his hand through his hair, he added desperately, "I've come to the end. Of course I'm going back a little later, but I must have a smoke and a drink."

"Why not take a nap?" Mrs. Archbald inquired. "The nurse told me you were at the hospital nearly all night. It is much better for Eva not to try to see her until she feels better."

"Yes, I know." He caught eagerly at the suggestion. "She won't have anybody with her when she is sick. As if a thing like that made any difference to me."

"Well, it's better to humour her. Will you come in and let me make you a julep?" Though Mrs. Archbald disapproved of a julep in the early hours of the day, she realized, being a broadminded woman, that there are exceptions to every rule of right living. "I am sure Father needs a thimbleful, but he never touches a drop until after sunset."

"Thank you, I'd better go straight home. I'm not fit company just now for anybody, and I know you both need a rest. I shall never forget how you stood by us." His voice was flat with fatigue, and the General saw that he was at last empty of words. In the recoil from overstrained emotion, all that mattered was a brief escape from too intense a reality.

When the car reached his gate, he muttered, "I shall never cease to be grateful," as automatically as if the words were spoken by a machine. A moment later he jumped out of the car, entered the gate without glancing back, and went rapidly up the path to the small grey porch, where the wistaria was just beginning to bloom.

"It is a pity," Mrs. Archbald sighed, as they drove on to the red brick house, set well within a black iron fence, at the other end of the block, "that strong emotions have so little staying power."

"If strong emotions had staying power, my dear, none of us could survive them."

Again Mrs. Archbald sighed and considered. "I sometimes wonder if two persons who love each other so deeply can ever be happy together."

"It is a question. Certainly, the great lovers of history are not often the happy lovers."

As the car stopped, and Jenny Blair waved to them from the window, her mother remarked uneasily, "Well, after to-day, I shall never doubt his devotion. Perhaps they might have been happier if she had been less jealous by nature."

"Or he more faithful. . . ." Baxter had opened the door of the car, and while the old man stepped cautiously to the pavement, he tried to remember that Eva had her faults as a wife, that she was exacting in little ways, as close as the bark on a tree (so Cora had said), and jealous of every look George turned on a woman. But it was in vain that he forced himself to dwell on her failings. A great love, he thought, is always exacting; it was for George's sake that she had learned to be penny wise; and every chaste woman, according to the code of his youth, is naturally jealous. No matter how firmly he recited her imperfections by name, he found that they scattered like specks of dust before the memory of her face above the grey blanket on the stretcher, with her two childish plaits brought forward over her bosom.

He stumbled slightly, and Baxter caught him under the arm and helped him into the house. Why did old men (women were different) dislike so much to be helped? In other civilizations, where manners were more gracious, old age was regarded as an honourable condition. But in America, even in the South, the cult of the immature had prevailed over the order of merit.

"Is there anything I can get for you, Father?" Mrs. Archbald persisted. "Would you like a dose of aromatic ammonia?"

"No, my dear, nothing whatever. All I ask is to lie down for an hour."

"You must go into the library. I'll shut the doors and keep every one out. Nobody shall disturb you till lunch."

"How did she stand it?" Jenny Blair and Isabella asked together.

"Wonderfully. She stood it wonderfully," Mrs. Archbald replied. "Of course she is gravely ill, and she will be sick from the ether; but John said they felt very hopeful."

"Oh, Mamma, I am so glad," Jenny Blair cried happily. "When do you think I may send her my kimono?"

"Not yet, darling. Not for a week at least. She is too ill to enjoy it. Now, your grandfather wants to rest. All this has been a great strain on him. He must be left perfectly quiet in the library."

While she spoke she was gently pushing them away and leading her father-in-law to the deep repose of his sofa. After she had placed him comfortably and had tucked the softest pillows under his head, she stood looking down on him with anxious concern. "Isn't there something else I can do, Father?"

The old man struggled up. "I'd better go to my room, Cora. I must get into my old slippers." For the pain had returned in his joints, and he felt that no torture could exceed the red-hot twinges of gout.

"Jenny Blair will bring them, Father. You mustn't get up. Jenny Blair, find your grandfather's old slippers in his closet. If you don't know them, ask Robert." Kneeling on the floor, Mrs. Archbald unlaced the old man's shoes and drew them off gently. "Is that better? Put your feet up. No, don't worry. Not a soul is coming into the room."

He breathed a long sigh of relief. "It's the right foot. I could stand the left, but the right foot is too much."

"I know." She stood up with the shoes in her hand and gave them to Robert when he brought the well-worn slippers. "Wouldn't you be more comfortable if you loosened your collar?"

He shook his head stubbornly, shrinking from so serious an infringement of habit. Though it was commendable to rebel in one's mind, it was imperative, he felt, to keep on one's collar. "No, my dear, no. As soon as I've rested, I'll go upstairs and brush up a bit." When he had glanced at the staircase, the flight had seemed to him endless. "I couldn't have made it," he murmured to himself. "Not with this pain, I couldn't have made it."

"Remember, Etta and I are on the back porch," Isabella was saying while Mrs. Archbald closed the green shutters of the French window. "The sun has come out and the air feels like summer. If you need anything, call me. The children have gone to play in the park, and I am going to make Cora lie down until lunch."

But Mrs. Archbald could not rest in peace until she knew that her father-in-law had been properly restored to himself. After leaving him for a minute, she returned with a glass of milk and a beaten biscuit, and he ate and drank to oblige her, while she watched him with a solicitude that failed now to annoy him. "You are a staff to lean on, Cora," he said, humbly grateful.

"Aren't you feeling better?"

"Yes, my dear, I'm feeling better."

"Are you sure you wouldn't like Jenny Blair to sit with you?"

"No, I can rest easier by himself. William is here, isn't he?"

"Yes, he is here." Looking up at the mention of his name, William thumped his tail and moved nearer. "If you need anything, don't get up to ring. Isabella is just outside the window."

After a last sympathetic pat, she took up the glass and plate from the table, and went out of the room with her springy step. Through the door into the dining-room and the open French window, he could catch a glimpse of the flickering sunshine in the garden. A watery green light filtered into the room, and the familiar objects appeared suddenly to be swimming beneath the waves of the sea. Outside in the trees birds were calling, and now and then he heard the lowered voices of Etta and Isabella. This was the homely texture of life, he thought presently, woven and interwoven of personalities that crossed without breaking, without bending, without losing their individual threads of existence. A good pattern, no doubt; but what of those who cannot be blended into a design? He had always been alone; he had always been different; yet he had not, except in periods of shock or strain, been unhappy. Unsatisfied, he had been, but not unhappy. Was this because unhappiness is as rare as happiness? Was the natural state of mind merely one of blunted sensation, of twilight vision? For he had had what men call a fortunate life. Only in war had he been hungry and cold. Impoverished, he had been after the war, but not actually famished, not actually shivering. His greatest sorrow had been, he supposed, what all theologians and many philosophers would describe as a moral victory. In other ways, he had prospered. He had had a just measure of those benefits for which revolutions are made, and yet he had not been satisfied. "But my life has been better than most," he murmured, thankful for the comfort of his slippers, as he sank into a doze.

An hour later he awoke with a sense of elation, of extraordinary well-being. "I've had a good nap," he thought, with his gaze on the watery green light drifting in through the slats of the shutters. "I feel rested." Part of his exhilaration may have been only freedom from pain, for the throbbing had died away in his joints; but there was something more, he told himself, than simple bodily ease. His mind, too, was eased of its burden. "Eva is over the worst," he mused; and yet there was more even than swift relief from dark apprehension. It was as if the April wind had blown through his thoughts and scattered living seeds over the bare places. Now and then in the past, especially in his youth at Stillwater, he had known this sensation in sleep, the sudden breaking off of a dream so blissful that the ecstasy had brimmed over into his life. "It is a good world," he thought drowsily, while consciousness sifted slowly in flakes of light through his mind. "I shouldn't wonder if my best years are ahead of me." Released from wanting, escaped from the tyranny of chance, he might settle down into tranquillity at the end. For age alone, he perceived, striving to grasp this certainty before it eluded him, is capable of that final peace without victory which turns a conflict of desires into an impersonal spectacle. "Yes, I shouldn't wonder," he repeated, "if my best years are ahead."

After another doze, he found himself thinking, "How attractive Jenny Blair looks in that blue dress with the white collar. Like a little girl playing that she is grown up." He saw the heart-shaped oval of her face mirrored in the greenish haze from the shutters—the rose-leaf skin, the short blunt nose powdered with freckles, the yellow-hazel eyes rimmed so strikingly in black lashes. If one asked nothing more than young innocence! Then the girl's face melted into the swimming light. He turned his head on the pillows and thought, with patience born of rest, that he must keep in touch with George for the next few days. He would go over to see him this afternoon. Perhaps Cora had asked him to drop in for lunch or dinner. Some men preferred to be alone; but George disliked solitude. Well, he would do what he had promised; he would stand by George until Eva was out of the hospital. And not only because of his promise. For he was fond of George in his heart, though he perceived as plainly as the sternest moralist could have done that George was deficient in character, in the kind of endurance that Cora so aptly called staying power. In place of character, he harboured a collection of generous instincts. A proof of weakness, no doubt; yet nothing in General Archbald's experience had astonished him more than the height that human nature sometimes attains without a solid foundation. A character like granite, he had observed, may prove as unprofitable to virtue as a succession of fine impulses. For it was true that character became warped quite as frequently as impulses ran wild.

Yes, it was possible, he found, to admire George's quality

while one disapproved of his conduct. A little later, after lunch perhaps, he would go over for a word with him. A little later, but not now while the birds sang in the trees and the scent of lilacs floated in from the garden. A vague shadow crossed the shutters of the French window, and the still air of the room was stirred by ripples as noiseless as the reflection of leaves in a pond. There was a breathless laugh, broken off on a pulsing note, like the call of a bird. Jenny Blair, that was her laugh. Had he ever laughed so musically, even when he was young, even before he knew what life is? What life is at best, with its ceaseless toil, its frustrated desires, and its meagre rewards.

When he called that afternoon, George had gone to the hospital, and only John Welch was at home.

"I'm on my way to see her now," the young man said, turning from the hall into the library, which opened on a porch at the back of the house. "Of course she doesn't need me. She has Bridges and Adams; but I feel better if I am within call."

"Then don't let me keep you. She has stood it well, hasn't she?"

"Yes, she has stood it well, though she is too sick now from the ether to feel anything else. If you don't mind missing George, I'd like to talk to you. There is no hurry."

"No, I don't mind missing George. That is the least of my regrets. But I cannot keep on my legs." He sat down in the Windsor chair by the desk, and stared with a fixed frown through the door of the porch. The back yard, which had once been a flower garden, was running wild with unmown grasses and weeds, and several old lilac bushes were in bloom by the steps. It was a pity the garden had been allowed to go to seed; but the Birdsongs were in straitened circumstances as usual, and they had not been able to afford a gardener since the death of Uncle Abednego. Few old gardens were left in Queenborough nowadays; yet he remembered the time when every well-to-do house in Washington Street was enclosed in borders of roses or evergreens.

The house, too, looked shabby, he observed, withdrawing

his gaze. Only persons who never read would call the room in which they were sitting a library. True, a few broken sets of books filled the lower shelves of the rosewood bookcases; but odd pieces of china, mostly of the Willow pattern, were arranged behind the glass doors at the top. Newspapers or light magazines littered the fine Sheraton table in the centre of the room and George's big mahogany desk by the back window. There were curtains of wine-coloured damask, faded by age and use into silvery purple, and a grey-green Axminster carpet with rubbed places. In one corner, between the desk and the door, a small cupboard was open, and he could see George's leather coat and golf-clubs, and, on a rack above, the guns and bags that were used in the shooting season. George was a famous shot. Every year he spent a part of November shooting ducks at a place on James River, and nothing else in life was important enough to interfere with this annual engagement. Since his game-bag was as open as his mind or heart, Mrs. Archbald often remarked that her butcher's bill was pared down to the bone every autumn.

"Is your sciatica troubling you again?" John asked, with sympathy, as he lighted a cigarette. "I had hoped you were rid of that for the summer."

"Worry brings it back, I believe; but my gout is worse at this minute. I had to come over in my old slippers," he added ruefully, as he glanced down at his right foot. "I see nothing ahead of me but a diet of bread and water." Then he asked abruptly, wondering if it could be the absence of Mrs. Birdsong that extinguished the brightness in the room and made even the flowered chintz look wilted, "I suppose you can't be sure yet?"

"Not perfectly sure, but the trouble was more serious than they thought it would be."

The General winced, "Poor girl, poor girl, she struggled too hard not to give up." For a moment, while he tried to distract his mind, he sat brooding in silence, with his eyes on the blue-and-white Willow plates on the top shelf of a rosewood bookcase. Why, he pondered, did women put china in such unsuitable places? No man would arrange a row of plates on end in a bookcase. Bare shelves would appear better to a masculine eye. "Well, I had my hands full—at least Cora had her hands full with George," he burst out at last; for he was very tired; his foot pained him; and the best years of his life, to which he had looked ahead so happily a little while before, were still far out of sight.

"I don't doubt it." John's tone was curt. "I sometimes think the whole trouble is too much George. George is not a restful person to live with. Nor, for that matter, is romantic love restful."

"She adores him, and she has always been his ideal, ever since she was a slip of a girl."

"That is a part, the larger part probably, of the trouble. Think what it must have cost her to keep up being an ideal for more than twenty years! You may talk about keeping up socially, but it doesn't touch the effort of keeping up emotionally. She must have known, too, in her heart, at least, that George wasn't worth it."

"You can't deny, after to-day, that he gives her the best that is in him. We ought not to ask more than that of any man."

"Perhaps not. But when the best in a man pulls one way and everything else pulls another way, the only end is catastrophe." He shook his head impatiently, while the light on his flaming crest and his sharply pointed features gave him the look of a crusader. His face held manliness and sincerity and rugged authority. To be sure, there were persons who distrusted his advanced, or as they insisted radical, opinions. Not only had he become a Socialist in an age when Socialism was still considered dangerous, but he held equally unsound views of suffrage, religion, and the scheme of things in general. The names they called him in conservative Queenborough were not meant to be flattering. However, names are only words in the end; and the old man, who had been called by many different names, though never by the right one, in his own youth, could no longer be frightened by labels. Even names with stings in their tails were only stinging words. "My generation felt about social injustice," he thought. "John's generation talks about social injustice; and perhaps, who knows, the next generation, or the generation after the next, may begin to act about social injustice." Not that it mattered to him now, for that throbbing had begun again in the joint of his toe.

"Tell George I came over," he said, rising heavily to his feet. "I suppose you will find him at the hospital."

"I don't know. She doesn't like to have him about when she is sick. Did you notice how unnatural she became the minute he entered the room?"

"I saw that she made an effort to seem bright and cheerful."

"The strain told every time. I watched her pulse, and finally I asked him to stay out of her room as much as he could."

"Well, it's hard on him too. After all, he doesn't want her to make an effort. He'd much rather she'd be natural. I believe he is perfectly sincere when he says it doesn't make the slightest difference to him how she looks."

"It's too late now to hammer that into her mind. He fell in love with her, as you say, because she was an ideal, and she has determined to remain his ideal until the end."

"Well, I hope George will keep his nerve, and, I may add, his capacity to feel anything. There is, I suspect, a limit to feeling for every human being. Some are able to stand more than others; but whenever the end of endurance is reached, each one takes his own way of escape. Well, give her my love, and tell her I'm ready to come whenever she wants me."

Walking with an effort that exasperated him, he left the house, descended the steps, and made his way slowly past the intervening front yards to the end of the block. At the door Jenny Blair met him, and he told himself, startled, that he had never seen her so lovely. "She looks as if she were in love," he thought shrewdly. "I wonder if she can have a secret fancy for John. You can't tell the way a woman feels by anything that she says."

"George was not there," he said, "but I was talking with John." He looked at her closely as he spoke, and it seemed to him, though his old eyes may have been mistaken, that her gaze faltered.

"Oh, were you?"

"She is still suffering a great deal from the ether; but he says everything has gone as well as they could expect."

"I am so glad. I know she will get well. She has so much to live for."

"Well, I hope she will always have that. Are you going out, my dear?"

"I promised Mrs. Birdsong I'd go over every day to see her canary. You remember Ariel? She keeps him upstairs in her bedroom, and she worries about leaving him when she is away. Servants are so careless. Is John there by himself?"

"He is going up to the hospital; but he said there was no hurry."

"After all, I think I'd just as well wait till to-morrow. I saw Berry give Ariel his bath and clean his cage this morning."

"Would you rather not see John alone, my dear? If you feel that way," he offered gallantly, "I'll crawl back with you, in spite of my toe."

"Oh, no." She laughed at the idea. "What difference does John make? But I can see Ariel just as well in the morning."

What did she mean? he wondered, as he followed her into the hall. Of what was she thinking? No matter. Whatever she thought now, she would probably think something entirely different to-morrow.

That night he slept brokenly and was wide awake with the dawn. As the sun rose, he lay motionless in bed and watched the elm branches mounting upward like the inner curve of a wave. Hours must pass before Robert would bring his early coffee, and he knew that he should not be able to drop back to sleep. Rising presently, he slipped into his dressing-gown and went over to the front window which looked down on the street. Though he still occupied the large corner room he had shared with his wife, there were days in summer when he wished for at least a single window that opened on the flower garden. True, there was a plot sown in grass, but too deeply shaded by trees, just below his side windows; but when he rose early, as he had fallen into the habit of doing, he preferred to sit in his wife's old chair with deep wings in the front corner. Erminia had been dead so long now that he had ceased to associate her with any particular chair. Though he thought of her frequently, and missed her presence more than he had ever enjoyed her company, her figure and even her features had faded gradually into a haze of tender regret.

Overhead, there was a pale aquamarine tinge in the sky, and long pulsations of light quivered up from the sunrise. On the earth, mist was dissolving; birds were cheeping; the rumour of life was awaking, now far off, now nearer, now in the house next door, now in Washington Street. As the light throbbed into his mind, he seemed to become, or to have been from the beginning, a part of the dawn, of the earth, of the universe. Girdled about by the security of age, he felt again that his best years might still be ahead of him. For the first time in his life, he might make the most of the spring; he might enjoy the summer splendour with a mind undivided by longing. His daughters, his daughter-in-law, Jenny Blair, his grandchildren, William—all these were dearer because they were no longer necessary. And dearer than all, though she, too, had ceased to be necessary, was Eva Birdsong. . . .

It was at this moment, while that quiet happiness was filling his thoughts, that his look dropped to the street, and he saw George Birdsong passing along the pavement on the way to his gate. For a single heart-beat, no more, the old man was shocked into wonder. Then, as quickly, astonishment faded. Florid, refreshed, invigorated by his escape, George glanced with a slightly furtive air at the houses he passed. A few hours later, after a cold shower and a hearty breakfast, he would return with replenished sympathy, no doubt, to Eva's bedside.

After he had entered his gate and disappeared behind the boughs of the trees, General Archbald sat plunged in meditation from which happiness had strangely departed. The world of good intentions had not altered; yet, in some inexplicable way, it was different. Virtue—or was it merely philosophy?—seemed to have gone out of it. "I wish Robert would come," he thought. "I'll feel better again as soon as I've had my coffee."

The sun rose in the heavenly blue; the birds called in the trees; and the vague discord of life, swelling suddenly louder, drifted in from the streets. With inexpressible relief, he found that the ripple had passed on, but the deepened sense of security, that tideless calm of being old, had not wavered. At eighty-three, he could still look ahead to the spring and the summer, and beyond the spring and the summer to the happiest years of his life, when nothing, not even life itself, would be necessary.

IT WAS the end of June before Mrs. Birdsong was well enough to leave the hospital, and then, after a few days at home, she went for a long visit to her uncle, Frederick Howard, who lived at the family place near Winchester. The morning before she left, Jenny Blair ran in with a little gift, and found her weeping in front of the oblong mirror on her dressing-table.

"Oh, I'm so sorry," the girl cried, with passionate sympathy. "Is there anything I can do?"

"Nothing, dear, nothing. You've been an angel." Turning away from the mirror, Mrs. Birdsong wrapped Jenny Blair's kimono, with the design of trailing wistaria, about her, and sank into a wicker chair by the window. "You are always giving me pretty things," she added, untying the package and taking out a nightgown of blue crêpe de chine, "but you ought to keep them for yourself."

"I'd rather you had them," Jenny Blair said, and she meant it. "I'd give you anything I have if it could do any good."

"It is too pretty," Mrs. Birdsong answered softly, while the tears welled up in her eyes, and she turned her face to the window.

In the neglected garden below the old perennials were blooming again. The grass had grown too high; but pink roses and larkspur and pale purple foxglove survived in the flower-beds, and a cloud of blue morning glories drifted over a broken trellis to the window-sill by which Mrs. Birdsong was sitting. Against the luminous warmth and colour her brilliant fairness looked worn and tarnished. Illness had left her cheeks drawn and haggard, and her skin, which General Archbald had compared to alabaster, was tinged with faint yellow on the temples and about the mouth. In the darkened hollows her eyes were veiled and remote, and when she lost animation, there was the flicker of some deep hostility in the blue fire of her gaze. Even her lips, touched carelessly with red, looked straight and hard, and her fixed smile seemed to change with an effort. Only the pure outline of her head and profile was as lovely as ever.

"It is nothing but nerves," she said presently, with a sob that turned into a laugh. "I sometimes think the nervous breakdown has been worse than the operation. It has left me more unstrung and at the mercy of everything that goes wrong. Doctor Bridges and John both say I'll be well again if I have patience—but it is so hard to have patience."

"You're getting well. You will soon be strong again," Jenny Blair answered, while her heart was wrung with emotion. "Let me turn down your bed. You have been up too long, and you look so lovely in bed with your curls on your neck. Have you noticed," she asked cheerfully, "how beautifully everything in the room matches your kimono?"

The colours of the room were blue and mauve, and the chintz curtains, faded by many washings, held a shadowy design of wistaria and larkspur. A flowered paper, worn but still bright, covered the sunny walls, and there was a coverlet of blue silk, a present from Mrs. Archbald, on the foot of the bed. The morning sunshine fell in a chequered pattern over Ariel's cage at the window.

Mrs. Birdsong shook her head, while her tears flowed over features so inanimate that they might have been carved in ivory. "I can't stay in bed all the time. I must use my strength. I am going away to-morrow, and I must use my strength," she repeated despairingly.

"It will be cool in the mountains, and you will soon begin to improve. Anybody would be weak after that long illness."

"Nobody knows, nobody knows what I have been through."

"But you're getting well. You're getting well, only you must be careful. The doctor told you to go very slowly at first."

While her arms enfolded her friend, Jenny Blair felt that she was aching with sympathy and compassion. How she loved her! Not for anything in the world would she betray her trust. It was true that she loved George, too (she had begun to call him "George" in her thoughts), in a different way—oh, so different! —but that wasn't her fault. She had not chosen to fall in love with him. Some winged power over which she had no control had swept her from the earth to the sky. Since it was useless to deny her love, she could only remind her conscience (near enough to the nineteenth century to make scruples) that she did not mean the slightest harm in the world. All she asked was to cherish this romantic love in the depths of her heart. "Nothing could make me hurt her," she thought passionately, "but it can't harm her to have me love him in secret." And, besides, even if she were to try with all her strength, she could not stop loving him; she could not destroy this burning essence of life that saturated her being. "When you can't help a thing, nobody can blame you."

Kneeling on the floor, crumpling her pink linen dress, with her arms about Mrs. Birdsong, and her hard young heart dissolving with pity, she said aloud, "You must get well soon. You must get well soon because there is nobody like you."

Within her arms, she felt Mrs. Birdsong relax and give way, as if courage had failed. She looked straight before her into the sunshine, and her eyes were like blue hollows in which the light quivered, sank, and was drowned. Yet even in despair, Jenny Blair thought, she was more vital than any one else. Though her radiance was dimmed and sunken, it infused a glow into the room, into the house, which borrowed life from her presence, into the summer wildness and stillness of the garden.

"I shall never be well again," she said suddenly. "Something tells me I shall be like this always."

"But you won't. The doctors all say that you will be well again."

"They say that, but I know better."

Jenny Blair kissed her hand. "Let me put you to bed. You are sad because you're tired."

"In a minute, dear. I'll go in a minute." Pushing the hair back from her forehead, Mrs. Birdsong sat up very straight and wiped a moisture like dew from her lashes. "Only let me get a breath of air. I must be in bed before George comes home. It depresses him terribly when he finds me like this. I know I am selfish; but, somehow, for the first time in my life, I can't think of anything but what I've been through. Self-pity is a contemptible thing," she added, with an empty laugh, and asked abruptly, "Has it turned very much hotter!"

"No, it has been hot all the morning. Shall I turn on the fan? I wish you could have gone away before this last hot spell. Poor Aunt Etta is feeling it dreadfully; but Grandfather doesn't seem to mind the heat as much as we do. Old persons don't suffer with heat, do they?"

"I don't know. Perhaps their blood is thinner, or they take less exercise. But your grandfather ought to have gone to the White as usual. He can't do Etta any good by staying at home."

Poor Etta, who had suffered for weeks with an excruciating pain in her head, was being treated every day for an infected sinus; and since Mrs. Archbald was obliged to remain in town with her, the General had refused to open his cottage at White Sulphur Springs.

"He simply won't go anywhere without Mamma," Jenny Blair explained, "and of course she couldn't think of leaving Aunt Etta. We're all going just as soon as the doctor thinks she is well enough."

"I thought you were going abroad, dear, with the Peytons."

Jenny Blair shook her head. "I've been abroad twice already, and there wouldn't be a bit of fun in going anywhere with Bena. That is why I gave up the idea of living with her in New York and studying for the stage. She has her head full of boys, and I never liked them."

"But that isn't natural. You're young and you're pretty."

"I don't care. I like older men best, even very old men like Grandfather."

"How absurd, darling! I remember you used to talk that way about John when he was a boy; but I thought you'd outgrown that long ago."

"I haven't. I don't like him any better than I did years and years ago."

"Then you ought to be ashamed of yourself." Mrs. Birdsong was laughing, and her voice sounded natural and gay. "John has a brilliant career ahead of him. Every one says so, and in a few years, as soon as he begins to succeed, he will settle down in his views."

"I don't care. In his heart he doesn't like me any more than I like him—and that is not at all. You know as well as I do that John adores the very ground you walk on."

"But that's different. That's not being in love." A flush of pleasure dyed the delicate texture of Mrs. Birdsong's cheeks, and she looked suddenly animated and young.

"Well, he's not in love with me either. He says romantic love is a mental fever, and I don't care what anybody says, we don't really like each other. He thinks I'm selfish, and I think he's perfectly horrid. I'd rather be an old maid all my life than marry anybody like John."

"But you must marry. Every woman ought to marry. If she doesn't, she is sure to miss happiness." Though the accents were those of genteel tradition, the voice trailed off slowly on a note of broader humanity. "Not that marriage always brings happiness. I don't mean that; but I do think that every woman ought to have the experience of life."

"Well, I haven't seen a boy yet I'd like to be married to, and, most of all, I'd hate to be married to John."

"I can understand that, but you will have other chances. You're the kind of girl men fall in love with. I don't mean because you're pretty. There is something else in you that attracts, and I believe this something else counts more than real beauty in the long run. I'm not sure that great beauty, the beauty that brings fame while it lasts, is wholly a blessing. They used to call me the Virginia Lily because they said I was like Langtry," she added pensively. "There was one photograph in profile that was sometimes mistaken for a picture of her when she was young."

"I remember that one. But you were—you are far lovelier. Grandfather says her eyes could never compare with yours. Once, when I was a little girl, I asked him what the Mediterranean was like, and he answered, 'Like Mrs. Birdsong's eyes!' "

"That was dear of him, but he is always too kind."

"He says that there will be no great beauties, as democracy increases, just as there will be no more great men or great heroes. Do you believe that? Grandfather has very queer notions. Mamma told me he was so queer when he was young that everybody was surprised when he made a good living. I asked him about that, and he laughed and said that he made a good living by putting an end to himself. Do you see what he means?"

"I think I see," Mrs. Birdsong murmured in a wistful voice, "but you couldn't, dear, not until you are older. It may be better, I'm not sure, if what he prophesies does really happen and everything is made level. Any difference, especially the difference of beauty, brings jealousy with it, and worse things than jealousy."

"But it must be wonderful," Jenny Blair sighed enviously. "People love you without your having to take the least bit of trouble." Her eyes dwelt on the romantic contour of Mrs. Birdsong's head, with the soft twist of curls on the nape of the neck.

"Oh, you do take trouble if you have a reputation to keep up, and no fame on earth is so exacting as a reputation for beauty. Even if you give up everything else for the sake of love, as I did, you are still a slave to fear. Fear of losing love. Fear of losing the power that won love so easily. I sometimes think there is nothing so terrible for a woman," she said passionately, while her thin hands clutched at the blown curtains, "as to be loved for her beauty."

"But you have so much else. You have everything else. Grandfather says——"

"Ah, yes, your grandfather. . . . Men never know. Men know many kinds of fear, but not that kind."

How she loved her! Jenny Blair thought, how she pitied her! If only love, if only sympathy, could help one to bear pain! "Oh, you must not, you must not!" she cried, while the shadow of tears that did not spill dimmed the light.

"No, I must not make you sad." When Mrs. Birdsong smiled, the rouge on her cheeks and lips seemed to glow, too, with life. "You are a darling child, and I wish I could tell you the way to feel a great love and still be happy. But I cannot. I have never learned how it can be. I staked all my happiness on a single chance. I gave up all the little joys for the sake of the one greatest joy. Never do that, Jenny Blair." Her voice dropped to a whisper, and she brushed the hair from her forehead as if she were trying to brush away a cobweb of thought. "Never do that." Putting the girl's arms aside, she rose and stood with her gaze on the azure drift of the morning glories. A bird outside called twice, and the canary answered gallantly but hopelessly from the cage. "I sometimes wonder," she said, turning away, "if it is fair to keep a single bird, even a canary, in a cage. If I let him out, what would become of him?"

"He would fly away. You would never find him again."

"Yes, when a bird flies away, you never find him again."

Walking across the room as delicately as if she were made of glass, she looked into the mirror with a scornful expression. Though she stopped only a minute, she winced and hesitated before she lifted her hand and tucked a silvered lock of hair beneath the bronze waves on her temples. Then, withdrawing a few hairpins, she shook her head and released the profusion of bright curls, which rippled over her shoulders and over the haggard line of her throat. "It is too hot," she complained fretfully.

"Curls are so becoming." Jenny Blair glanced round admiringly while she removed the coverlet from the bed and turned down the cool old linen sheets, which were scented with dried rose-leaves and lavender. "They make you look very young."

"And that I'll never feel or look again. Will you pick out a fresh gown, dear, or shall I wear the pretty one you've just given me?"

"Oh, wear mine, wear mine. I know it will look lovely on you. I told Mamma it was made for you."

Tossing her kimono aside, Mrs. Birdsong slipped the folds of blue crêpe de chine over her head, while her crumpled night-gown of batiste dropped to the floor.

"Is that right?" she asked listlessly, as she stooped to pick up the gown at her feet. "Have I put it on straight?" Then, without glancing at the mirror, she stretched herself between the sheets with a sigh of infinite weariness. "Will you lower the shade, dear, just a little. Yes, it is good to be in bed again, to lie flat and let everything, persons and shadows, go by without caring." For a moment she seemed scarcely to breathe, and in the mellow light, tinged with gold and ivory, she looked pale, serene, almost transparent. Her eyes were closed, she seemed to be dropping into a sleep of exhaustion, when suddenly her eye-lids quivered and opened, while she started up and listened attentively. "George has come," she said softly, for she had heard his step on the walk. Her thin shoulders trembled erect, and she waited motionless, unnatural, and extraordinarily vivid, with her eager gaze on the door. "This is his afternoon for golf, and we are having lunch a little early. Can't you stay, Jenny Blair?"

"No, I must go in a minute. Mamma is expecting me." What was the meaning? Jenny Blair asked herself. What was the secret? "I will not speak to him," she determined, as she heard him ascending the stairs. "No matter how hard he tries to make me, I will not speak to him." When he came into the room, she thought, "He must have been out of doors, for he smells of summer. He smells of summer when the sun is hot, and your face is buried in red clover." Something had happened. The air of the room had become restless with animation, with suspense, with a delicious excitement. A glow flamed over her, as if her whole body were blushing. Life was filled to the brim with possibilities of adventure. All her senses were awake, only her will was caught and held fast in the net of emotion.

"Have you been out already?" Mrs. Birdsong asked, smiling.

"Yes, I've had a round. There was nothing to do at the office, so Burden and I slipped away and played nine holes." He was bending over his wife, and, for a moment only, she seemed to surrender. Her shoulders drooped again, but more softly; the wave of energy flowed on into her raised arms, which clasped his shoulders, and into her upward adoring glance. Then, as swiftly as it had risen, the ardour in her look wavered and vanished. Her head sank back on the pillows, while the expression of weary indifference dropped like a veil over her features.

"Are you worse again, Eva? I had hoped you were better."

"No, I'm only tired. I had to tell Berry about the packing. Then I rested a little. You haven't spoken to Jenny Blair."

"Why, I didn't recognize her!" He spoke in a tone of airy banter. "The Jenny Blair I know is a little girl, but this is a young lady." And he did not look at her! Though she had stood there, waiting in the same spot ever since he had entered the room, he had not even glanced in her direction. He was treating her as if she were still a child. "I don't love him, I hate him," she thought. But this sudden hatred was more intense, was more burning, than love. She felt it quivering over her, and even trembling in her elbows and knees. Never had she been so angry before, not even with John Welch when he teased her. That had been temper of a different sort. Then she had only wished to turn and walk away; but the rage she felt now seemed to bring her nearer to George than she had been when she loved him. "I must go," she thought, while she lingered. "I shall take no more notice of him," she told herself, while the devouring innocence of her gaze rested mutely upon him.

"Don't be a tease, George," Mrs. Birdsong remonstrated. "Jenny Blair is a darling. Haven't you eyes to see that she grows prettier every day?"

"She was always pretty enough," he rejoined flippantly. "I remember when she was ten years old, or perhaps it was nine, telling her that she had the eyes and hair of a wood-nymph. I meant, of course, yellow eyes and green hair."

"Don't mind him, dear." Mrs. Birdsong looked very tired and worn now. "He never teases anybody he isn't fond of."

"I don't care." With amazement, Jenny Blair heard her own voice speaking defiantly. "I don't care what he thinks." To herself, she added, "I must go, but I can't go until he has looked at me."

"You ought to be ashamed, George," Mrs. Birdsong said in a reproachful and faintly agitated tone. "Please don't quarrel. I am so nervous."

"Well, we shan't. We aren't going to quarrel, are we, Jenny Blair?" As the girl did not answer, he continued, almost plaintively, "But you look all right, Eva. She looks all right, doesn't she, Jenny Blair?"

"Oh, yes, she looks all right." Still he did not turn to glance at her, and still she lingered.

"I look," Mrs. Birdsong said bitterly, "a perfect wreck."

"No, you don't. You look all right. I mean it, and Jenny Blair thinks so too."

"No, Jenny Blair doesn't. She knows better."

"But you do think so, don't you, Jenny Blair? Don't you honestly think she looks well?"

"Of course she does. She looks lovely." Never would he meet her eyes, never, never! How could she bear it? How could she go away when he had not given her so much as the barest glance? Anything was better than indifference. Anything was better than the dreadful suspense of not knowing if he remembered.

Then Berry came in with a glass of milk and a powder, and Jenny Blair knew that, for the day at least, waiting was over. To-morrow, everything would begin again; but there was a whole long night to be endured between to-day and to-morrow. Crossing over to the bed, she stooped and kissed Mrs. Birdsong.

"Oh, do get well quickly. Grandfather and I are coming to the station to see you off."

"Are you, darling? That's lovely. Take care of yourself and go away as soon as you can."

"Why didn't she go abroad with the Peytons?" George asked, without turning his head.

"She didn't wish to go," Mrs. Birdsong replied. "Jenny Blair and Bena are not very congenial."

"Aren't they? I thought they were inseparable."

"No, they have never been really congenial. Bena has her head filled with boys and parties, and Jenny Blair is a serious person." Though she spoke playfully, the lustre had faded from her smile and her mouth looked strained and insipid.

"A serious person!" His tone was mocking. "Why, Jenny Blair has been an incorrigible flirt ever since she was nine years old."

"Don't mind him, dear," Mrs. Birdsong murmured caressingly, and fell back exhausted.

A shiver of indignation pierced Jenny Blair's heart like an icicle. Never had she disliked any one so intensely. Never, not even if he were to beg on his knees, could she be persuaded to notice him. "I'll never look at him again," she resolved vehemently, and looked again in the very act of resolving.

"Write to me, darling," Mrs. Birdsong called after her.

"Oh, I will, and I'll take good care of Ariel."

"When are you going away, Jenny Blair?" George asked, as she ran out of the room. "You ought not to stay on in this heat."

Even if she had wished to reply (and nothing in the world could induce her to open her lips!), the swelling anger in her bosom would have made speech impossible. As she ran to the staircase, Mrs. Birdsong's voice floated after her like a dying echo, "If Etta is well enough, they are all going to the White the first of August."

Her feet flew down the stairs, and at the front door, still flying with an inward gaze, she ran into the arms of John Welch, who appeared more annoyed than pleased by the encounter.

"Are you running away from a fire?" he asked in an amused tone that failed to amuse her.

"I know I'm a fright. Is my face very red?"

"Rather. Has anything put you out?"

"Nothing but the heat and this bad smell again. Aunt Etta is trying to make Grandfather move up to Granite Boulevard."

"Why, it hasn't bothered me. I thought it was better, or perhaps we have got used to it. Has Cousin Eva said anything?"

"No, but Aunt Etta complains all the time. She says it makes her head ache."

"She imagines that. The smell only comes now and then when the wind is in that direction. There isn't a breath of wind to-day anywhere."

She bit her lip in annoyance as she slipped through the door and out on the porch. No, there wasn't any wind. It was a pity she had thought of the odour as an excuse. "Mrs. Birdsong is having lunch early," she said hurriedly. "You needn't go home with me."

"Oh, I don't mind." His eyes blinked thoughtfully behind his rimless glasses. "Can't you tell me what the trouble is? Has Cousin Eva said anything to hurt you? You mustn't mind if she has." He opened the gate while he spoke, and shut it without a sound when they had passed into the street.

"Oh, no, she hasn't said anything. She is as patient as an angel, but I am dreadfully worried about her."

"So am I." His face clouded with anxiety. "I don't like the way she looks. Adams doesn't either; but Bridges is the only one of us who knows how to handle her, and Bridges is a blockhead about nerves."

"She thinks he's wonderful."

"I know she does. He has a way with women. All the same, she needs somebody else."

"She doesn't——" Jenny Blair began, and held back the words until they stood under one of the old sugar maples on the corner. "She doesn't seem real. There are times, just fleeting instants, when she looks like death. Sometimes I wonder if it is her smile. She doesn't seem able to stop smiling, not even when she thinks she is alone."

"That's what I meant. I wonder what your grandfather would say."

"He wouldn't say anything. Only that she's perfect. I'm sure he doesn't know it," she added, with the insight of thwarted impulse, "but he has always been in love with her in his heart. I shouldn't admit this to anybody else, but it is really true."

She had expected a laugh, or at least a smile, but he answered gravely, "Well, it can't do any harm, I suppose. Not at eighty-three."

"Oh no, it can't do any harm."

"You haven't told me anything I didn't know. But you think you're observant, don't you?"

"I think more than that," she retorted angrily. "I could tell you of some one else who I think is in love with her." It was wrong, she knew, to say that, but she couldn't help striking back when he teased her. Never could they be together ten minutes without a quarrel! And it wasn't make-believe, as Grandfather tried to pretend. She had disliked John Welch even when she was a child, and she had known, without knowing why or how she knew it, that he disliked her. Then, because she felt that she had gone too far, she continued, "But I don't care. I want to go away. I'm tired of Queenborough. I'm tired of everything," and she was indeed for the moment. Already she was regretting that she had given up the struggle to go to New York and try to be an actress. "I sometimes wish I were a suffragette. The only natural human beings seem to be those who are making trouble."

"Well, there are plenty of ways to make trouble. You won't have to look far if you want to do that."

"I gave up going to New York because of Mamma and Grandfather," she said, and really believed that she was speaking the truth.

"I'd go myself like a shot," he answered, "but for Cousin Eva. I couldn't leave Cousin Eva when she is like this."

"I thought you liked it here. I thought you were perfectly happy."

"No, you didn't think that."

"Well," she hesitated, trying to keep a note of vexation out of her voice, "I did think you liked Queenborough. Of course I know you are always fussing about things."

"I'd fuss anywhere. That's the way I'm made. But there's no opportunity in a place like this. All the young men are going away. As soon as a man begins to make a name, he packs up and takes the first train for some other place. That's especially true in my profession. If you stay here, it means arrested development."

"Then I shouldn't stay. I'd go as soon as I could."

"There's Cousin Eva."

"Yes, of course there's Cousin Eva. But she may get well."

"If she gets well, I'll go. I'll go the first of next year. There's a place waiting for me with Burdette in New York. He's one of the very best men in the Neurological Institute."

For the first time she looked at him with animation, almost with interest. "It's good of you to wait," she said, "and I know that she depends on you." Feeling that this perfunctory praise was not sufficient, she added, "I wonder if people always want to go away and be something else? Grandfather thinks they do."

"As long as they're young, and sometimes after they're middle-aged. The trouble is we imagine we can change ourselves by changing our scenery. I feel that way, though I ought to have learned better. I'd like to go away and be free, and I know perfectly well the kind of freedom I am looking for has not yet been invented. After all, Queenborough is only a small patch in the world. It is the same everywhere. People who have tradition are oppressed by tradition, and people who are without it are oppressed by the lack of it—or by whatever else they have put in its place. You want to go to New York and pretend to be unconventional, but nothing is more cramping than the effort to be unconventional when you weren't born so. It is as hard on the nerves as pretending, like Cousin Eva, to be an ideal."

"But all places are not like Queenborough."

"Some are worse, and some are bigger. It is all nonsense to talk as if Southerners were a special breed, all wanting the same things and thinking after the same pattern. There are as many misfit minds here as anywhere else. Washington Street used to be a little Mayfair at the tail end of the procession, and Queenborough has all the foul or stale odours of civilization. If we have our false sense of security, so have New York and London and even Moscow. It looks, by the way, as if England's sense of security is about to be tried. Her next war will probably be with Ulster, and it may come any day."

"Grandfather was telling us that last night. It was dreadful, too, about the killing of the Austrian Crown Prince."

"Yes, but that didn't excite me. Somehow, if anybody has to be sacrificed, I prefer that it should be a crown prince. There are few persons I can spare easier. The thing that pricks through my skin is when some hundreds of poor devils are blown up in a mine owned by philanthropists."

She smiled vaguely. "You are very advanced, aren't you?"

"Perhaps. That depends on the way you're going, I suppose, and on how far you've gone."

"Well, you're different, anyway. That's the reason Grandfather likes you so much, though you never seem to agree about anything. But he says all the Archbalds are eccentric. I suppose it began with his great-aunt Sabina, who was a witch. There were only two witches in the Colony," she added proudly, "and she was one of them. I don't mind that a bit. I think it's nice to be different. Grandfather thinks it hurts dreadfully. That's what he means when he says he made a good living by putting an end to himself. Mrs. Birdsong understands, but I don't."

"You wouldn't, not with your sparrow vision. But it's true, nevertheless. You must be a slave or starve in this damned world. That's the trouble I'm facing now, and it is as true of medicine as of everything else. Conform, or be kicked out."

"If I felt like that," she said when he paused and looked

at her with a frown, as if he dreaded yet expected an answer, "I'd go as far away as I could."

"Where? There isn't any place far enough away for a man who asks more civilization, not less. It's silly to talk, as some people do, about seeking an opportunity outside the South, unless, of course, he is merely seeking more patients to experiment on, or more clients to keep out of prison. Our civilization is as good as the rest, perhaps better than most, because it's less noisy; but the whole thing is a hollow crust everywhere. A medical man is expected to take it easier when he calls it anthropology, but I can't see how that helps. They forget that living in anthropology may be quite as disagreeable to a sensitive mind as living in civilization."

She laughed a little vacantly, because she was wondering how she could hurt George at the station to-morrow. Would it be better to behave as if she didn't know he was there or to nod disdainfully when she told Mrs. Birdsong good-bye? "That sounds like Grandfather," she said. "But, you know, he's much happier now than he was in his youth. He thinks you will be less vehement about wrongs when you are older."

"That's easy to say when you are eighty-three; but what are you going to do about living while you still have to live? Of course if you happen to be either a primitive or a pervert, it's a simple problem. Then you can escape to the South Sea Islands, eat breadfruit, and debauch the natives. But suppose you're neither a primitive nor a pervert, but merely civilized. Suppose you ask a better social order, not a worse one——"

"Oh, John, don't say things like that," she broke in hurriedly; for she had seen the curtain at Mrs. Birdsong's window blow out in the sunlight, and that blown curtain had started a strange flutter in all the nerves of her body. Was he standing there at the window? What had happened? Was he really as indifferent as he appeared? Or was he only pretending? Aloud she said in a vacant tone, "You ought to be careful how you talk. People won't want you for a doctor if they think you're not normal."

"You're right," he assented moodily. "I've never talked this way before, not even to your grandfather. Most people would tell you that I'm no worse than a crack-brained Socialist. But something upset me this morning. There was an accident down at the chemical plant, and the helplessness of the poor always makes me see red when I come up against it like that. Especially when there's a fool of a philanthropist standing by who has learned nothing more from two thousand years than 'ye have the poor always with you.' No, I'm not joking. That actually happened. She thinks I'm disqualified as a physician because I told her that poverty is a social disease and should be wiped out like smallpox."

"I must go now. There's Mamma looking for me." She smiled plaintively, as she turned away, and looked back to say over her shoulder, "I'll ask her to find out his name and send some soup to the man who was hurt. Mamma is always doing something for somebody." Oh, yes, she knew, she knew; but she couldn't (and it wasn't her fault) find the poor interesting. She loved life, and she wanted to be happy; and if John called that the sparrow vision—well, there was nothing she could do about it. If attending to your own happiness meant the sparrow vision of life, that vision seemed to her to have its advantages. But the poor, and John also, had been different before she had fallen in love. Perhaps when this ache of hope that was not hope passed out of her heart, she might feel sorry for other people again.

"Well, that's all. Good-bye!" he called derisively.

"Good-bye. I'll see you at the station to-morrow."

On the steps she turned again and looked after him as he walked away from her. "I despise him," she said in a whisper; but she was not thinking of John Welch, she was not even seeing him.

I DIDN'T speak to him," Jenny Blair said to herself while the train moved away. "He couldn't make me speak to him, not even at the very last minute."

A wave of exultation swept over her. She heard again, with a difference, that strange whisper of excitement among the images in her mind. These images were still vague, but they had ceased to be colourless. Glow and rhapsody were in this thrilling suspense, this burning light that streamed into her thoughts. Though she had not spoken to him, though she had not even looked at him until the last, she had known that he remembered. Without glancing in his direction, she had felt that he was seeking her eyes, that he was asking her to forgive him. But she had resisted. Gravely and tenderly, she had kissed Mrs. Birdsong; gravely and kindly, she had shaken Berry's hand and told her to take care of her mistress; gravely and indifferently, her eyes had wandered from John Welch to her grandfather and from her grandfather to the train that was waiting.

"Good-bye, Jenny Blair," George had called as he stood on the platform. "Good-bye, Jenny Blair, will you look after my mint bed?"

Though she did not reply by a glance, she knew, without seeing him, how attractive he looked, and how young for his forty-odd years. She knew how fresh and gay he always seemed on a summer morning, with the ruddiness of health in his face and the mockery in his near-sighted eyes narrowing down to an imperative flash. "I know he's old," she thought, "but I don't mind. I don't mind about anything. He will be back in three days. I have only three days to wait." She did not ask herself for what she was waiting. Beyond the glowing sweetness of the present there was a virgin wilderness of mystery and delight. "Three days," she repeated, "three days are not long. In three days he will be back in Queenborough, and then I may see him. Even though I never speak to him, I shall be able to see him again." Then, as the train moved out of the station, she raised her head and looked after him, with eyes that were grave, questioning, unabashed, and eager for life. She looked after him until, smiling back at her, his figure melted, with the flying train, into the blue distance.

"What do you think of her this morning?" General Archbald inquired of John, as they turned away and walked back through the station. "Do you feel easy?"

For an instant John hesitated; then he parried defiantly, "Do you, General?"

The old man flinched. "I was shocked to see her," he replied, and pressed down on his walking-stick.

"Well, you had seen her only in bed. She always looks better in bed. I hope," he added briskly, "this change will be the very thing that she needs."

"It may be," the old man assented, and then, as John did not speak, he continued in a troubled tone, "There is a look in her face I don't like. I had never seen it until to-day. The look of defeat."

"So you've noticed that. Yes, I can't understand it. But then, one never knows everything."

"I've seen that look often before, but there was always some cause I could explain. I saw it in many faces after the war, and in many more faces while Reconstruction lasted. But those were times that shattered men's nerves."

"I don't know and I refuse to guess," John said slowly. "If I did guess, I should put it down to the long strain, the unnatural life she has led. She was not meant for poverty and insecurity, and yet she has had both." He shook his head as if he were trying to rid himself of a gnat. "Yes, I hope this change will be the very thing that she needs."

When they reached his car, General Archbald climbed in with an uncertain step, and put his arm about his grand-daughter, who had not spoken a word since she had watched the departing train. His knees were still shaking from the effort to walk straight without help.

"Will you go up with us, John?"

"No, thank you, General, I must rush off to the hospital. Jenny Blair is looking well, isn't she? Or is it that pink lining under her hat?"

Turning to glance at the girl, as the car moved away, the old man was startled by the change in her expression. What was the meaning? he asked himself. Was it only the pink lining under the transparent brim of her hat? Or had she sprung up in a night with the dew on her freshness? The tender contour of her features was still empty; but there was a burnished glow on her skin and hair, a richer and deeper gloss, as if some shining fluid saturated her body. Yet her eyes, more golden than hazel in their dark setting, were unabashed and exultant beneath the shallows of innocence.

"Are you all right, my child?" he asked, pricked by an uneasy presentiment. "Nothing is wrong, is there?"

"Oh, nothing." She seemed to be waking from sleep.

"You look unusually well, but you seem quiet."

"I've been thinking——" She broke off, suppressed a yawn as she looked out of the window, and left her sentence unfinished.

"Did John depress you? Are you anxious about Mrs. Birdsong?"

"Oh, yes!" She grasped the idea with eagerness. "I am dreadfully anxious about Mrs. Birdsong."

"Well, you must remember that all young physicians are inclined to be serious."

"But she looked so ill, Grandfather. I heard old Aunt Betsey tell Berry this morning that death was in her look. She hadn't seen her since she left the hospital. You know Aunt Betsey went to live in Goochland after she got too old to work."

"She ought not to have said that." The General was disturbed, and he showed it. "That's pure superstition. Coloured people see entirely too much."

"Yes, I know." Jenny Blair sighed and looked at the houses they were passing. "Oh, Grandfather, I do hope she will get well!" she said passionately, after a long pause. "I couldn't bear it if anything happened to her!"

"Naturally we feel anxious, my darling, but we have every reason to hope."

"I couldn't bear it if she were never to look like herself again. I couldn't bear it."

So that was the trouble! How unjust it was that youth should be condemned to bear so many vicarious burdens. As one grew older and age hardened the imagination, as well as the arteries, a comfortable numbness protected the heart and the senses alike.

"There, there, my dear," he said, patting her hand; and he repeated gently, while a tear stole over the violet pouch beneath his bad eye, which had lost that last amenity of civilization, the power to control emotion, "We have every reason to hope."

"John seemed," she hesitated for a word, "so angry about— about everything. He talked to me yesterday just as if somebody or something had injured him."

"He is young yet, and most young minds think, if they think at all, with a sense of injury. He wants to blame something, but he has lost his bearing and can't decide where the blame ought to rest. I know that because I went through it myself. That is why I am thankful that age has closed, like the shell of a clam, over my nobler impulses. I can't fight for lost causes, I can scarcely condemn successful causes, any longer."

"But, Grandfather, life is so beautiful."

"I hope you will always find it so."

For a moment she was silent; then she asked in an agitated voice, "Do you suppose she still cares so much, Grandfather?"

"Cares, my dear?"

"I mean," the words were spoken with a stammer, as if she were overcoming an impediment in her speech or her mind. "I mean Mrs. Birdsong. Do you think she still cares as much as she used to care?"

"For her husband? Why, of course she does. Have you any reason to think otherwise?"

"No, no reason in the world. Only I wondered. Can you see why she ever fell so madly in love?"

"You asked me that once before. No, my child, one is never able to see a reason in love. But do you really dislike George? Has he done anything to annoy you? If he has," the thick eyebrows beetled angrily, "I'll speak to him as soon as he returns."

"No, no." She looked at him with terror, a look that reminded him of a rabbit. "He hasn't done anything. He doesn't take any notice of me. But I can't abide him. I wish I never had to see him again as long as I live."

"Well, well, my faculties must be growing rusty." Anger softened while he spoke into perplexed wonder. "Why I thought you and George were friendly enough." After all, one could trust to the intuitions of youth. When he was young himself, he had disputed the truth of this precept; but as age fastened upon him, he had returned to the worship of adolescence and other myths of primitive culture. Yet he had believed that he was still young for his years. Young, except in his legs, and in the way important things sifted out of his mind and left an accumulation of rubbish. Curl-papers, and the look in his grandfather's face when he blooded him, and the stench of that runaway slave he had found in the forest at Stillwater. Queer how trifling impressions, the merest snatches of sensation, flickered to life again. Even now, he could not walk in a dim light through a negro quarter, he could not stumble upon the acrid smell of old sweat anywhere, without having some dark corner of his memory unfold like the radiating sticks of a fan, and that autumn scene spread out before him as vividly as if it were painted.

"Are you tired, Grandfather?" Jenny Blair asked, as they crossed the pavement on the way to the house.

"Not tired, my dear, only feeling my years."

"But you aren't really old. You don't act old—not very old."

The General laughed. "Thank you, my dear. You are almost, but not quite, as tactful as your mother. Well, we'll go in and see if William is still alive. He's approaching the end, too, and he knows it."

As they stood in the hall, the girl inquired in her softest tone, "Do you need me any longer?"

"Why, no, I don't need anybody. I'll speak a few words to your mother, and then William and I will go out into the park."

"I was going to do a little shopping, but, of course, if you want me——"

"Not a bit. I know my own way about."

Flying upstairs, Jenny Blair remembered, with an exquisite suspense, a joyous abandonment, that she had only three days to wait. Safe within her own room, she collected her faculties, paused on a note of pure rapture, and asked herself uneasily, "Waiting for what?" For she did not mean anything, she insisted, gazing through the back window down on the garden, where little Erminia was building a house of pebbles and sticks in the deep roots of the sycamore. All she wanted was to live her own life and be happy, without hurting anybody or making the least bit of trouble. Nobody, not even her mother, could reproach her for that. Suddenly her heart cried out, and she spoke in a whisper. "I want to be happy! If I can't be happy, I'd rather be dead!" Even though she despised him, she knew that she couldn't be happy again so long as he was away. "I hate him so much that I cannot bear it if he does not come back. It is just like love, only it isn't love." Nothing could be more amazing than the way love and hate ran into each other, and melted and blended, and felt so exactly alike when they caught fire and flamed up.

The door into the hall was ajar, and Aunt Etta's voice floated plaintively from the back room on the opposite side of the house. "Is that you, Jenny Blair?"

"Yes, I'm going out." Crossing the hall, she entered the room and stood beside the couch on which Aunt Etta was lying. "Do you need anything?"

"Nothing but some thinner nightgowns. But I told Isabella. She is going to look for them."

"Has she been here this morning?"

"Yes, she's just gone out shopping. All the children are downstairs, and they make such a noise I can't hear myself think. They must drive Isabella out of her senses."

"Oh, she doesn't mind. She always liked noise."

"I know she does. It's a pity Joseph doesn't talk more."

"Well, I like Joseph. I always did."

"Do you know where little Erminia is? She is quiet for once."

"That's because she is playing by herself. She is building a house in the roots of the sycamore. Isn't your head better this morning, Aunt Etta?"

Aunt Etta sat up on the couch and smoothed the hair from her forehead. She held a novel with a yellow back in her long thin hands, and her eyes, the colour of frosted plums, were fixed on the feathery blossoms of a mimosa tree. When she came home every day from the doctor's office, her nostrils were packed with an ointment which was supposed to relieve her pain, but had never done so except for a few minutes. She was interested now, Jenny Blair knew, in the strange young physician who treated her every morning, and then forgot all about her until he saw her again. Poor Aunt Etta's infatuations began always with this kind of false dawn and ended in a sultry twilight of disappointment. It did not seem fair that she should have exactly the same mistake happen over and over again; but, then, did anything ever seem fair? Mamma said she had fallen into the habit of being disappointed in love, and that it was one of the very hardest habits to break.

"Perhaps," Jenny Blair said, trying to sound sympathetic, though, as she told herself impatiently, one could not go on feeling sympathetic for ever, "perhaps Doctor Pembroke will really cure you."

With her thumb keeping the place in her book, Aunt Etta lay back on the high pillows and withdrew her moody gaze from the mimosa tree. There were times, her look said, when she preferred ugliness, when ugliness hurt less than beauty, which was too much alive. For ugliness demanded nothing, had no exactions, left one, without effort or excitement, in the long peace of futility.

"He is simply wonderful," she replied. "I've never seen any one so skilful. He thinks he can cure me if I give him time."

"Oh, I hope so. Please give him all the time he needs. Has he said when he thinks you may go to the White?"

"He doesn't know. Not until the first of August anyway. But I wish you would take Father. Cora might go, too, perfectly well. I don't mind being left with the servants."

"Well, I'd just as soon stay with you. I don't care about going."

"But you ought to go. It is dull for you in town. Father is feeling the heat dreadfully. Won't you try to persuade him to go next week?"

"I thought old people didn't suffer from heat. He is always insisting that he finds the summers pleasant in Queenborough. He says he has even got used to that bad smell."

"He is just saying that on my account." Aunt Etta's tone was almost peevish. "He thinks he has to stay with me; but I don't need him. The house is so much quieter when I am here by myself, and Isabella's children aren't making all that noise in the garden. Besides, Doctor Pembroke will look after me. He says he'll come any hour, day or night, that I need him."

"I know," Jenny Blair assented. "But it isn't any use trying. Families are like that. They are always there, whether you want them or not. Aunt Isabella is going Saturday, and all the rest of us will go the first of August, if the doctor is through with you."

"I wish," Aunt Etta complained querulously, "that I might sometimes do as I please."

"You can't. Nobody can. I don't believe even Grandfather ever did as he pleased. I suppose coloured people do," the girl added desperately, "but I'm not sure. It seems to me everybody is bent on crossing everybody else. Now, I'm going. Are you sure you don't want anything? There are some old men talking to Grandfather downstairs, and I want to slip out before they see me. Old men are so silly. Not just older men, but really old men, the sort that come to see Grandfather and are always wanting to kiss you."

"No, nothing at all." Aunt Etta's face sagged like an empty pouch, and she opened her French novel with a gesture of spiritless defiance.

"I wonder," Jenny Blair thought, turning away, "why her face stays so puffy when she is thin everywhere else? When she gets old, she will look exactly like a pudding. Oh, well! I do hope when I'm old I shan't have a face like a pudding. Not that she's really old. Oh, well——"

But she had never thought about Aunt Etta with her whole mind; and by the time she had crossed the hall and entered her room, her own inner self absorbed her attention. Obeying a confirmed habit, of which she was entirely unaware, she walked straight to the mirror and gazed at herself with admiration and a kind of unfailing surprise. There was a little smile tucked in at the corners of her mouth, and she tried to keep it there as long as she could, for it seemed to her very attractive, as if it were saying to men, "Come and catch me! Come and catch me!"

No, she wouldn't go out yet. There was no reason for going into the street on Saturday morning. Everything there seemed stale, dusty, unexciting, and strangely deserted, just as it looked after a parade had gone by and left only orange rinds and peanut hulls and flat toy balloons. A vague dissatisfaction stole into her mind, and her youthful features borrowed for an instant the hardened look of a woman who is disenchanted with life. She yawned slightly, not from drowsiness, but because she could think of nothing she wanted to do. It was too hot for a walk or a drive and, besides, Mamma would have the car for her Saturday marketing. If she went to see Bena, there would be only more talk of boys, and of the girls who had gone too far at the Whites' garden party last week. Boys, she thought angrily, dropping down into a chair by the window, are the most stupid things in the world. They never see when they are in the way; they never see anything but themselves. Older men are nicer, even if they are horrid and do try to tease. But they have some sense; they are more like her handsome father, who had been simply too wonderful to live in the world. Older men didn't just giggle and chaff and fling bread-crumbs across the table into one's face. Yes, older men knew something. They knew how to behave.

Outside, heat rained down like light from the metallic dome of the sky. From the garden end of the house, away from the street, the whole world appeared, not flat and dusty, but over-ripe and juicy and dripping with summer. As the sunshine poured down over the flower-beds, a sleepy fragrance floated up to the window. Now and then, after a long stillness, a faint breeze stirred the sensitive leaves of the mimosa; and then, for a minute only, an evil odour tainted the air and the sunlight.

OWNSTAIRS on the back porch, sheltered from the sun by the grey-and-purple awning, General Archbald sat with a group of old men who had dropped in for a smoke. Though all were upwards of eighty, there was nothing impressive about their long lives except that they had been able to live them, that they had been young once and were now old. On the surface they were alike and yet not alike. Each face was engraved, as all old faces are, more by habit than by character or emotion. Only the expression of the eyes was indistinguishable—a look that was patient, uncertain, apologetic, and clinging. As they had accepted fate without thinking about it, so they clung now to the empty hours that were left over from life. If they stayed through the morning until one o'clock, Mrs. Archbald would send out mint juleps in silver goblets; and the old men would drink slowly, with a lingering delight in the quality of Bourbon or Bumgardner, and a moderation that would have amazed their grandchildren in the next decade.

Light footsteps sped through the hall, and Jenny Blair, still wearing her white straw hat with the pink lining, opened the screen door and glanced out. "Good-morning! I know you're having a lovely time!" she said, and darted away in time to escape being kissed.

Outside, in lower Washington Street, the sun blazed down on asphalt and dust and motor cars and a few hucksters' carts drawn by tormented horses. Several fine old elms were still left, preserved by the ceaseless vigilance of General Archbald and George Birdsong; but on the blocks beyond, where property was held in greater esteem, the trees had been cleared away before office buildings, shops, and garages. In front of the shops, people were passing in bands, colourless yet perspiring, slouching, giggling, untidy. The men slipped by rapidly, driven by the fetish of time; only the women, in bright stained dresses that clung to their ankles and flower-garlanded hats skewered to projecting masses of hair, dawdled to gaze in the windows with eyes that were absorbed, empty, pathetic. Many of them were old, and both old and young dragged whimpering, resisting children through the dust and the merciless sunshine. These were the unsheltered women, Jenny Blair knew, unsheltered everywhere, not only in places like Queenborough, but all over the world. They were the women, and the men too, of whom John Welch talked so long and so tediously.

Well, even if life were unfair to them (and Mamma insisted that they were all happier than Aunt Etta, who had been sheltered so tenderly), what could she or John or any one else do about it? "I suppose they are better off than they were in the Middle Ages," she thought cheerfully, "but I'm sure their faces could never have been more empty than they are now. Empty and sullen, John may say what he pleases. No matter," she thought, impatiently, turning back into the shade of the trees. "Life is like that, and you cannot change things by thinking." Why had she come out? It would have been better to stay in the house. Or, perhaps, she ought to have gone with Mamma to market. There wasn't anything to do out of doors on Saturday morning, and if she went to see Bena Peyton or Grace Bertram or Amy Jones, she would simply have to listen while they ran on about nothing. To be sure Bena always had caramels (it was the way she stuffed sweets that made her so fat); but it was silly to eat caramels when one might look ahead to Zoana's blackberry roll for lunch. No, she would not go anywhere until late afternoon. She would only stop at the Birdsongs' a minute to ask Maggie if she had remembered to give Ariel his bit of lettuce.

But the Birdsongs' house was so lonely she could scarcely bear to stay a moment inside. Life, air, colour, animation, all had melted away since yesterday morning. Was it being lived in that made houses alive? she asked herself, gazing at the silent canary. Or did Mrs. Birdsong possess some peculiar enchantment, some living magic of personality? Never, never had she felt such loneliness, such stillness, such vacancy. "When he comes back, and I know he is in town, everything will be different," she thought. "Then I shan't mind coming over here every morning. Even if we never meet, it will be something to feel that he will soon be in the house." The garden, too, was as flat and glittering as if it were seen under glass. Looking out, as she went through the library, she saw the overgrown flower-beds, the web of blue morning glories, and a bent old coloured man cutting the tall grass with a sickle. Nothing looked natural. Every tree, every shrub, every flower, and even the monotonous rhythm of the sickle and the pale swaths of grass all seemed to be swimming in loneliness. "I've only three days to wait," she thought. "Not quite three days, because a part of one is already over." But, after three days, what did she expect? For what was she waiting? She could not answer. She did not know. Suddenly, she thought with a rush of emotion, a welling up of delight, "Just to see him again! After all this loneliness, just to see him again!"

As she turned back into the library, the door of the cupboard swung open, and she caught a glimpse of the brown woolen sweater he had worn for golf on cool days. Going inside, she buried her face in the knitted thickness and roughness and the intoxicating smell of sunshine on red clover. Little pointed flames flickered over her cheeks. Almost she could.bring him back to her. Almost she could feel his arms about her and his eager kiss on her mouth. If only she had known sooner! Now, as long as he was away, she could steal over every morning, when nobody suspected, and bury her face in the brown wool while she pretended that she was clasped in his arms. Then, as she heard the sound of Maggie's step in the hall, she slipped out of the cupboard, shut the door carefully, and ran out of the house.

For three days, and then three other days, she kept this joy secret. Not to her mother, not to her grandfather, could she let the slightest sign of it escape. For they, of course, could never understand how she felt. They would think that she hoped to be happy, when all she wanted was to love in vain and for ever, to feel this longing hidden safe away in her heart. For her feeling had altered once more. After six days of waiting for nothing, of passionate silence, all the bitterness was drained out of her thoughts. He might tease her now; he might mock her as much as he pleased, if only he would come back.

But he did not come back for another week, and when he came, she did not see him alone. Though the General brought news of him or of Mrs. Birdsong every day, George came to the house only for a few minutes before or after his game of golf. He was always either just going out to the club, or just going home to change before dinner. Then, at last, he dropped in quite casually one Sunday evening and asked Mrs. Archbald if he might stay to supper. Jenny Blair was wearing her prettiest summer dress. At the first sound of his voice in the hall, she had flown upstairs to her room; she had seized her rose-coloured chiffon from the closet; she had shaken the flounces until they were smooth; she had slipped them over her head; she had wrapped the sash of blue ribbon round her waist and knotted it in a flowing bow at her left side. In five minutes, scarcely more, she was down again in the drawing-room, with her hair as lustrous as satin and her face glowing like a carnation. Her heart was beating all over her body. Not only in her bosom and in her ears, but everywhere. The drumming was so loud that it frightened her. Suppose her mother, who missed so little, should ask her what was the matter. Then, she felt, she should die. She could not live if she were dragged out into the light and her agitation exposed.

But nobody noticed. Nobody heard her heart, though it sounded, she thought, as relentless as the breaking of waves on a beach. Though she shivered in the heat when George, who was fresh and bronzed and ruddy, said carelessly, "Why, Jenny

Blair, you look like a doll," she was able to toss back flippantly, "Not in this old thing. I've had it for ages."

"But it is one of your new dresses," her mother corrected.

"Well, it feels old. I put it on because it is cool."

"It's a nice colour," her grandfather observed, peering over his glasses with a puzzled expression. "Those thin, frilly dresses are very becoming."

At last they went in to supper, and afterwards (how had she been able to live through it?) George had talked to her grandfather for the rest of the evening. Even on the back porch in the moonlight (which was so living and savage that it stole into her mind, and made her more unhappy than she had ever been in her life) he still talked to her mother and her grandfather. They spoke of politics (all were Democrats but they disapproved of both parties and agreed that there was nothing to be done about them); they spoke of foreign affairs, of Austria and Servia, of the Liberals in England, who were not so very liberal, after all, and of the Irish question, which was becoming more and more Irish; they spoke of the suffragettes in other places and the suffragists in Queenborough (though George was inclined to make fun of them, Grandfather felt that the easiest way to avoid trouble was to give women what they wanted whenever they wanted it); they spoke of the heat wave, which they called the worst of the summer, and George insisted it was better to pay no attention to it, while Grandfather and Mamma believed that one should stop eating meat and move about as little as possible. Then, at last, after hours of misery, they began, just as George was leaving, to speak of that evil odour, and to wonder if it would end by driving them out of the neighbourhood, which, Mamma declared, was rapidly becoming impossible.

"You don't notice it to-night," George said. "There's not a whiff of it out here. The scent of mimosa is delicious."

"It doesn't bother us often," Mrs. Archbald admitted. "Weeks go by, and nobody but Etta complains of it. Then something happens, either the wind turns or they are careless down at the plant, and the smell is quite disagreeable."

"I've never been positive," the General insisted, "that it isn't mere imagination, or the emptying of garbage cans somewhere in the alley. I've tried my best, and I'm never able to detect it. Not more than once or twice, anyway, and then only for a minute or so."

"That was when it was very strong, Father."

"Maybe you're right, my dear, and my senses are less keen than they used to be."

"Oh, I didn't mean that, dear Father," Mrs. Archbald put her hand on his arm with an affectionate pressure, "I didn't mean that."

"Well, it would be funny if it drove us all out of the neighbourhood." George could no more help smoothing things over, Jenny Blair knew, than he could help the sanguine tone of his voice. That was his charming way, and she asked herself vehemently if any man in the world could compare with him. "It would be funny," he repeated, standing there in the moonlight, with the open door at his back, "if, after having lived most of our lives here, we should be driven away at last by a smell."

"I shall hold my ground a little longer," the General declared, "in the hope that Cora's idealism, which John insists I share also, may pretend the nuisance away."

"It's amazing, isn't it, how the town, or our part of it, has run off and left us? A few more years, and industrialism will have swallowed us whole. Nothing can stop it, except another war, and that isn't likely. Not for us at least. It wouldn't surprise me any day if Ulster were to begin fighting in earnest, and trouble may come, though I doubt that, of this affair on the Continent. But we aren't apt to go far enough out of our way to start fighting in Europe."

He was going without a glance at her; he had said, "Good-night!" in his usual light-hearted voice; he had turned at the front door and smiled at the three of them, with an impartial wave of his hand. Now he was gone and the evening was over.

Never had she suffered like this! Never before had she known how much easier it was to give him up than to be given up by him!

"Are you sleepy, Jenny Blair?" her mother asked. "You were so quiet."

"Yes, I'm sleepy. I'm so sleepy I can scarcely hold my eyes open."

"Then run straight upstairs. I suppose it was dull for you." Mrs. Archbald paused to bolt the front door. "I wish you would ask some nice boys to Sunday supper."

"I don't want to ask any boys. I despise boys," Jenny Blair replied fretfully, for she was on the point of tears. Yes, it was true, she had never, in all her seventeen years and ten months, been so unhappy. As she went slowly upstairs, after kissing her mother and her grandfather, she felt that savage loneliness stealing like moonlight into her mind. And downstairs in the hall her grandfather was saying cheerfully, "Time to turn in, William. I hope we'll get a breeze later on." "Why is it," she asked herself, with tragic intensity, "that only young people are ever really unhappy?"

A week went by, then a fortnight, and she was still asking this question. Why did she have to suffer such anguish when she expected nothing? Nothing but that glow, that flame, that ecstasy, which beat over her in waves whenever she looked into his eyes, whenever she heard his voice, whenever she stole into the cupboard and buried her flushed face in the brown wool. "It isn't my fault," she thought resentfully. "Nobody could wish to suffer like this. I didn't want to fall in love with him. I didn't want him to kiss me."

And now, after more than ten days of longing, of vacancy, of parching thirst for the sight of him, her mother inquired, in a tone of anxious tenderness, if she felt a pain anywhere.

"Do you feel let down, darling? Has the heat been too much for you?"

What could she answer? How could she tell her mother that she suffered because she was in love (though she expected nothing) with George Birdsong, whom she had known all her life? He was old enough to be her father; he was the husband of her mother's dearest friend; and he was the last man in the world, even had he been unmarried and above reproach in his conduct, that her mother would have desired as a son-in-law. No, she could not confess. She would endure anything, she would suffer every torture of hopeless longing, before she could be forced to confess. For her mother would only laugh, and worse than any pain would be the humiliation of her mother's laughter, which was wise and dry, like the sardonic laughter of age.

"No, I haven't a pain anywhere. I'm just tired."

"I don't like the sound of that, Jenny Blair." How brisk her mother was, how firm, how capable, and how undiscerning! "You may be feverish. Whether you like it or not, I'm going to take your temperature. I never thought it was safe for you to stay here in this terrible heat."

"There's nothing the matter. Anybody would be tired when it is so hot." But she was made to sit down and hold the thermometer in her mouth, while she shivered with fear lest the tiny glass tube should betray the passion of love.

"No, you haven't any fever." Mrs. Archbald appeared relieved, as indeed she was. "You will be all right, I hope, as soon as we get to the mountains. Etta is doing so well—her illness is the only thing hot weather seems to agree with—that the doctor thinks it will be safe for us to go the end of this week."

"Not this week? Why, to-day is Thursday." Jenny Blair's lips dropped apart, while her empty little face, with its flower-like colour and softness, was transfixed by dread.

"You needn't worry, dear. I've had my things, and your grandfather's too, packed for days, just waiting until the doctor said Etta was well enough. It won't take me two hours to get you ready, and Cindy, who is going with us, can easily look after Etta. We shall all feel so much better as soon as we are out of this heat and settled comfortably in our cottage. Remember to shut your mouth," she commanded sternly; "when you hold it open like that, you look as if you hadn't a particle of sense."

"But I don't want to go, Mamma. I'd much rather stay here all summer."

"Jenny Blair!" Mrs. Archbald's voice was cool, crisp, and commanding. Though she seldom lost her serenity, and had acquired a commendable adroitness in handling both the old and the young, there were moments, she sometimes said, when everything seemed too much. The intense heat of the last fortnight, Etta's incessant demands for sympathy and service, and her daughter's inexplicable spells of caprice,—all these things had tried her, she felt, beyond anybody's enduring. True, she looked cool; but the coolness of her skin, which was naturally dry and did not flush easily, was as deceptive as the rosy cast of her philosophy. For one instant, scarcely longer than a drawn breath, she appeared almost disagreeable; then the artificial sweetness of her expression sprang back, as if it were held in place by an elastic band. "Jenny Blair," she repeated, "are you out of your head?"

"Not day after to-morrow, Mamma! Not on Saturday!"

Mrs. Archbald, who was hemming a napkin, fastened the square of damask over her knee with the fierce thrust of a black-headed pin. Not until the work was securely pinned to her lap was she able to bestow her undivided attention upon Jenny Blair.

"I wish I knew, my child, what is the matter with you."

"Nothing is the matter, Mamma. Only, please, please, don't go next Saturday. I can't get ready in time."

"You won't have any getting ready to do. I shall attend to all that, and you know perfectly well you have never lifted a finger to help with the packing. As soon as you are out of Queenborough, you will begin to feel better. Sometimes," she added gravely, biting her lower lip, "I think that it is a mistake to bring up girls as we do. We make them entirely too self-centred. If I didn't know better, I should be tempted to believe that you have some foolish notion about a boy in your head."

"Oh, Mamma, you know I haven't!"

"Yes, I am sure that you haven't. That is what I can't understand. Have you had a quarrel with John?"

Jenny Blair tossed her head. "No, I haven't—but suppose I had. What difference in the world would it make?"

"Then there's Fred Harrison. I hope you haven't made any trouble with Fred. His mother was my bosom friend when we went to school."

"Well, I haven't. He's only twenty-two, and I've always told you I couldn't abide boys."

"You're too young to have notions," Mrs. Archbald said sternly. "Why, you aren't even out yet, and it is the greatest mistake for girls to fall in love before they're old enough to know their own minds." Then, as she unpinned the napkin and gathered up her work-basket, her scissors, her thimble, and her needle and thread, she added warningly, "The trouble with you, Jenny Blair, is that you do not know the first thing about life. It is only by knowing how little life has in store for us that we are able to look on the bright side and avoid disappointment."

Long after she had gone, Jenny Blair stood gazing out of the window into the golden dust of summer. As if anybody but Mamma had ever found that there was a bright side to disappointment! That was the way people talked when they embraced resignation—and if there was a single virtue she disliked more than any other, she thought bitterly, that virtue was resignation. Hadn't she, when all was said, a right to a little happiness? A stab pierced her heart, and she knew that she could not—she simply could not go away without seeing him. No matter what her mother said or did for her good, no matter what any one else said or did, she could not go away without seeing him. If only he had not avoided her! If only he had shown her by the slightest sign that he had not forgotten! The faintest sign would have sufficed. The faintest sign that he remembered would have driven away this torment of longing. Her thoughts fluttered like living things in her mind, and while they fluttered and dropped and fluttered again out into the stillness, she changed into a prettier dress, and settled the hat with the flopping brim and the wreath of cornflowers at a more picturesque angle on the scalloped waves of her hair. Then, at last, after a questioning glance in the mirror, she picked up her beaded bag and a fan that was decorated with bluebirds, and ran downstairs and out of the house. "Anything is better than this," she thought, as she walked down the block to the Birdsongs' gate. "It isn't," she changed the bag and fan to her left hand, and opened the gate, "as if I were to blame. It isn't," she stooped to detach a muslin flounce from the thorn of a rose, "as if I had chosen to suffer like this."

✻ ✻ ✻ ✻ ✻ ✻ ✻ T H E R ring Maggie opened the door, hurriedly ✻ wiping her free hand on a crumpled apron. ✻ She was a kind, fat, slow old body, blacker, as ✻ Mrs. Birdsong once remarked, than God made ✻ them now. Her sponge cake was delicious, and ✻ ✻ ✻ ✻ ✻ ✻ ✻ ✻ completely refuted Mrs. Archbald's theory that sponge cake requires the hand of a lady. She was also the only surviving cook in Queenborough who could be per-suaded to make beaten biscuits, which she beat for half an hour with the handle of an axe, and salt-rising bread, which must rise four times, and was put down by the kitchen stove at four o'clock in the morning. But Mr. Birdsong enjoyed beaten bis-cuits and salt-rising bread; and though Maggie loved her mistress in moderation, she adored the ground her master walked on and was proud of all the extra trouble he made.

"I'm going away, Maggie," Jenny Blair explained, flushing and paling because her heart thudded so fast and loud under her lace bertha. "I'm going to the White day after to-morrow."

Well, all news was good news to-day, Maggie declared. She was happy because Miss Etta was mending; she was happy because they had had a cheerful word from Miss Eva (who was doing as well as could be expected, though naturally she was homesick and missed Maggie's hand in the dough); she was happy, too, because Jenny Blair would have a good time and catch all the beaux at the White.

"I don't care for beaux, Maggie." There was no use, of course, in saying that. Maggie would not believe her; and whether she believed her or not made little difference. "I've run over to say good-bye," she added, as she entered the hall. "Is Mr. Birdsong at home?" The question was out. She had spoken his name to Maggie and the empty house, and nothing had happened. "Who? Marse George? Yas, ma'am, he's heah. He's settin' right out dar on de back po'ch." Berry, who belonged to the new school, would never have called Mr. Birdsong "Marse George," and this, Jenny Blair suspected, was one of the reasons he preferred Maggie—this and the way she spoiled him and never minded slaving over her stove on hot summer evenings, if only he rewarded her with an appetite and praise of her dishes.

So he was really there! Already, even before she knew, her senses had warned her that he was near. "You needn't wait, Maggie," she said boldly. "I'll see you before I go, but I want to run upstairs and look at Ariel a minute. Is he all right to-day?"

"Yas'm, but I'se moughty feared he's gwinter mope w'en dar ain' nobody but me left in de house."

She went back to the kitchen, untying her apron as she passed out of sight, and Jenny Blair, spurred by a sense of panic, darted through the library and out on the little square porch beyond the lattice-door.

"I've come to tell you good-bye," she called, before she descended the single step from the door to the porch. "We're going to the White on Saturday morning."

At her step, at her voice, he spun round. "If it isn't Jenny Blair!" His kind and charming face beamed down on her. She looked into his smiling grey eyes and thought, in an ecstasy shot with terror, "This is what I was waiting for. This is what I expected." As he took her hand in his, she saw his eyes and his smile, and beyond his eyes and his smile, she saw the blue of the sky, the wind whitening the leaves of the mulberry tree, and the sunshine that struck downward like a blade of light on a border of red lilies.

"So you're going away, Jenny Blair?" He had drawn her to a bench, and stood gazing down on her, sunburned, eager, glowing with pleasure; yet, in spite of his pleasure, a little reserved, distant, inscrutable. Never had he seemed so gay or so splendid. All the lustre was there, but something was wanting. Oh, well, what did life, what did anything matter? She was blissfully happy. She knew that he remembered. The sky fell; the red lilies soared; and a radiant spray of sky, sun, flowers, saturated her mind. "Here, now, at this instant," she felt without thinking, "I know what ecstasy is." Not to-morrow, not next year when she was grown up, but while she stood here, while she looked into his eyes, while he held her hand, she was living her moment.

"That's nice, my dear child," he said quietly, standing very straight in the last sunbeams. "That's very nice for you. I hope you'll have all the fun in the world."

She looked up at him reproachfully. "Are you glad?"

"Of course I'm glad. I want you to have all the happiness there is anywhere."

His voice was firm and gentle, but it killed ecstasy. With his first words, ecstasy paled, flickered, died, and was lost. In a flash so brief that it was gone before she had seized it, the light was over, was done with, was nothing more than a fog of unhappiness. "I'm only seventeen," she thought, sitting on the bench, with her bag and fan in her lap, "and I may live for ever. I may live to be seventy." She might even live to be ninety. One of her grandmothers (she couldn't have been in love) had lived to be a hundred and one.

The shock was more than she could bear. "I can't—" she began suddenly, "I can't——" Sitting on the bench, with her hands clasped over her beaded bag and her fan, she began to cry quietly, without sound or movement, as a child cries when it has been punished. Her eyes were filled with reproach; her mouth fell open; her features were so immobile that the tears might have flowed over a painted mask.

"God!" he exclaimed, more in anger than invocation. For a breathless second he stared at her as if he expected her to burst like a bubble and vanish. Then he asked sharply, "Why are you doing that? What is the matter?"

A whimper broke from her, but she cried all the faster. Without lifting her hand, without making the slightest effort to check her tears or wipe the drops from her lashes, without even twitching her lips, she sat motionless on the bench and looked up at him.

"What do you want, Jenny Blair?" he demanded again more angrily.

"I don't want anything." The words rushed out in a low whimper of distress. "But I can't bear it. I can't bear it if you treat me this way."

"If I do what?" A sound that resembled profanity but may have been an endearment burst from him. "You're an idiot," he groaned softly. "You're a precious little idiot."

"I don't care." She was sobbing now, and her features were convulsed. "I can't bear it."

"Can't bear what?"

"Can't bear—everything."

He caught his breath sharply. "But don't you see how childish, how perfectly absurd all this is? Why, I'm old enough to be your father; I've known you ever since you were born; I am devoted to your family, especially to your grandfather. You're in love with love, you little goose."

"I don't care. I don't care how old you are." She looked up at him with her wide, shallow, devouring gaze. Beneath the stains of tears, her face was as soft as a baby's, and her small, vivid mouth, which was round and open and insatiable, was as innocent of meaning as if the hole had been drawn with two hasty strokes of red chalk.

"It isn't as if I wanted anything," she said presently. "I'm not asking for anything in the world." Her lips closed, relaxed, and then dropped back into that look of incredible vacancy.

"Oh, yes, you are." His tone was aggrieved and roughened by a sense of injury. "That's the way with all you young things. You never think of a human being but yourselves. I don't want to hurt anybody. I never wanted to hurt anybody. The trouble with you, my dear little girl," he added, unconsciously repeating her mother, "is that you don't know the first thing about life."

Her eyelids flickered and a single tear on her lashes trembled and fell. The taste was as sharp and salt as the sea. She had forgotten that tears were so briny. "I do," she replied, with an obstinate whimper. "I know more than you think."

"Well, you don't act like it. If you could see what a baby you look, you'd stop whimpering. Can't you stop it?" he exclaimed, with sudden exasperation. Still watching her, but drawing no nearer, he added resentfully, "And there are some fools who think men make all the trouble in life!"

Without lowering her eyelids, which might have been plastered back by her wet lashes, she fumbled in her bag and brought out a wisp of a handkerchief. While she dabbed aimlessly at her eyes and cheeks, she rose from the bench and made a single faltering step toward the door. As he did not try to detain her, she stopped of her own accord and turned round. "I am not," she retorted in vehement despair, "I am not trying to make trouble."

"Oh, yes, you are." Big as he was, his tone was one of injured helplessness. "You're not only trying, you're making it as fast as you can." The heat—or was it anger?—had whipped a dark wine-colour into his face; there were moist splotches round his mouth and under his eyes; and it seemed to her that his features had swollen, as if his lower lip had been stung by a hornet. But there was no hornet about, there was not a mosquito, there was not even a gnat; and she decided, while she looked up at him, that it must be either the hot spell or that curious resentment which made him appear suddenly so much less attractive. Yet it astonished her to discover that his overheated face made not the faintest difference in her desire to be close to him. "You're tempting me," he added hoarsely, "and you know it."

"I'm not. I'm not tempting you." Her anger flashed out to meet the challenge of his. "I hate you. I've always hated you."

"Do you?" His abrupt laugh quivered through her senses, and poured itself like joy into the shuddering beats of her heart. "Do you hate me, Jenny Blair? Do you hate me now?" He had bent toward her; she was in his arms again; she was enveloped in his strength, his vitality, his hardness and roughness, in the summer smell of his clothes and his skin, and, above all, in that lost feeling of security, rightness, fulfilment. "Do you hate me like this, Jenny Blair?" he repeated softly, with his cheek on hers and his lips seeking her mouth. As if he also were lost in the moment, he began kissing her mouth and throat, at first lightly and slowly, and then faster and deeper and more roughly until it seemed to her that her breath was extinguished. Ecstasy over again! Oh, what ecstasy! Once more the world was alive without and within. Once more the shower of light rained through her being. Once more the sky fell, and the last sunbeams crashed and splintered over the red lilies. For this was life, not pain, not longing, not inner loneliness, but this ecstasy.

Then, while she still clung to him, he released her and drew back. As abruptly as he had embraced her, his arms dropped away, his lips tightened and grew stern, his face closed and darkened. In a second he was reserved, severe, distant.

"Now you'd better run home," he said. "Be a good child, and have all the fun you can at the White."

"I don't want to go to the White." She was shivering in her muslin flounces. "I don't want to go anywhere."

"But you must. You must enjoy youth while you have it." He had walked to the other end of the porch, and was holding a cigar in fingers that trembled. "You don't know what it means to be growing old—to be growing old and to know that youth is the only thing in the universe."

At the change in his voice she seemed to shrink back within herself, and a yearning look awoke in her young face. Why did he talk like this? What did all these things matter? What did anything matter? "I don't care," she said stubbornly. "I don't care, and I can't help it. I didn't ask to suffer this way."

His smile, as he looked down on her, was tender, ironic, and faintly wistful. "You ask, my dear, without knowing it. But how long have you had this—this extraordinary fancy?"

"Oh, always!" She spoke with courage and vehemence. "Ever since I was little. Ever since that afternoon, years ago, when I met you in Memoria's house and we sat on the pile of lumber together."

"In Memoria's house?" His voice was so breathless that she glanced up in startled suspicion. Was he mocking at her again? Or was he merely surprised to find how long, how very long she had cared? "Have you ever," he inquired after a pause, "told any one of our meeting?"

"Didn't we promise? If I'd told any one, even Mamma or Mrs. Birdsong, it wouldn't have been our secret any longer. It was keeping our secret that—that——"

"But you were only ten. Why, you weren't even ten!"

"I was nine and a half. Of course I didn't know how I felt until—until—" she choked, bit back a sob, and went on with an air of gallant surrender—"until that afternoon in the yard at the hospital."

A frown drew his smooth brows together, and for the first time since she had known him, his face appeared almost forbidding. "You make me feel that I was a cad," he said slowly. "There is no excuse for a cad—only—only I never imagined." He came a step nearer, while his charming smile enkindled his features, "Oh, well, you're a dear little girl. Run along now, and have all the fun that you can."

Terror seized her again, terror alone, without ecstasy. He was glad, he was even eager to send her away. "I am not a child," she answered resentfully. Because she could not keep back the impulse any longer, she broke out desperately, "I thought you cared! Oh, I thought you cared when it happened!"

"Of course I care. Can't you see?" He was frowning again. "I adore youth, and you are—well, youth adorable."

Her face cleared; summer rained into her eyes; a smile trembled like an edge of joy on her lips. Life was marvellous again, or unendurable! "I want everything," she thought swiftly. "I want everything before I am too old." Aloud she said in an exultant tone, "I can be happy if I know you haven't forgotten."

"Well, we'll make another promise, and a better one this time. If you will go away and be happy, I will promise not to forget you. John is coming now. I hear him at the front door."

"Then I'll go. That's a promise, but—" she smiled up at him joyously—"I am coming back again in six weeks."

"In six weeks? By that time, you will have lost your heart and your head too. Good-bye, and God bless you." Then, raising his voice, he asked quickly, "Is that you, John? Jenny Blair is waiting to tell you good-bye."

That was not true. Turning away quickly, she went through the library to the hall, and met John before he had time to put down his papers and take off his hat. "I haven't a minute to stay. I'm going straight home."

"I'll walk over with you. You won't mind?"

Oh, no, she did not mind. Dazzled, blissful, floating on air, she descended the steps and passed out of the gate. Though she was vaguely disturbed by the presence at her side, John existed for her more as a moving shadow than as a man. Nothing mattered but George's promise not to forget her. Nothing mattered but this central bliss which diffused light and warmth through her being.

"You don't look natural, Jenny Blair," John said abruptly.

"What?" Her mouth dropped, and she stared up at him.

"You've looked different for the last few weeks. Has anything happened?"

"What could happen here in summer?"

"What couldn't? Life, death, falling in love, falling out of love."

How provoking John was! Even as a boy he had had a way of seeing too much. "How could anybody fall in love in this heat?"

"If you think this is hot, you ought to go down to the chemical plant."

She shook her head. Why was he always dragging in disagreeable subjects? "I don't want to go. I can smell it up here."

"Oh, no, you can't. You haven't the faintest notion what it really smells like. I saw a family down there today that hadn't had any ice all summer. There is a baby six weeks old and three other children."

"Why don't they go to the Ice Mission? Mamma works awfully hard making people give money to her Ice Mission." Her voice trailed off pensively. It was all distressing, she knew, and she wished she could make the whole world happy and good; but she wanted to be alone and to think, she wanted to be alone with her insurgent emotions.

He was watching her attentively while he mopped his face. Why did men always look so hot? "You don't care about anything but yourself," he burst out angrily at last, for, like other fine characters, he imagined that people could be made over by scolding. "Oh, I know you better than you think! You are like every other young girl who has grown up without coming in touch with the world. You are so bottled up inside that your imagination has turned into a hothouse for sensation. I can look into your mind—I can look into any young girl's mind—and see every one of you busy faking emotion. Good God!" (What did he mean? Was he really beside himself?) "As if passion didn't do harm enough in its natural state, without trying to fake it!"

"I don't see," her tone was airy with insolence, "why it should matter to you what we do. It isn't your affair anyway."

"I'm not so sure of that. Everything seems to be my affair sooner or later."

"Well, I'm not." Why couldn't they be together ten minutes without plunging into a quarrel? Why did he feel that he was inspired to improve her? "And I'm never going to be that, so you may make your mind easy."

Her words were emphatic, but they had barely left her lips before they dissolved into vapour. Again she floated up into the shimmering haze of her illusion, beyond sight, beyond sound, beyond touch of reality. When at last he spoke, she was obliged to sink down from the clouds to his flat and prosaic medium.

"There's one thing certain," he said abruptly. "If there's a real war, I am not going to be left out of it. But for Cousin Eva, I'd sail to-morrow."

"Do you think England will fight?"

"Who knows? Your grandfather says human nature has never turned its back on a war that comes this near."

"Well, I hope they won't fight; but if they do, I hope they will stay in Europe. It's bad enough hearing all the old men tell about the Civil War over and over."

They had stopped before her gate, and he was looking down on her with a troubled expression. "You will be careful, won't you, Jenny Blair?"

"Careful?"

"I mean about everything, now that Cousin Eva is ill." Then he frowned. "It may be just my imagination, but—oh, well, you know why I am speaking."

"No, I don't, and I don't want to! I don't care what you say about anybody."

Rushing ahead of him, without glancing back or heeding his voice, she opened the gate and hurried up the walk to the porch. Her heart choked her, and she felt as if she were smothering. Then, as she looked round and saw that John had not followed her, that he was already returning to the Birdsongs' house, the tumult died down, and she waited there in the twilight, with her eyes on the thinning red of the afterglow. Gradually the storm passed and was followed by the exultant joy of her earlier mood. Nothing had happened. Everything was still as perfect as it had been before John cast his shadow of ugliness. "In six weeks I shall be back again," she thought. "In six weeks I shall be back again, and I shall see him." And it seemed to her that these weeks of absence stretched in a dark hollow between the illuminated peaks of the past and the future.

CHAPTER 11

WELL, the summer went by quickly," General Archbald said, leaning back, with the head of William clasped between his knees, as the car turned the corner.

"Oh, Grandfather, it was an eternity," Jenny Blair responded, with one of the broken sighs of youth which come and go without reason. "And we stayed so much longer than we expected to. Why, to-day is the first of October."

"But you had a beautiful time," Mrs. Archbald remonstrated; for it seemed ungrateful to Providence not to acknowledge occasional blessings. Then she also sighed, but her sigh was drawn out to its fullest dimension, since all the effort and burden of moving had been hers, and her mind and muscles ached with fatigue. "It was a very successful summer," she added. "The change has done your grandfather and Aunt Etta a great deal of good. But I am glad to be home again. It is always a relief when a pleasure is over." While she lost control of her thoughts for a moment the sanguine expression of her mouth might have been etched on blank parchment.

"I feel much stronger," Etta admitted, "and I'm glad I learned to play cards. This winter, if I can keep free from that sinus infection, I'm going to have some card parties."

"And we'll all be very busy over Jenny Blair's coming out." Mrs. Archbald recovered her sprightliness. "Old Mrs. Montgomery thinks we're bringing her out too soon; but the child has such a dread of a finishing school. Nobody knows, anyway, what may happen next year, and this war in Europe will keep us from going abroad."

"If Mother hadn't made me wait two years because Uncle

Powhatan died, I might have had some pleasure before I lost my health," Etta murmured, forgetting, after a fortunate habit, that she had been a failure before she was born. As the car passed into the lower end of Washington Street, she poked her long thin nose out of the window and sniffed the dusty air of the town. "There is that smell again, Father. It seems too bad to come back to it."

The General, who was pulling William's ear, looked more annoyed than sympathetic. In the last few months, ever since Mrs. Birdsong's illness, even Jenny Blair, wrapped up in the impenetrable egoism of youth, had noticed that he flushed easily and was irritated by trifles. Once she had called her mother's attention to the old man's altered disposition. "What is it that makes his features twitch like that, Mamma? He never used to lose his temper, but now the slightest thing seems to upset him."

"He is showing his age, my child. You must remember that he was eighty-four this summer. Try to have patience. He has had a hard life, and that always tells at the end. After the war it was uphill work for a man in his thirties to take up a new profession and begin all over again. Never forget that old age is more trying to him than to any one else."

Now the old man was saying testily to Etta, "If you'd had to stay at home, perhaps you would not have noticed the smell so much. Suppose you were one of that throng streaming down to the tobacco factories."

"I was just watching them," Etta replied tartly. With less cause, since she was only thirty-three, she also was easily irritated. "The faces are all exactly like insects. Anyway, nobody minds the smell of tobacco."

"The smell will be gone in a minute," Mrs. Archbald said briskly. "It never lasts. There! You don't notice it any longer. And Father is perfectly right. We ought to remember our blessings and be thankful that we aren't working in a factory."

"No, Cora, I didn't put it that way." General Archbald's face was beginning to twitch. Then breaking off with a gesture of hopeless impatience, he turned his head and looked out on the other side of the street.

"How many of those girls, do you suppose," Etta inquired moodily, "are as unhappy as I am?" As nobody answered her question, she leaned back in her corner and very furtively (since the General and his daughter-in-law both retained the prejudices of good breeding) used a bit of powdered chamois-skin she had concealed in her handkerchief.

Watching her, Jenny Blair thought lightly that ideas must skim over Aunt Etta's mind without touching the surface. Poor Aunt Etta, it must be dreadful to be like that, for she also, though she wasn't aware of it, had a face like an insect. It would be better to be young and pretty and work in a factory than to be old and ugly and tormented by a sinus infection. "I'm glad I'm pretty," she continued, flitting back to herself. "I'm glad people love me because I'm pretty."

Mamma, she felt, had spoken no more than the truth; they had had a beautiful summer. White Sulphur had been so gay and so wonderful that she had very nearly, but never quite, forgotten George for a whole evening. Very nearly, but not quite, she had fallen in love with somebody else—with somebody years and years younger. There was a love letter, her first real love letter, hidden now inside her chemise, next her skin. If she had stayed longer (she had met him only three days before she left), she might have fallen in love all over again in an entirely new way, which was even more exciting because it was vocal and unafraid.

But here everything was unchanged. It might have been summer still, so little impression had the last two months, which were packed for her with adventure, made on the arid scene she had left. Only the long straight street, rising and sinking with the hills, had accumulated a thicker deposit of dust, and the leaves on the elms hung brittle and tarnished, with curled edges, from the motionless boughs.

"I had almost forgotten," she thought, starting slightly. Almost, but not quite. As the car slowed down in front of the Birdsongs' gate, the sunshine was suddenly troubled, and the small bronze leaves stirred, rustled, turned on the stems, and came quietly to rest again in the stillness. A transparent curtain at an upper window blew out and was sucked in, as if a door had opened and shut in the room. When she looked back, it seemed to Jenny Blair that the old quiver started to life in the nerves of her memory, while a door in her mind also opened and shut, and the anguish she had left in Washington Street rushed in and consumed her. How had she lived through the summer? How had she so nearly forgotten? When the car stopped, and she waited for her grandfather to step to the pavement, that one instant, with the troubled sunshine and the blown curtain, seemed to hesitate and enclose her before it sped on again into the past. Everything was alive and aching once more. Not only her heart, which was filled again with unsatisfied hunger, but the houses and the street and every person and object. Even Mamma and Grandfather and Aunt Etta were all more real than they had been when she was living on the surface of herself in the mountains.

"Well, it's good to be back." They had entered the house, and after kissing Isabella and the children, stood gazing, like wistful strangers, through the hall and under the awning on the porch, to the scarlet sage and purple asters in the garden. From an immeasurable distance (so far off that the voices were as timeless as the breaking of waves on a beach) Jenny Blair heard and yet did not hear that Mrs. Birdsong had not come home because her nerves were still shattered.

"I had hoped she would be well by autumn," Mrs. Archbald said in an anxious tone, and Isabella replied, "Nobody seems to know what is the matter with her. She won't have anybody but Doctor Bridges, and he is too much of a surgeon to be good for anything else."

"When is she coming home? There are doctors enough in Queenborough."

"Yes, but she refuses to have any one else. She likes Doctor Bridges because he keeps telling her nothing is wrong. George is going to see her on Saturday, and he will bring her home if she is able to come."

"Poor George," Mrs. Archbald sighed. "He has really been very good."

"Yes, he has been very good when you consider——" The rest of Aunt Isabella's sentence was lost to Jenny Blair as she turned away from the porch.

In her own room upstairs, with the door shut, she felt that a mood had waited there since July to recapture her. The flower pattern on the wall-paper, the cream-coloured furniture decorated with garlands, the mirror so like a silver-green pool, the chintz curtains, the blue-and-grey rugs, her favourite books in the bookcase, the china figures of a shepherd and a shepherdess on the mantelpiece,—all these objects were drowned in that savage loneliness as if it were an invisible sea. It was extraordinary, it was incredible, that she should so nearly have forgotten the pang of desire, that she should so nearly have fallen in love with somebody else.

Stopping before the mirror, she took off her hat and gazed at her reflection. Yes, she looked well; she was prettier; her lips were riper; her eyes were deeper and more golden. While she stared into the glass, it seemed to her that the shadows of some meaningless words rippled over the surface. How long had they trembled there, blown out and sucked in again when a door opened and shut? "Suppose I were never to see him again! Suppose I were never to see him again!" As if the words had released an inarticulate longing, she felt the old torment of restlessness spring out of the silence. She felt it racing in her veins; she felt it stinging her flesh, as the wind stings one after a dip into the sea; she felt it shudder and pause and shudder again in her heart. No, she couldn't bear it alone. She had never learned how to bear things alone. Pain that she did not understand, secret and mysterious pain, plunged into her like the beak of a hawk, swept her, helpless as a wren, out into the void. Just those empty words, so meaningless a few minutes ago (how could it be possible for her never to see him again?) awoke this sudden terror, this sense of being alone, lost, estranged, and forgotten.

But, even if she saw him, she might find that he had not remembered. She might feel again the vague hunger of that July evening, when the moonlight stealing into her mind had made her wish that she were dead. Millions of years before she was born, it must have lain somewhere, that hunger, waiting, wanting, as dumb as the earth or the rocks. Millions of years, and now it came to life and sprang out at her. All the waiting, the wanting, of millions of years! She was too young to bear all that weight, the weight of earth and rocks for millions of years. Yet a few careless words brought it back again. "It isn't my fault," she said aloud to the mirror. "I didn't ask to suffer like this. Nobody could possibly choose to suffer like this." Then, as suddenly as it had come, the dark mood flitted over her. While she slipped out of her clothes in the bathroom and scattered aromatic salts into the water, she thought proudly, "I am young and pretty. I am almost beautiful, and I am in love. Life is so wonderful. . . ."

Late that afternoon, when she had changed to a red Eton jacket over a white silk frock with short sleeves, she came slowly downstairs and glanced into the library at her grandfather, who had fallen asleep in his chair. Outside, on the back porch, Mamma and Aunt Isabella were still talking (she believed they would talk in an earthquake!), and their voices, even, placid, monotonous, buzzed on and on like the droning of bees in the flowerbeds. Moving softly, for fear they should stop her, she opened the front door and went out, shutting it lightly behind her. As she did not wish to be seen, she stole down the path to the gate with a furtive air, and walked very close to the black iron fences on her way to the Birdsongs' house.

Here the gate was wide open, and without lifting her hand, but carefully edging her white skirt away from the iron, she entered the small front yard, and passed round the side of the house to the overgrown garden. This was the way she had come long ago, on that afternoon when she had fallen and hurt her knee in Canal Street. What scraps and scraps of things, what loose odds and ends of life, had gathered in her memory. For years she had not thought of that afternoon, and now an inner light picked out a detail, an outline, a splash of colour, until the whole scene emerged into view. There was Mrs. Birdsong placing a bowl of flowers on the table, and yellow Harrison roses blooming over the fence, and the tame bullfrog, as solemn as a preacher, on the moss-grown log in the lily-pond.

But she had never seen the garden look so overgrown, so neglected. All Mrs. Birdsong had meant, the charm, the spirit, the blossoming wildness, could be measured by the blight that had fallen over the place. For three months, or nearly three months, she had been absent, and in all that time weeds had sprawled like drunken stragglers over the grass walks and flower-beds. A pile of bricks had collected in the hollow of a box-bush; a broken saucer and an empty tomato can lay in the middle of a border; an old broom with a broken handle was rotting away at the foot of the steps; the leaves on the untended shrubs were curled and dry, as if the edges had been eaten by caterpillars.

"It is no better than a common back yard," Jenny Blair thought. "Men never seem to notice how things look, and you can't expect coloured people to be tidy." Maggie, whose, memory was failing though her motives were still above reproach, had forgotten to take in the week's washing. On a clothes-line, stretched between the kitchen porch and the mulberry tree, empty garments were swinging back and forth, like human beings deflated of vanity. Cup-towels with red borders. Jenny Blair had helped Mrs. Birdsong with the tedious hemming. A blue gingham; a black uniform, they were Maggie's; and a row of soft shirts and pyjamas. These, she knew, were George's, for she had heard his wife say that he would never let his clothes go to the laundry. And then, with a start of surprise, she realized that while she looked at these swinging shirts and pyjamas, so helpless, so grotesque, yet in some way so much a part of him, she was no longer in love. For an instant only her passion yielded to the shock of reality. Then the blow passed and was gone; the faint sting of aversion faded out of her mind.

How Mrs. Birdsong would have hated, she thought, to see the clothes left hanging out in the afternoon. She could imagine her impatient voice calling, "Maggie, you have forgotten to take in the washing! Berry, you can't have swept the back porch since yesterday! Oh, the weeds must be cut! Why am I the only one who ever sees anything?" But that was George all over. He would never care how much trash was left in the yard; he would never see the clothes on the line, not even if they were swinging under his nose. Careful as he was about his own appearance, he never noticed how his surroundings were kept.

The lattice-door between the back porch and the library opened and slammed. There was a step on the porch, and he came down into the yard, with a cigarette in his mouth and the evening paper still in his hand. A moment later, he had seen her behind the trellis; and she heard his voice calling her name, "Jenny Blair! Is it really you, Jenny Blair?"

He had reached her; the cigarette and the newspaper dropped to the ground; and without moving, without knowing why or how it happened, she was in his arms, while the sense of security, of ecstasy, of perfect rightness, flooded her being. Again he kissed her, at first lightly, slowly, as if he were savouring the joy, and then with sudden hunger and violence. But it was right. Nothing so true, so safe, so deep as this happiness could be wrong.

As her heart was melting with love, his arms fell away, and he drew back hastily and glanced round the trellis. "You took me by surprise," he said, with a laugh that sounded abrupt and confused. "I wasn't expecting you. Nobody told me you had come back."

"We came this morning. Grandfather is so tired he has been lying down all day." Emotion fluttered from her throat into her voice.

"Well, you startled me." Stooping, he picked up the newspaper and turned away to light a fresh cigarette. His colour was high and clear, and his look flying over her awoke the quiver of suspense in her nerves. "You startled me," he kept repeating. His tone was thicker and more muffled than she had remembered it. "You were away two months, weren't you?"

"More than two months. We went in July."

"Well, a lot has happened since then. There's this war in Europe, and John has forgotten he ever hated war, and is trying to get into it. I don't blame him. If I were younger, I'd go myself. Perhaps I shall, anyway, if it lasts long enough."

She sighed impatiently. Why, when ecstasy was just beginning, did it always break off? Why did he persist in dragging in, at the wrong moment, something that did not matter? "Everybody was dreadfully excited at the White," she replied in a small, flat voice. "Only Grandfather says he has heard it all too often before. In every war, he says, there is a Belgium, and Belgium is always invaded."

He had drawn farther away, and stood leaning against the post of the trellis, while he smoked nervously in quick puffs. His hand, she saw, with surprise and a sudden faintness, was trembling. "Well, you're lovely. You're really lovely. I suppose you had a beautiful time and fell in love as I commanded?"

"You know I didn't." For it seemed to her now that she had not, after all, had a beautiful summer, and she had never, no, not for a single minute, been in love with any one else.

"I do, do I? Why are you so sure about that?" Again he glanced round at the house, and she knew that he was scarcely aware of what he was saying, that his mind was occupied with some idea he could not put into words.

"Because you do, you do." Her mouth curved in a sullen droop, but she was thinking, "Oh, how wonderful it is to be alive and in love!" With a shiver of memory, she leaned nearer and put her hand on his arm, "Because you do, you do," she repeated.

Something bright and inscrutable (was it anger? was it fear?

was it love?) flickered and died in his look. Without moving, without touching her, he stood gazing down at her hand on his sleeve. He did not speak; his mouth was guarded; but his eyes never left her fingers, which began to play up and down over his arm as lightly as the brushing of rose-leaves. Then, as her touch slipped from his sleeve to the veins on the back of his hand, he aroused himself from his trance, and drew away so suddenly that her outstretched arm dropped to her side, and she stared up at him with a reproachful frown. "Oh, you know," she repeated.

"I don't know anything." He was fumbling again for a match. "I don't know anything about women. I thought you were a child."

"I was eighteen in September."

"You look younger. I never thought of you as grown up."

"Was that why you promised? You did promise."

"I promised?"

"You promised when I went away that you wouldn't forget."

"Well, I haven't forgotten. But I don't want to hurt you. I don't want to hurt anybody." The familiar sense of injury ruffled his words, as if he were suffering beneath an immense injustice which he had not deserved.

But she had seen that startled look in his eyes (was it anger? was it fear? was it love?) and a glow of exultation had driven the suspense from her heart. Through a secret wisdom, which she obeyed without understanding, she knew that, for this solitary moment, he was at her mercy, that he was the victim of some mysterious power which made her the stronger.

"You aren't hurting me." Her voice was soft, pleading, and as ruthless as innocence. "It isn't as if there were anything wrong. You don't think it is wrong just to tell me you haven't forgotten."

"Wrong?" He laughed shortly. "No, but it's natural. We mustn't be natural."

"Why not? Why mustn't we be natural?"

"Because you're dangerous. You're as dangerous as—as a lighted fuse. Whether you know it or not, innocence when it lives to be eighteen is wicked."

Though she pretended to be indignant, she was still surprised and exultant. For he cared. She knew now that his eyes, not his words, told her the truth. "You sound like John," she said coldly. "John always preaches. That's why I don't like him."

"Don't you like him?" He looked relieved because someone else was dragged in between them. "I thought you liked John very much."

"I don't. I never liked him. He says it is because he tries to make me think of somebody besides myself."

George's laugh was so natural that immediately, as if a spell were broken, the tenseness of the scene scattered like vapour, and the autumn air seemed to ripple and change and flow by them. "So he's trying to make you safe, is he? I didn't suspect that John knew that much about life." Then, with a lighted cigarette in one hand, he held out the other as naturally as if she were her mother or even Aunt Etta. "Well, for once, he is right. You are dangerous and adorable, and you must go home. There's Maggie coming to take in the clothes, and it is time I picked my few sprigs of mint. Promise me that you will never tell my wife how careless Maggie and I grow when we are left by ourselves."

"I won't." She smiled up at him, for, in spite of everything he said, she knew—oh, she knew! "That will be another secret between us."

"Another secret." He frowned, but she saw that he was angry with himself, not with her. "We'd better forget all our secrets."

"But I don't want to forget. Shall I come back to-morrow to see Ariel? There are only three days before—before——" Not until she checked herself in confusion did she realize that she had started to say, "before you bring Mrs. Birdsong home."

He looked down at her, torn, as even she could see, between two sides of his nature. "I ought to say no, but I can't. After all, I'm going away in three days, and when I come back we'll settle down quietly. We'll settle down and be chums again. We'll be the best chums in the world, darling."

Darling! Though the word did not escape her lips, she clung to it as fiercely as if it were hidden treasure. For the first and only time, he had called her, not "my dear child," not even, "my dear," but "darling." Tremulous with delight, she turned away and hastened round the side of the house, just as John's substantial figure passed up the front steps and into the hall. John, she felt, would spoil everything. He would begin to preach; he would harp on the prose of living when she asked him for rhapsody; he would scold her because people were poor, or even because Belgium was invaded; he would, as usual, she told herself, act his inevitable part of a kill-joy. "After to-morrow, I shan't mind so much," she murmured, every quivering thought, it seemed to her, fringed with suspense, "after to-morrow . . ."

CHAPTER 12

ENNY BLAIR,'' her mother called from the library, "have you been to the Birdsongs'? Is there any news?"

Was there any news? Had she heard? Had she forgotten to ask? Spinning round at the question, Jenny Blair hesitated, suffered a throb of self-reproach, and answered defiantly, "Yes, Mrs. Birdsong is coming home. She is coming home in three days." Why was it, she wondered resentfully, that life so often tripped her into falsehood or evasion? She liked as much as anybody to speak the truth, though it seemed that the privilege of speaking the truth was seldom accorded to her.

"Then she is better," Mrs. Archbald said thankfully.

"Yes, she is better."

"When is George going? Did you hear?"

"He is going on Saturday. He is going to bring her back."

"I hope her canary is all right."

"Yes, he is all right." She had forgotten to ask. She had forgotten to ask after Mrs. Birdsong; she had forgotten to ask after Ariel. For all she knew, Ariel might have died in the summer. There was the throb again, only this time it was a sharper stab. "I can't help it," she thought indignantly. "I can't help anything."

"Come here, Jenny Blair," Mrs. Archbald said mildly but firmly.

"I was just going up to dress, Mamma. Do you want anything?"

Entering the library, the girl stopped by the threshold, and swayed restlessly on her small feet in red shoes. Every minute seemed to her a solid barrier between the tiresome actuality and her own palpitating delight.

"Stop fidgeting, my child. What is the matter?"

"I'm not fidgeting, Mamma, but I'm awfully tired. I want to rest before dinner."

"Well, I shan't keep you a minute. But I am not quite easy about you in my mind. Are you sure, Jenny Blair," her voice was very grave, "that you are not keeping something from me?"

"Oh, Mamma, you know I'm not."

"Are you thinking about any boy you met at the White? Did you let yourself take a romantic interest in that good-looking Agnew boy?"

"I never thought of him for a minute."

"Of course I admire your reserve, my dear, but I've sometimes wondered if you were not just a little bit too stand-offish with boys—nice boys, I mean. Times have changed since I was a girl. Not that some girls were not fast in my day. Even then, we used to say that it was hard to be a belle and a lady too. Of course I don't want you to be bold like Bena Peyton; but you might be the least bit more encouraging."

"I can't help it, Mamma. I am made that way."

"I know, darling, and I like your reserve. It shows that you were well brought up. Are you sure, then, that you are not holding anything back?"

"Nothing, nothing. May I go now and lie down?"

"Yes, run away. I suppose, after all, it is only your youth that makes me think you lack something. In a few years, after your character is formed, I may feel safer about you."

Escaping at last, Jenny Blair flew upstairs to her bedroom, and while she flew her whole being seemed to recoil from the hard surface of facts, and to fold, depth on depth, into the happier world of her memory.

The evening passed, the night, the next morning; and slowly, after an interminable waiting, after starts and pauses of expectancy and disappointment (she had been obliged to read to Aunt Etta, and to drive with her grandfather), the day declined, and she watched the shadows of the elms begin to slant over the pavement. Afternoons, thank Heaven, were shorter now! It would have been distracting, she thought, as she entered the Birdsongs' yard, to wait through one of the endless days of summer. But no sooner had she turned the corner of the house than she saw that much had happened since yesterday. The swinging garments and the clothes-line had disappeared. Decrepit old Jacob was cutting the weeds very slowly, for his arm was rheumatic, but with the utmost precision, for his stroke was still accurate. In the overgrown borders, which had looked so straggling, the few autumn flowers had been rounded in and neatly confined. "They are getting ready for Mrs. Birdsong," she told herself, with a sigh. "How she would hate all that untidiness." What Mrs. Birdsong meant to her, she felt vaguely, was order, beauty, perfection, an unattainable ideal of living.

While the thought touched her and was gone, she turned back to the house, and saw, after a breathless instant, Mrs. Birdsong in the flesh looking down on her from the porch to the library. So changed was the face she remembered that she asked herself with a shock of fear, "Is she there? Is she really alive? Or is it only a vision?" Then, as she hesitated and drew back, her name was called joyfully, "Jenny Blair! I was just thinking of you and wishing you would come over."

Very swiftly, almost as if she were running, Mrs. Birdsong came toward her, with her thin arms held out, and her wasted features illumined by pleasure. "Jenny Blair, my darling child!" she exclaimed, while her voice revived the old fervour, the animation that had always been so strangely exciting. How lovely it was to see her again, the girl thought, as she ran up the steps into the open arms. In that thrilling embrace everything else slipped away. Her own visit needed no explanation; there was no suspicion, no question, in her friend's pleasure at seeing her; there was not the faintest shadow over the unaltered confidence, the old fascination.

"How did you know?" Mrs. Birdsong held her away and gazed tenderly into her face. "Oh, you're lovely, Jenny Blair, you're far, far lovelier! But how did you know I was here? I came so suddenly. All summer I had waited, hoping to be well again, hoping some miracle would happen. Just waiting until they said I might come home. Then, when it came to just three days longer, I felt I couldn't stand any more waiting, not a day, not an hour. After waiting three months, three days seemed too much for me. So I decided only yesterday, and took the night train down. I didn't tell anybody. Even George didn't know I was coming home until I walked in on him this morning at breakfast. I might have been a ghost. I really believe he thought at first that I was dead and he was seeing an apparition." While the words gushed out she seemed to regain colour and energy. "Come upstairs with me," she added, with her arm on the girl's shoulder. "I made George go to the club and tried to do something to this poor forlorn house. Never have I seen such a sight as it was! Maggie is a faithful soul, but she has no sense of order, and George never notices anything so long as he has good food and his shirts are washed right. I started them all working, but it has worn me out, and I look worse than ever. Come upstairs with me while I rest. I want to hear all about your wonderful summer and how many men fell in love with you."

At least he wasn't here, Jenny Blair thought desperately, that was a blessing. She couldn't have borne it if she had known that he was still in the house, if she had been obliged to listen with one ear to Mrs. Birdsong and the other strained to catch the sound of his footsteps. No, she couldn't have borne that, she repeated to herself, as she followed Mrs. Birdsong upstairs and into her bedroom, where the colours of blue and mauve looked softer and the pattern less distinct than she remembered. So the canary was still alive! His cage hung in the paling light by the window, and beyond it, she could see the withered brown leaves of the morning glories.

"Now, at last, I may rest for a minute." Mrs. Birdsong had flung herself down on the couch, and when Jenny Blair looked at her, the glow of pleasure died in her face, and her eyes, which seemed the only animated part of her, were filling with tears. With tears, and with the desperation of a mind that has given up hope. Though she had never seen this look before, some intuition told the girl what it meant, and dropping on her knees by the couch, she cried passionately, "Oh, don't! Oh, don't! It isn't over!" For the old fascination had reasserted its power; and while she knelt there on the floor, Jenny Blair told herself vehemently that she would sooner die than hurt Mrs. Birdsong. To see her changed, stricken, defeated by life, with all her glory dragged in the dust, was too terrible. It was not that she had lost youth alone, but that she had lost everything. Her face was tragic and burned out by suffering, as if she had passed through some great sorrow which had left its blight on her hair, in her eyes, and at the corners of her sensitive mouth. Yet, even now, she was lovely, with the loveliness not of hope but of despair, a loveliness which, pared down to the bone, was still indestructible. How ill she must have been, how terribly she must have suffered!

Collecting herself with an effort, Mrs. Birdsong pushed the straying locks from her forehead and forced a smile to her lips. "You must not worry about me, dear. Tell me of yourself. Did you have a happy summer? Did you fall in love with any one? I have a fancy—or I used to have when I was happy—that only love makes a woman bloom like this."

Jenny Blair shook her head. "No, I didn't fall in love, but we had a wonderful summer. Everybody was so nice to me. Only I missed you. I always miss you."

"Do you, darling? That is sweet of you. So few people miss one in illness. It may be my fault. I have been ill so long, but I have a feeling that I have worn out patience, that I've worn out affection." With a gesture of agony, as if she released her hold on faith, on hope, on illusion, she turned away, hid her face in the pillows, and broke into long convulsions of weeping. Her hidden features shuddered with grief; a spasm jerked its way through her thin body; and while Jenny Blair watched her, she seemed to lose herself in some violent but inarticulate horror.

"Oh, Mrs. Birdsong, dear Mrs. Birdsong, what can I do? I love you, I love you. Do let me help you."

"It is nothing, darling." Checking her sobs at the sound of

the frightened voice, Mrs. Birdsong struggled up on the pillows, and pressing her hands to her cheeks, forced a vital spirit back into her flesh. "It is just nerves. I try to keep up, but sometimes, as quickly as that, a panic sweeps over me, and I feel that I have lost everything. Everything," she repeated slowly, with drenched eyes and convulsed mouth, staring at vacancy.

"But you haven't, you haven't. You will be well again. I adore you. Everybody adores you." If only she could help her, Jenny Blair thought, if only she could give her back what she had lost. "I'll do all I can," she thought, in an anguish of pity. "He must love her best. Oh, I want him to love her best!"

"The fear comes and goes," Mrs. Birdsong said in a whisper, while the vacancy at which she stared was reflected in her fixed gaze, in her twitching mouth, in the blank misery of her expression. "It comes and goes in a kind of wild panic. Just nerves, they say; but while it lasts, whether it is for an hour or a second, I am alone in a void, in the darkness, alone, and lost utterly—lost——" Her voice failed, and she put her hands to her throat as if she were strangling. "I can't tell you—I can't tell any one the images that come to me out of darkness—out of nothing. Things so dreadful I never even imagined them. I never dreamed they could enter my thoughts. But I can't keep them away. They come buzzing in like insects—like gigantic insects—that drive me to do things I never thought of before. I never so much as thought of in all my life——"

"Don't think of that now. You will get over it. What can I give you?" Glancing round, Jenny Blair saw a decanter of Madeira and a plate of biscuits on a table by the bed, and pouring out a glass of the wine, she put it into Mrs. Birdsong's outstretched hand. "You are too tired after that long trip. You ought not to have gone downstairs."

"I know, but I had to. I couldn't stand things as they were. George brought me that Madeira before he went out, but I forgot to drink it. His father's finest Rainwater Madeira, and I can't taste it. I'd as soon have aromatic ammonia. . . ." A bewildered look crossed her face while her words sank to a murmur. For a few minutes she lay there, supine, crushed, empty, flattened out by despair. Then she struggled up, with a quiver of pain, like some bright winged creature fluttering helplessly on the earth, and gazed curiously about the room, as if she were in a strange place and could not remember whether she had ever seen it before. "What were we talking about, Jenny Blair?"

"About so much that needs to be done. But you must not bother. You must try to get well. Of course it is nothing but nerves."

"It is queer, isn't it, that some people should seem to have all the nerves, and others none? George hasn't a nerve in his body, or if he has, they behave properly."

"Oh, but he has. You've forgotten how upset he was when you were in the hospital. He said his nerves were all shot to pieces."

"Yes, I'd forgotten," Mrs. Birdsong assented, and looked round the room again with her bright wondering gaze.

"It will take a long time to get well," Jenny Blair said. "You must go very slowly. But when you are over the shock, you will be stronger than ever. Doesn't Doctor Bridges tell you that?"

"Yes, he tells me that. After a long time, perhaps a year, I may be well again. I may even be a wife again. Or, better still, I may be a nice comfortable old woman, with a face like a damp sponge, who doesn't want to be a wife any longer." A sound between a laugh and a sob broke from her lips. "But you can't understand, Jenny Blair. You are too young to know what trouble is. I sometimes think that all the cruelty of youth—and nothing in the world is so cruel as youth—comes from not knowing what trouble is."

"I do understand. Oh, I do."

"Do you know why I came home, seized by panic, because, after three months of waiting, I had three days longer to wait?" Was she looking for something? What had she missed? Or was she asking herself if she had ever been here before? "In terror lest I should lose something I had already lost——"

"But you haven't lost anything! Not anything that you wanted. When you are well again you will know that nothing is lost."

"When I'm well again. Then I may find that I haven't lost it, that I never had it, that it never really existed. Women are like that. What they value most is something that doesn't exist. Nowhere. Not in any part of the world. Not in the universe." Her voice was wild, and there was a wild look in her face, which was haggard and exalted by anguish into a beauty more significant than the beauty of flesh. No, Jenny Blair could not understand. All she could do was to share pain without understanding. Her heart, her very bones, she felt, were dissolving in pity. But what, after all, did it mean? What did anything mean. Did Mrs. Birdsong suspect? Did she know? Or had she been driven home, as she said, by a blind panic? Her face, with its blankness, told nothing. It was as if she had thrown herself against life and been broken.

"Yes, you're too young," she began presently, after a pause. "You're too young to know what it means." Then, while her voice was still despairing, her lips smiled, and that swift smile diffused warmth, charm, a subtle magic of personality. "Whatever you do, Jenny Blair, never risk all your happiness on a single chance. Always keep something back, if it is only a crumb. Always keep something back for a rainy day." Still smiling, she held out her arms. "Now, you'd better run away, darling, and I'll ring for Berry and have my bath. You will come back early to-morrow?"

"Yes, I'll come early to-morrow. I'll come whenever you want me."

"In the morning, then. Come in the morning and read to me before I dress. I missed people so in the country. You know I always like people about me."

"Well, you've plenty of friends."

"Yes, I've plenty of friends still. But people don't like to be depressed. You must not let me depress you. Have all the joy you can while you are young." As Jenny Blair looked back from the door, Mrs. Birdsong sat up on the couch and threw a kiss after her. "You've been the greatest comfort to me, dear," she called cheerfully. "Come early to-morrow."

The staircase was dim, but the front door was open, and the sallow flush of the afterglow streamed into the hall. "I must not see him alone. It is all over," the girl said to herself. "I shall never, no, never think of him again." Driven by the thought, she ran down the walk and out of the gate before she saw that John was stopping his car by the pavement.

"Wait a minute, Jenny Blair. I want to speak to you," he called in a tone that sounded resentful. "I tried to see you last night," he added, as he reached her and held out his hand. "Did you really have a headache? Nobody ought to have headaches at your age."

"Of course I had a headache. Didn't Mamma tell you?" How awkward John was! How crude honesty became when two human beings disliked each other. Perhaps, after all, her mother's way was the best. At least it kept the surface of life smooth and agreeable.

"Yes, she told me," he answered, but his tone had not altered.

"Then I don't see why you blame me. Nobody wants to have headaches."

"You oughtn't to have them."

She tossed her head defiantly. That was the difficulty with John, and with the scientific mind in general, she was beginning to perceive. It was never satisfied, after the milder habit of philosophy, to let anything rest. Always it insisted on tearing excuses to pieces to see how they were made. "Well, I can't help it," she said, "and neither can you. When are you going to France?"

"As soon as I can. Whenever Cousin Eva is better."

"I thought you hated war."

"Well I did until this one came. You see there's Belgium——"

"I'd like to go, too. Don't you think," she asked, lowering her voice, and speaking for the first time with genuine feeling, "that Mrs. Birdsong looks worse than ever?"

"Worse? Yes, but of course the trip told on her. What brought her home so suddenly?"

He turned to look at her closely, and she felt a senseless blush stinging her cheeks. "Just a feeling. She said she couldn't stand it any longer. Ill persons have those fancies."

"She is very ill," he said in a low voice, as if he feared that his words might be caught by the autumn dust and blown up from the quiet street to the window of Mrs. Birdsong's room. "She needs all the help we can give her. She needs more help than we are able to give her."

"I'd do anything for her."

"So would I. Anything. It is easy to see that she is ill, but there is something else. There is something I feel but cannot reach in her mind."

"Something more than illness? More than the operation?"

"Well, they were bad enough, God knows——" He uttered an abrupt exclamation. "The trouble with women is that they tell everything but the one thing it is necessary to know." His eyes behind his glasses were perplexed and sad, and it seemed to Jenny Blair that his freckles reddened until they matched the crest of hair over his high forehead. Yes, John was fine, but he was not lovable.

"Perhaps there isn't really anything." She spoke brightly, prompted by an inherited impulse to make the best of a bad situation. "You never can tell about nerves. I know because poor Aunt Etta is always having panics like that, and waking us up in the night."

A smile twisted his lips. "I suppose you call that view looking on the bright side; but that may be after all what is really the matter."

"The matter with Mrs. Birdsong?"

"I mean not facing things, trying to pretend that anything you don't wish to look at doesn't exist. It is a false attitude, of course, even if it is a noble one. I may be a crank. Sometimes I think the only use I can be put to is to be shot. But, whether I go or stay, you'll help her through, won't you?"

Stirred by his distress, she looked up at him with eloquent eyes. "I'll do anything. There isn't anything I wouldn't do for her."

Hurrying away from him, she entered the house and ran upstairs to her room. Though her mother called her as she went by, she did not answer. Her breath came and went with a fluttering sound; tears were welling into her eyes and trickling over her cheeks to her lips. "He must love her best," she thought, while her heart seemed to quiver and fail, "I want him to love her best. I shall never, never think of him again as long as I live."

CHAPTER 13

SO IT IS beginning again, thought General Archbald, while he shielded his eyes from the November sunshine and sank down in his wicker chair in the garden. Once more life was coiling back on itself. Once more the process men call civilization had swerved aside, and was seeking a new outlet through violence. Was it in a dream that all this had happened somewhere in the past? Or by the time one was eighty-four did every event, every emotion, turn into a platitude? Far away as yet, but growing nearer and louder, he heard the throbbing of old hatreds, the drumming of primitive impulses. In every war the noble savage returned. He remembered not only the *Maine*, that symbol of national vengeance, but the Civil War, the Spanish War, and all the legends he had heard in his childhood of the Indian Wars and the Revolution. None of them seemed now to differ by so much as a grasshopper's chirp in its shrilling. But he was old. He was old; he was looking ahead to his best years; he was enjoying the end of his life as an aged lover enjoys his last embrace. One could not, of course, make the young understand this; for the young, so tragically ignorant, believed that they knew. They confused sensation with happiness; they mistook violence for adventure.

And not the young alone, but the old also, were seeking a false youth in recovered sensation. All the old men who came, with trembling knees and enfeebled loins, to sit with him in the sunshine were excited, noble, indignant, because a virgin was ravished. Like other old men in walled gardens all over the world, they were reliving, through memory and instinct, the happiest years of their lives, the years when they were more completely male in spirit and sinew. All the unrest had united in a solitary resentment. Even John, since he had found something to blame, had begun to feel happier. What the world needed, it appeared, was the lost emblem of evil. Yet he had spent a year in Germany in his youth, and he had believed, he still believed, that kindness was a distinguishing trait in the German character. People said that modern Prussia was different from the Germany of his youth. Perhaps. He did not know. But fear drove nations, as well as animals, and the look of driven fear is not, he told himself, unlike malevolence. He had seen that look too often not to remember it. He had seen the mortal alone defying the nature of things, the atom seeking an escape from the current of life, the grain of dust blowing into the void.

"Are you feeling better to-day, Father?" Mrs. Archbald was descending the steps of the porch to the square of sunlight between the border of scarlet sage and the boughs of the sycamore. In the centre of the square, the old man was sitting, with William stretched at his feet. As he looked up at her, his fine old head reminded her of a picture she had seen somewhere (it must have been in Europe, since she never looked at pictures in America) of Saint John—or it may have been Saint Joseph. Older, much older (she had a bad head for such matters), but there was the same contour, the same quality.

"Will you come down a minute, Cora, if you have time." He lifted his right hand, once so smooth and hard, but as withered now, he thought in disgust, as the paw of a monkey.

"Haven't I always time for you, Father?" When she smiled, the corners of her eyes puckered and her thin lips appeared to sink deeper. Yet her indomitable will to believe the best had never been broken.

"I know, my dear, and I appreciate it. I only wanted to ask you if you had heard from Eva since this morning."

Drawing out her handkerchief from an embroidered bag, Mrs. Archbald pressed it to her lips as if she were making up her expression. "I was just talking to John," she replied. "He did not sound encouraging, but, then, John always takes too dark a view. That doesn't seem right in a physician. I wonder why he ever decided to study medicine."

"He is honest, anyway, and he has the rare gift of moral indignation. The longer I live, the more I realize that we lack moral indignation. Not moral hysteria, which springs from cruelty, but sober indignation."

"Yes, but there are different kinds of honesty, don't you think?" Mrs. Archbald inquired in a conversational tone. "I suppose, too, moral indignation is all right in its place, but I can never understand why everybody who makes life unpleasant is regarded as a public benefactor. That doesn't mean, of course, that I am easy about Eva. Something is wrong, I know. George told me yesterday that twice in the last ten days she had got up before breakfast and dressed herself and wandered off somewhere. He didn't know where. When she came back, she couldn't remember where she had been. He seems dreadfully discouraged, and that isn't usual with George. I couldn't just make out what he is afraid of. Men are so vague," she ended, with a sigh disguised in a cough, "but he has shown more character than I ever gave him credit for."

"He means well. Most people mean well. I hope Jenny Blair is a comfort to her. She is a sympathetic little soul."

"Sympathetic? I used to think so, but recently I've begun to wonder. I have a feeling, only a feeling, nothing more, that the child is keeping something back from me. She goes about with that moonstruck air young girls have when they fall in love. I asked her if she had taken a fancy to anybody—it might well have been that good-looking Agnew boy at the White—but she positively denies it. There isn't any one else, except Fred Harrison, I can think of at the moment. I really believe she is telling the truth when she says she dislikes John. But I sometimes think," she added, letting anxiety break through, "that I know nothing about Jenny Blair."

"Every parent feels that at times, my dear daughter. She is at the empty age now. Be patient with her while the springs of character begin to fill. Perhaps Eva knows her better than we do. She seems to find her companionable, and Jenny Blair shows that she is devoted. Hasn't she been spending every night over there?"

"Only when George is away. He has been down at Fairmont for several days, shooting ducks, and Eva doesn't like to be alone when John is called out in the evening. That reminds me," Mrs. Archbald bit her lip and appeared to calculate hurriedly, "that I shan't need to order any meat for the rest of the week. George is coming home this afternoon, and he will be sure to send us more ducks than we can possibly use."

"Will Jenny Blair be there to-night?"

"Not unless George stays away. She is going to take Eva some of my currant jelly; but she won't spend the night again. Shall I tell her to stop and speak to you? She is really very unselfish about it, and she insists that she is willing to give up her whole winter if she can help Eva get well. Still, I am opposed to the child's sacrificing her youth. When you give up a year of youth, it seems impossible ever to make up for it again."

"You're right, I think," the old man assented. "Let Jenny Blair have all her happiness."

After she had gone he dozed for a few minutes, and when he opened his eyes again the mood of earth and sky had softened into the mellow harmony of late afternoon. So still were the gauzy shadows and the faint sunshine that the drift of autumn seemed to be less a stir in the air than a part of the tranquil spinning of earth. Over the whole garden there was the powdery haze of November, so motionless that it might have been painted, yet as perishable as the bloom on a grape. Even the pale yellow leaves of the sycamore fell slowly, without turning, without rustle, as if they also were created by an illusion. Beyond the white boughs of the tree the deep blue sky was streaked with transparent green, and far above the solitary steeple of a church a thin trail of smoke hung suspended.

The autumn was passing, and more than the autumn was passing with this slow rhythm of evanescence. He was not aware that his era, the age of glory, was dying. All he knew was that he had been young and was now old, that when he had defeated every other antagonist, there remained time, the unconquerable. Yet he was too old to dread time. For it was time that had given him, sitting here in the warm sunshine, the happy end of his life.

But the age was drifting, he knew; the world was flattening around him; the heroic mould had been broken. Beauty, like passion, would decline to the level of mediocrity. With the lost sense of glory, the power of personality would change and decay. It was possible, it was even probable, he thought, that the individual would return to the tribe from which it had so lately emerged. Better so, perhaps. Who could tell? Who could tell anything? Of one thing alone he was sure,—life would never again melt and mingle into the radiance that was Eva Birdsong. "Personality," he thought, being old and sentimental, "could reach no higher." Beyond that triumph there was no other triumph. To go onward, civilization must fold back, must recoil from individualism and seek some fairer design. Though he did not suspect that his era was dying, he felt that both he and his age were drifting, not aimlessly like dust, but somewhere to an end. Somewhere? He was not greatly concerned. Whatever came, he could meet it; he could even endure not to meet it. Having lived his little hour of mortality, he had ceased to fear any form, he had ceased to fear any formlessness, of the Absolute.

For the calm of being old was strangely like happiness. While he dozed there, dreaming of Eva Birdsong, clinging, with the tenacity of age, to his last illusion, he was visited by a sense of fulfilment. The mind could play queer tricks, he thought, looking down at William, asleep on the grass. For there were moments when an image came to him, not of one woman alone, but of two women blended, when he could no longer separate the memory of the past from the sentiment of the present. In that fleeting hour before frost, before death, he felt that a presence was near him in the faint sunshine, motionless among the scattered powdery bloom of the autumn. A shape was there, less a shadow than a changeless outline of light, falling between the scarlet sage and the boughs of the sycamore. Was it the thought of a woman or of all women? Was it the poet who might have been and was still, perhaps, somewhere? Not that it mattered. Whatever it was, that vague outline brought happiness; it brought serenity of mood; it brought the courage of dying; it brought, even, acceptance of life. "After all," he found himself repeating aloud, "character may survive failure. Fortitude may be the last thing to go."

"Grandfather, do you want anything?" Jenny Blair was at his side, carefully holding the glass of currant jelly. "You were thinking aloud."

"Was I, my dear?" He looked round at her wistfully, for the still shape had dissolved in her shadow. "What was I thinking?"

"Something about character, something about fortitude."

"I remember now. I was dreaming of Mrs. Birdsong."

"I am going there. She likes to have me run in very often."

"Has George come back?"

"She expected him. If he doesn't come, I've promised to spend the night with her again."

"Well, I'm glad you are a comfort, my child. She needs comfort."

"She likes to have me," Jenny Blair repeated, patting his shoulder. "Is there anything I can do for you before I go?"

"Nothing, my dear. Give her my love."

"Shall I tell her you were dreaming of her when you said something about character, something about fortitude?"

"Tell her I am always dreaming of her. The old live in dreams."

"She says you must come to see her. You haven't been near her for days."

"I thought I depressed her." He was glad that she had noticed his absence; but the truth was, strange as it sounded, that he felt happier, he felt nearer to her when he was not with her. Here, beside this dim outline of light, his heart was suffused with pro-found tenderness. There were instants, lost in memory, when the glow, the warmth, even a breath of the old rapture, brushed him and was gone like the fall of a leaf. But when he was with her he knew that she was beyond reach of his love, that she resented his pity.

"Oh, you don't depress her," Jenny Blair insisted. "How can you say things like that, Grandfather?" Though the child's look was sweet and reproachful, he recognized the hollowness of the words, and it seemed to him that her voice was blown out of vacancy.

"Well, run on, darling. I must not keep you," he answered. "I have everything and more than a man needs at my time of life."

CHAPTER 14

"N o, it isn't my fault," Jenny Blair said aloud. She had not wished to fall in love. She had not, she repeated defiantly, even wished to be born. Something bigger than herself had swept her away in its claws. And even now, after all her struggle to escape, she was still tormented by restlessness. For days she had put him out of her mind; she had refused to think of him even at night in the dark; she had flung herself passionately into trivial amusements. Then, without warning, just as the hawk swooped and pounced on its prey out of the sky (she had watched one light on a bird in the summer), she was seized again with the suspense, the misery, the unsatisfied longing. If only he had been less distant, she thought, shutting the door behind her and descending the steps. If only he had let her see by a look that he cared, she could have borne it more easily, she could have been almost contented.

At the Birdsongs' gate she paused an instant, and practised, before she moved on, the careless smile and the innocent upward curve of her mouth. To give up may be hard, she told herself, summoning her resources, as she opened the door and went into the hall, but to be given up is far worse—oh, far worse than anything! "I can't bear it, I can't bear it," she thought, glancing from the stairs into the library, where she saw George showing his wild ducks to John. "I brought back twenty-five," she heard him say, "and I shot three times as many." He spoke with pride; she could tell that he had forgotten her; that his whole mind was filled with the whirring of wings and iridescent bunches of feathers! But he liked them dead. He was never so happy, she knew, as when he had just killed something beautiful. They were scattered everywhere, on the chairs, on the table, on his desk, with his gun and his game-bag beside them. She watched him pick up a duck here and there, look it over with boyish pride, and then lay it down again. He appeared to be perfectly happy. He was not troubled by love; he was not troubled by self-reproach.

Looking up, he caught sight of her on the stairs, and called cheerfully, "Jenny Blair, I'm sending some ducks to your grandfather. Come and see what beauties they are." But he was not thinking of her while he stood there, lean, vigorous, ruddy with pleasure. His mind was still on the ducks; he was still, she could tell when she looked at him, feeling his power. As he held out a large, handsome mallard, he barely glanced at her, and she told herself that this was what she had not expected. Had he looked at her in the old way, she would have known, she would have understood, and everything might have been smoothed over between them. But he did not look at her. He never looked at her now if he could help it. "Aren't they beauties?" he asked, as proudly as if he had created instead of destroyed them.

"Beauties," she replied in an indifferent tone, and felt resentfully that John had his eyes on her—John, who had told her not long ago that what she needed was to break the glass of her hothouse and get outside of herself.

"They were superb in flight," George said, while he drew back and looked down on the fine plumage. But he did not mean it. He enjoyed killing. He was possessed, she could see, by that strange exultation which comes to the sportsman when he has shot something that was alive the minute before. "I'm taking them to my friends," he added, pointing to a card he had attached to a splendid neck. "It's a good way to pay off scores. Eva scarcely touches them anyway."

How absurd it was, Jenny Blair thought suddenly, to send out these handsome dead birds in pairs, with visiting cards bearing playful messages attached to their necks. Well, we were like that. Men, especially, were like that. And all the time, while he arranged the ducks and wrote the messages and tied the cards, she said to herself, "If I knew he cared, I shouldn't mind anything. It would be so much easier if he would only show by a look that he has not forgotten." For she was again in the clutch of that misery. She could not help it; she had resisted with all her strength; but she was again in the clutch of unsatisfied longing.

Turning away without a word, she went out into the hall and upstairs. Her whole being was shaken as a pool is agitated by the sudden dropping of a pebble. Why? she wondered, with hot resentment. What had happened? Nothing. She had seen him; she had heard his voice speaking proudly of wild ducks. He had tried not to look at her. That was all; and yet she was in a quiver of emotion when she entered Mrs. Birdsong's room and found that she had just come back from one of her desperate flights into the street.

"Oh, you haven't been out by yourself!" the girl cried reproachfully.

"I had to go. I couldn't stay in the house." Mrs. Birdsong was slipping out of her street dress into a tea-gown. "George and John were so busy with the ducks they didn't hear me slip down the back stairs. I didn't go far, but when that terror seizes me, I am obliged to rush out of doors, to get away from myself—or the part of myself I leave in the house. No matter where I may be, I am obliged to start up and go to some other place. In the night, I go downstairs to the drawing-room, or the library, or even the kitchen. Half the time George sleeps so soundly he never knows I'm awake." While she talked she was busily hanging her dress in the closet, putting away her hat and gloves, and drawing the silk robe over her knees when she had dropped on the couch. "You don't know what it is," she continued, after a pause. "Nobody who hasn't felt it can possibly know what it is. You feel it is useless, but still you go. You are trying to run away, and you can't make yourself stop." Colour had flamed into her face, and her blue eyes were living once more. Though her beauty had frozen into stillness, she had not lost it. Nothing, not even death, Jenny Blair told herself, could take it away.

"You must not go out alone," she said caressingly. "Send for me, and I will go with you. I will go with you anywhere." For it was true that she adored her. She adored her until it was like a wound in her heart.

"When it comes, I can't wait, darling. I can't wait even for you. This morning, I was reading downstairs on the back porch. I was quite peaceful one moment, thinking about nothing, and then the terror rushed over me. That is the way people felt when they were fleeing from Pan. They couldn't wait. They dropped everything. But they didn't know, of course, that Pan was life. They were running away from life."

"You will get over it. All the doctors say you will get over it."

Mrs. Birdsong smiled listlessly. Her loveliness, so vivid an instant before, had died down into pallor, into apathy. "Yes, I may get over it. One gets over everything." She stopped, drew a long, slow breath, and repeated wearily, "Everything."

"But promise me you won't go out by yourself."

"Unless I go alone, I can never find myself. When you've never been yourself for forty years, you've forgotten what you are really." She had been pleating the thin silk robe into folds, but pushing it away with a gesture of irritation, she threw that bright searching look round the room and broke into a laugh. "I don't mean half I say, darling. Only I'm worn out with being somebody else—with being somebody's ideal. I want to turn round and be myself for a little while before it is too late, before it is all over. But I've frightened you enough for to-day," she added in a natural tone. "Did you see George when you came in? Did he show you his ducks?"

"Yes, he called me as I was coming upstairs."

"He brought them up here, every one of them. They were all over the couch and the chairs, and I had to stop his putting them on the bed. But I don't like to look at dead things. I can never understand why men enjoy killing, especially killing beautiful wild creatures."

"He likes it more than anything in the world. All men do. Now he is busy thinking of people to send them to."

"I know. He sends them with visiting cards." Her smile was

twisted with irony, but her eyes were still restless, watchful, searching.

"Grandfather sent his love to you," said Jenny Blair, who had forgotten the message. "He told me he had dreamed of you out there in the garden. He is beginning to show his age, but he insists this is the most interesting time of his life."

Mrs. Birdsong's face softened. "I wonder what he thinks of now that life is behind him."

"He says it isn't behind him, that he has just learned how to live with the whole of his nature. It's funny, isn't it, but he told me yesterday that all the rest was nothing more than an experiment. All day long he sits there in the sun. He says he is living with his mind. Only I can't imagine what he is thinking about."

"About wild ducks perhaps." Mrs. Birdsong lay back on the pillows and drew the robe over her bosom. "Nobody ever seems to think of what is really important. Though, I suppose," she continued mockingly, "ducks are more important to themselves than anything else. Do you imagine they would consider it an honour to be sent round to one's acquaintances with visiting cards tied to their necks? Oh, I hope he hasn't forgotten Doctor Bridges! I promised him the finest pair of ducks George brought back. I must go down and select them."

As she sprang up, Jenny Blair pushed her back. "No, lie down. Don't get up. I'll run down and tell him, or call John. Perhaps he has not forgotten."

"I'm not sure I told him. I knew there was something I wanted to do; but I couldn't think what it was. When that terror comes, it sweeps my mind bare." A frown knitted her forehead and her mouth worked convulsively. "It is dreadful to have no memory. But I knew there was something."

"Well, don't get up. I'll run down and remind him. He can easily change one of the cards." Bending over, she kissed Mrs. Birdsong's cheek. "It is so late, I shan't come up again, but I'll see you early to-morrow. You'll try to rest now, won't you?"

"Yes, I'll try to rest now." The frail arms fell away from the close embrace. Turning on the threshold, the girl watched Mrs.

Birdsong's eyelids waver and droop over the flickering glow in her eyes.

Downstairs, the house was very quiet, and the windows were filling slowly with twilight. The hall looked as if it were asleep, and the furniture wore the insubstantial air objects assume before daybreak. John must have gone up to his room, for he had left his hat and stick with an open book on the sofa. Maggie, she supposed, was in the kitchen; but since Mrs. Birdsong's return negro spirituals no longer wailed and sighed through the vacant rooms. In the the library the ducks were still spread on the table and the desk. She saw the cards attached with bits of narrow green ribbon to the superb necks; and she remembered that Mrs. Birdsong had ripped that ribbon from an old dress yesterday afternoon. Never could she bear to throw away scraps. Her work-basket was brimming over with odds and ends. When George was searching for a string, he must have picked up those loose ends of green ribbon. "Men never see things," the girl thought. "It is strange how they can go through life seeing so little." For there was something pathetic, as well as comic, in the picture the ducks made, lying there, with clots of blood in some of the proud beaks, on some of the noble breasts, decorated, as if for a wedding feast, with bits of green ribbon.

A shadow moved on the porch beyond the open lattice-door, and she saw that George was sitting on one of the benches, with a Scotch and soda beside him. As he sprang up and looked at her expectantly, she felt, without thinking, without speaking, that nothing made any difference. All the world throbbed with long-ing, and the old misery came to life again in her heart. So sharp was the realization that she cried out, though not in words, "I can't bear it! I can't bear any more!"

"Is anything the matter, Jenny Blair?" he asked quickly. "Do you want me?"

Did she want him? Her throat ached with desire, and she turned her head away because she could not bear to look in his face. She could not bear to see him hard, vigorous, ruddy, and indifferent to the suffering he caused.

"Do you want me?" he repeated, and came toward her, as if he were about to go into the house.

She found her voice, though it seemed scarcely more than a thread trembling there in the dusk. "Did you remember Doctor Bridges?"

"Bridges?" He looked puzzled. "She isn't worse, is she?"

"No, oh, no. It is about the ducks. She promised a pair to Doctor Bridges."

"Oh, did she?" Immense relief brightened his look. "No, she hadn't told me, but I'll make it all right. I can give him the pair I'd put aside for the Morrisons. I shan't even have to change the card," he added cheerfully, as he drew out his watch. "Well, it's time I was going on, if I'm to leave them all before dinner. Just a minute. There's no use, if you'll forgive me, in wasting this good highball." With an airy gesture, he drained his glass and put it down on the wicker table beside him.

He was about to leave her. In another moment, she knew, it would be too late to speak; and with the knowledge, her whole body was invaded by that sharp violence, that jealous despair. "You mustn't," she breathed in a whisper. "Oh, you mustn't."

"Mustn't? My dear little girl, what have I done? What is the matter?"

"You mustn't treat me like this. I can't bear it. You know I can't bear it."

He stared at her in silence, while a light flooded his face. "My dear child, what can I do? What can I do without hurting you?"

"You are hurting me. Oh, you are hurting me! If you cared——!"

"I do care. You can see that I care. Haven't I cared for months? Haven't I cared until I am almost out of my mind?" His arms were round her, and looking up she saw a single vein beating like a pulse in his forehead. "You know I care," he said over and over, as if he were suffocated by words, and in his voice, too, she felt the throbbing of anguish.

Then, suddenly, while her whole being vibrated, a shudder jerked through his muscles, and she was left there, alone and abandoned, as his arms dropped from her body. From the horror in his face, she knew, before she spun round, that Mrs. Birdsong was looking at them out of the dusk in the library. Frozen, expressionless, grey as a shadow, she smiled through them and beyond them to the empty horizon. For an instant time paused. Then she said in a voice that was as vacant as her smile, "George, I want you," and turned slowly back into the room. Without a rustle, as soundlessly as she had come, she turned away, and was sucked in by the twilight.

"No! No!" Jenny Blair cried, and flung out her hand, as if she were pushing aside a moment too terrible to be borne. She was alone and deserted in space. Without a word to her, without so much as a look, George had followed his wife into the house. "No! No!" the girl cried out again, thrusting Mrs. Birdsong's smile back into the dusk, into the nightmare of things that could not have happened. Breaking from the trance that held her, she ran down into the garden, far down by the old lily-pond, and circled round and round, like a small animal that is looking for the hole in a trap. Round and round, and always back again to the place from which she had started, as she had fled in one of her old dreams that she had never forgotten. After a few minutes of violent flight, she sank down on the ground behind the mulberry tree, crouching in the shadow and straining her ears for any sound from the house. In the centre of a vast loneliness, she listened to sudden noises from the street, to the long reverberations of crashing things within and without. Then, abruptly, the rattle of crashing things, of falling skies everywhere, stopped. Except for the tumult in her mind, and the distant sound of motor cars, the garden was as still as if it waited for the coming of thunder. The dusk was sultry with vapour, and a tarnished light was burning far down in the west. Presently, while she lay there, this light stole into her mind, and everything in her thoughts was discoloured, while that evil odour poured up from the hollow below and tainted the air. "Nothing has happened," she said aloud, sitting up in the damp grass. "Nothing has really happened."

A lamp flashed on, then off and on again, in the house. She saw a figure pass and repass the library window, and she thought, "That is John. John will know what to do." An instant later, the figure came to the door and she heard her name called sharply. "Jenny Blair! Are you out there, Jenny Blair?" The voice was so unlike John's that it might have been a stranger calling her name in a tone of distracted impatience.

Rising from the ground and pressing her damp skirts about her legs as she walked, she went across the grass and out of the dusk into the square of light on the porch. For the first time, she felt that she was shivering and that her knees and elbows were twitching. The passage from the dimness into the light seemed to strip her stark naked. She felt her clothes torn away and the illumination pricking her flesh.

She had expected to find John waiting for her; but when she reached the house, he had turned back into the library. As she crossed the threshold, he looked over his shoulder and said, "There has been an accident. I am trying to get your grandfather. There has been an accident," he repeated in a smothered voice, as if he were struggling to cry out in his sleep.

Her steps dragged into the room, and stopping before she looked round her, she thought, "I know what I shall see." But, at first, when she raised her eyes, she saw only the dead ducks on the desk and the table. One pair had slipped to the floor, with the bit of green ribbon holding the outstretched necks together. Drops of blood were still in the beaks, as if they had been nibbling, and the heads rested on the sweeping lace flounce of Mrs. Birdsong's tea-gown. With an effort, pressing her eyeballs, Jenny Blair looked at Mrs. Birdsong, who sat very erect, and gazed, with her fixed smile, into the twilight beyond the window. Her face was so vacant that her expression and even her features were like wax. The waves of her hair clung to her scalp; her skin was as colourless as the skin of the dead; and her eyes and mouth were mere hollows of darkness. On the rug at her feet the ducks were huddled together over George's gun, as if she had just kicked them away.

While she stared at the splotches of dried blood on their breasts, Jenny Blair heard herself thinking, "She killed him. And he will have blood on him. When I look, he will have blood on him." Her eyelids were as heavy as lead, so heavy that she could barely lift her lashes. Turning slowly, she looked, and there was blood on his lips. Fallen slightly against the desk, he lay back in the Windsor chair, and seemed to watch her with the look of helpless reproach he had worn so often in life.

After an eternity, she still stood there. She had not thought; she had not felt; she had simply stood there and stared at the flecks of blood on his lips. John was speaking to her, she knew, as if she were deaf or an idiot, repeating over and over words without sense, without meaning. "He shot himself. It was an accident. Do you hear what I say? It was an accident." Then she saw that her grandfather was looking down on Mrs. Birdsong, was stooping over to lift her. How he got there, when he came in, she did not know. One moment there was nobody, and the next, her grandfather stood looking down on Mrs. Birdsong.

"Cora wasn't at home," she heard him say, "but I've sent for her." And, in a louder tone, as if his throat hurt him, "It was an accident." There was fear, there was despair, in his voice. "But how could it have happened? How was it possible?"

Then John's answer, low, intense, determined, "It did happen. It was an accident."

As if the hammered phrase had released some spring by which she moved and thought, a spasm shuddered through Jenny Blair's mind. Dropping into a chair, she threw back her head and began to scream with the thin, sharp cry of an animal caught in a trap.

"Stop that!" John called angrily. Crossing the room with a stride, he seized her and shook her into silence. "Stop that noise! General, can't you make her keep quiet?"

Turning away from Mrs. Birdsong, the old man spoke in a wandering tone, with an effort to separate his words as he uttered them. "Don't be brutal, John. The shock has unnerved her. Remember how young she is, and how innocent." Stretching out his old arms, he added gently, "It is too much for you, my darling. You had better go home and wait for your mother."

Springing to her feet, Jenny Blair stared at him with eyes that saw nothing. Desperately, as if she were about to run round and round in the same circle, she flung herself into his arms.

"Oh, Grandfather, I didn't mean anything," she cried, as she sank down into blackness. "I didn't mean anything in the world!"

❧ AFTERWORD ❧

In 1929 her contemporary Allen Tate said, "She writes an abominable prose style" and "is one of the worst novelists in the world." In 1953 literary critic John Edward Hardy said she "always lacked" "the aesthetic sense," any "sense of form," and even good storytelling skills. In 1982 historian Daniel Joseph Singal argued that she "plainly belonged to the nineteenth century," not the modern age.[1]

Yet Ellen Glasgow received the Howells Medal from the American Academy of Arts and Letters in 1940, the Southern Authors Prize and the *Saturday Review of Literature* award for Distinguished Service to American Literature in 1941, and the Pulitzer Prize for fiction in 1942. In an essay published in 1976, Louis D. Rubin, Jr., the recognized dean of Southern studies, declared, "She was, simply, the first really modern Southern novelist." Julius Rowan Raper echoed that view in 1990: "She . . . set the form that Modern Southern Fiction has followed."[2]

While it's not unusual for readers to hold different opinions of a writer's work, the differences with regard to Glasgow's work are notable for the fervor of some of the negative reactions and for the length of the debate. Almost fifty years after her death in 1945, the debate goes on.

What accounts for the conflicting views of Glasgow's fiction? For one thing—a small thing, perhaps, but a striking one—many critics have found Ellen Glasgow a difficult person to love. Their reaction to the woman may color or intensify their reaction to her fiction. For example, in the letter in which Allen Tate calls her "one of the worst novelists in the world," he also writes, "Miss Glasgow has everything that I have learned to detest in the transformation of the Virginian character—the feeble and offensive assumption of past superiority along with casting a vote for Hoover: she exhibits the 'aristocratic' manners of the South and shows how ridiculous they are: she is an incredible old snob."[3] Her high seriousness about the craft of fiction, particularly her estimation of her own works, irks some readers, who find her immodest. In a valuable study in which he undertakes to demonstrate Glasgow's significance to American literature, Louis Auchincloss nonetheless returns continually to weaknesses he perceives in her fiction. He repeatedly has to argue against himself to make his case. One wonders if he resists his own thesis because Glasgow the person offends him:

> It puts one off a bit that Ellen Glasgow struck, again and again, so high a note for herself. As she conceived of her personal suffering as more intense than anyone else's, so did she conceive of herself as a novelist on a Tolstoian scale. She did not hesitate, in the preface to *Barren Ground*, to nominate it as the one of her books best qualified for immortality, and in her memoirs she described it further, together with the Queenborough trilogy and *Vein of Iron*, as representing "not only the best that was in me, but some of the best work that has been done in American fiction."[4]

But obviously reactions to Glasgow's personality cannot alone account for the criticism she has frequently received. John Edward Hardy never touches on the personal in his essay on Glasgow, yet he is disdainful throughout. Ellen Glasgow's repertoire is, in fact, uneven. Of her nineteen novels (her few short stories and poems are rarely mentioned), only six are commonly praised today by even her admirers. Moreover, her apprenticeship was long: her best works came in the second half of her nearly fifty-year writing career.

Born in Richmond in 1873—a place and time in which

the only serious artists were expected to be men—Ellen Glasgow received little encouragement and no guidance as an aspiring writer, and the popular models around her were of the sentimental Southern school that she recognized as inferior. She had to find her own way as a writer, discover worthy models on her own. That she would master her craft slowly should not be surprising. That the flaws of her early fiction should rob her of the status she deserves because of the later fiction, however, is a shame. Had she written only *Phases of an Inferior Planet* (1898), *The Wheel of Life* (1906), *The Ancient Law* (1908), and *The Builders* (1919), Louis Auchincloss would be correct in saying, "She was unable sufficiently to pull the tapestry of fiction over her personal grievances and approbations" and thus "does not stand in the very first rank of American novelists."[5] Had she, on the other hand, published only *Virginia* (1913), *Barren Ground* (1925), *The Sheltered Life* (1932), and *Vein of Iron* (1935), she would likely rise unopposed to the first rank. Yet for all the merits of these later novels, Glasgow is rarely taught in courses on American or even Southern literature. What a loss. Mark Twain wrote only one really great book, but we don't let the weaknesses of *The Connecticut Yankee in King Arthur's Court* or *The Tragedy of Pudd'nhead Wilson* keep us from returning again and again to the pleasures of *The Adventures of Huckleberry Finn*.

Glasgow poses one additional difficulty for critics that helps account for the tenuousness of her position in the literary canon. It is that her long career spanned two so-called schools or periods in the literature of the South, and her fiction shows characteristics of both. Categorizing her—a practice literary critics are prone to—is thus troublesome. Does she belong, with her fellow Virginian Thomas Nelson Page, in the sentimental school of Southern fiction still popular at the end of the nineteenth century? Or is she more akin to the Faulkners, Warrens, and Weltys of the so-called modern Southern Renaissance, who presented a more realistic and honest view of the South? As we have seen, Hardy and Singal are sure she belongs to the nineteenth century, whereas Rubin and Raper place her with the modern writers.

Yet Rubin clearly is uncomfortable with that placement. Early in his influential book *Writers of the Modern South: The Faraway Country* (1963), he calls her "the first really important modern Southern novelist," but then in the Postscript in the same book he retracts that claim: "The Southern Literary Renascence may be said to have begun with the formation of the Fugitives [a group of poets in Nashville] just after the First World War. . . . Ellen Glasgow and James Branch Cabell were really of the previous generation, and though in the 1920's, when the Fugitives were first meeting, their popularity was very high indeed, it has since receded, and when one thinks of modern Southern Literature, one is likely to have in mind the generation of Faulkner, Wolfe, and the Fugitives."[6] A few critics straddle the fence: rather than placing her in one or the other school, they see Glasgow as bridging the two. That's Auchincloss's ultimate position. C. Vann Woodward states the case positively: "'When eventually the bold moderns of the South arrested the reading and theatrical world with the tragic intensity of the inner life and social drama of the South, they could find scarcely a theme that Ellen Glasgow had wholly neglected. She had bridged the gap between the old and the new literary revival, between romanticism and realism.'"[7]

But to see Glasgow as bridge is to invite neglect of her as surely as does assigning her to the now-seldom-read nineteenth-century sentimental school. For why, except for historical interest, would one turn to a precursor of the "bold moderns" when one could turn to the bold moderns themselves? At any rate, those who would exclude her from the modern canon have had the final word. In introducing and defining the Southern Renaissance in *The History of Southern Literature* (1985), a monumental work sponsored by the Society for the Study of Southern Literature and produced under the general editorship of Louis Rubin, Jr., Thomas Daniel Young writes, "Ellen Glasgow and James Branch Cabell, because their literary careers were launched before World War I, are not included in the Southern Renascence, though some of their most important work was done in the twenties, thirties, and even later."[8]

I have suggested elsewhere that the orthodox view that the Southern Renaissance began following World War I with the Fugitives at Nashville is arbitrary.[9] As Woodward says, Ellen Glasgow anticipated virtually every theme to which the "bold moderns" would turn, so perhaps the Southern Renaissance in fact began with her. But that's not an argument I want to make here. Instead, I want to demonstrate that, whatever one thinks of the rest of Glasgow's fiction, her novel *The Sheltered Life*—which has rarely been available in paperback—is a jewel of American literature and deserves recognition as a masterpiece of the Southern Renaissance. Not only does its publication date qualify it for consideration in the modern canon, but it treats familiar themes with a distinction that makes Glasgow's a progressive voice at the forefront of the renaissance. With no traces of sentimentality, yet with understanding and sympathy, it presents fully realized characterizations that embody a stunning critique of the exalted Old South legacy. Moreover, it is exquisitely structured as a bildungsroman, or novel of education, and may be the first such in modern Southern literature to have a female protagonist.

Born in 1873 into a comfortable, middle class family in the capitol of the former Confederacy, Glasgow was raised by an attentive black maid and protective parents, was largely self-educated because she was considered too delicate physically and emotionally to attend the public schools, and, by her own accounts, enjoyed a brief career as a popular Southern belle. She would seem an unlikely candidate not only to become a writer but also, as a writer, to revolt against the sentimental or romantic vein that characterized much of Southern fiction in the late nineteenth century. But write, and revolt, she did.

In her autobiography, *The Woman Within* (1954), Glasgow reports that she became a rebel at an early age: "I cannot recall the time when the pattern of society, as well as the scheme of things in general, had not seemed to me false and even malignant."[10] Her thinking was formed in part by some controversial theories of the time, including those of John Stuart Mill, Gibbon, and Darwin, whom she read, despite her father's displeasure. She became a suffragist at age eighteen.

Once she dedicated herself to the writing of fiction (she had considered herself a writer since age seven), she rebelled consciously against "the evasive idealism" that she perceived running through Southern society and Southern literature: "I would write, I resolved, as no Southerner had ever written, of the universal human chords beneath the superficial variations of scene and character. I would write of all the harsher realities beneath manners, beneath social customs, beneath the poetry of the past, and the romantic nostalgia of the present."[11] Her first novel, *The Descendant* (1897), published when she was twenty-four, was recognized immediately as daring. As her protagonist, Glasgow had chosen not the usual hero, a member of the old aristocracy, but an illegitimate poor white who was a radical social scientist. Yet the story is burdened by didacticism, a setting (New York City) about which the author had little knowledge, and an amateurish, heavy-handed prose style. Years later, Glasgow would judge *The Descendant* honestly: "If only I had learned to write before writing, my first book might have been not entirely unworthy of my idea."[12]

By the time she had written her tenth novel, she had come a long way as a writer. Several scholars as well as Glasgow herself have judged *Virginia* (1913) to be the best of her early fiction. She now was writing about something she knew well: "I analyzed the whole tradition of the Southern lady."[13] And she did so with irony and restraint. She would continue her study of the Southern woman in some subsequent fine work, most notably *Barren Ground* (1925) and *The Romantic Comedians* (1926). And then would come *The Sheltered Life* (1932). All three of these novels, as well as *They Stooped to Conquer* (1929), *Vein of Iron* (1935), and *In This Our Life* (1941), fit into the time period the Southern Renaissance is conventionally said to encompass.

The Sheltered Life was published only three years after the watershed year of the Southern Renaissance, 1929, which saw the publication of three novels usually deemed to be the first major novels of that renaissance: William Faulkner's *Sartoris* and *The Sound and the Fury* and Thomas Wolfe's *Look Homeward, Angel*. It followed closely on the heels also of the agrarian manifesto *I'll Take My Stand* (1930), which has been called the formal announcement of the renaissance and is generally taken to reflect major tensions in the region that influenced the post–World War I flowering of a serious literature. Written by twelve Southern white male scholars, including several of the Fugitive poets whom the orthodoxy credits with being the first artists of the renaissance, *I'll Take My Stand* is a collection of essays that champions the Old South's agrarian way of life against the encroaching industrialization of the modern age. That image of a South at the point of change, and Southerners torn between the past and the future, recurs frequently in modern Southern literature. Whereas Thomas Nelson Page, writing in the decades immediately following the Civil War, sentimentalizes the Old South, treating it defensively and nostalgically as a golden age, the authors of the Southern Renaissance rebel against such sentimentality and generally manage to bring some detachment and realism to their treatments of character, customs, change, and place. With *The Sheltered Life*, Ellen Glasgow succeeds as well as any of them, and better than most.

Hers is a progressive voice in the renaissance. In "The Dynamic Past," an essay published in 1921, she had criticized the South in much the same terms that satirist H. L. Mencken had a few years earlier in his essay "The Sahara of the Bozart," in which he asserted that, artistically, the South was as sterile as the Sahara desert. Saying that she could tell the truth about Virginia because she herself was "a Virginian in every drop of my blood and pulse of my heart," Glasgow then faulted the South for its backward, self-centered vision and its failure to cultivate a high art: "There are few places in the world richer in color and inspiration than our own South—yet because of the stagnant air, the absence of critical values, the flaunting of borrowed flags, the facile cult of the cheap and showy, art has languished among us." Whereas in 1930 the backward-looking authors of *I'll Take My Stand* would hold up the Old South as a model for the good life as they protested the industrialization of their region, Glasgow almost a decade earlier spoke for the future: "For the glory of men as of nations is measured not by the strength with which they cling to the past, but by the courage with which they adventure into the future.... [Genius] means a departure from tribal forms and images. It means a creation of new standards and new ideals of beauty and new rules of conduct."[14]

In *The Sheltered Life*, she portrays the remnants of the Old South as a society that has become stagnant and ingrown—a society that blindly holds to past ideals and past rules of conduct while the future knocks at the door.

Ever since the War Between the States had transformed opulent planters into eminent citizens, a dozen old country families had clung to the lower end of Washington Street. Here they had lived, knit together by ties of kinship and tradition, in the Sabbath peace that comes only to those who have been vanquished in war. Here they resisted change and

adversity and progress; and here at last they were scattered
by nothing more tangible than a stench. . . . Only the Archbalds and the Birdsongs. . . stood their ground and watched
the invasion of ugliness. (6)

The time is 1906; the setting, Queenborough, a fictional-
ized version of Glasgow's Richmond.

In her honest treatment of progress, Glasgow does acknowledge, through images and selective choice of verbs,
that undesirable elements accompany it: not only does the
chemical factory produce a stench, but "the old houses
[have been] demolished, the fine old elms mutilated," and
"telegraph poles slash[ ] the horizon" while "furnaces . . .
belch[ ] soot" and "newspapers . . . litter[ ] the pavements"
(6–7). But by suggesting a parallel between the characters'
resistance to change and the South's fighting the Civil War
to resist change, she implies not only that the resistance is
doomed but also that it reflects an arrogance and a refusal
to face reality: "Still undaunted, the two families held the
breach between the old and new order, sustained by pride
and by some moral quality more enduring than pride. After
all, they might have asked, were they not defending their
homes from a second invasion?" (7). The Birdsongs can't
afford to move, "and the Archbalds stayed because the General, in his seventy-sixth year but still incapable of retreat,
declared that he would never forsake Mrs. Birdsong. Industrialization might conquer, but they would never surrender" (6).

Early on, Glasgow symbolizes the new-age industrialism
in the stench from the chemical factory and the remnants
of the old order in the Archbalds' walled garden—the wall
itself symbolizing the family's attempt to hold at bay the
new order and to make time stand still in their small world.
The walled garden is "a small place, but it held beauty.
Beauty, and that deep stillness through which time seems to
flow with a perpetual rhythm and pause. . . . Only at long

intervals . . . was the tranquil air brushed by a roving taint, a breath of decay, from the new chemical factory" (5).

While Glasgow's frequent references to signs of modernization indicate that she is portraying the South at a time of change, the novel's action does not rest on a conflict between the old and new ages. Like the stench from the chemical factory, the other evidences of the new age waft in only occasionally. Though John Welch, the one character who speaks for change, plays an important role toward the end of the novel, he appears in only a few scenes. Rather than the changing times, Glasgow's focus here is the Old South tradition itself. Whereas the authors of *I'll Take My Stand* hold up that tradition as an ideal, Glasgow presents it with no traces of nostalgia. She shows that the Old South's values, enforced by a strict code of behavior, stunt individuals.

General Archbald is himself an emblem and a product of the Old South, though, ironically, he has always "known that he was not a part of his age" (31). That he is different, too sensitive to be a man of his time and place, was first suggested to him when, as a child, he realized that he could never be, like his father and grandfather, a hunter: he could not stomach killing an animal for sport. Yet the only time in his long life that he violated the code of behavior expected of him was when, in his youth, he had assisted a runaway slave. Even so, when war came, he loyally fought for the South, and in all other things, he walked the line laid out for him as a gentleman of the South: he had lost the woman he loved because of appearances (though unhappily married to someone else, she had children), married a woman he did not love to save appearances (he had proposed, and she accepted, because their sleigh had broken down during a snowstorm and they had had to spend the night together), and then, after his wife's death, had denied himself the possibility of happiness with another woman also because of appearances (his daughters and daughter-in-law expected him to remain loyal to his wife's memory and to devote himself to them). He realizes that he has lived "in an age when marriage was an invisible prison" and that his own marriage was "thirty years of heroic fidelity" during which "he had sacrificed his youth, his middle age, his dreams, his imagination, all the vital instincts that make a man, to the moral earnestness of tradition" (33). He has seen the evil of the system, but he has denied his insights, denied himself, and fulfilled the role of the Southern gentleman to perfection.

For the Southern woman of the old tradition, appearances are even more vital, for the ideal for womanhood, the Southern belle, is defined by both her physical appearance and her actions. Just as General Archbald embodies, in spite of his feelings, the ideal of the Southern gentleman, so is Eva Birdsong the Old South's ideal of womanhood.

> Mrs. Birdsong was one of those celebrated beauties, who, if they still exist, have ceased to be celebrated. Tall, slender, royal in carriage, hers was that perfect loveliness which made the hearts of old men flutter and miss a beat when she approached them. . . .
>
> She had been, at eighteen, the reigning beauty of Queenborough. . . . The Victorian age, even in its decline, worshipped beauty; and she was as near perfection in her girlhood as if she had stepped out of some glimmering antique horizon. (19)

In her middle thirties when the novel opens in 1906, Eva is still worshipped by Queenborough, "still regarded less as a woman than as a memorable occasion." According to legend, "Not only had her beauty delayed wedding processions, but once, it was said, she had even retarded a funeral when she happened to enter Rose Hill Cemetery just as the pall-bearers were lowering a coffin into a grave" (7).

Though Queenborough romanticizes Eva, Glasgow does

not. Through several characterizations and that of Eva especially, Glasgow exposes the cult of beauty worship as a cruel legacy of the Old South tradition. With the society expecting so little, yet so much of her—that she be unceasingly beautiful, young, and vivacious—Eva is under constant stress. She can never relax and be herself.

> Thinking herself alone in the street, unaware of the row of admiring spectators, Mrs. Birdsong had permitted her well-trained muscles to relax for a moment, while her brilliance suddenly flickered out, as if the sunshine had faded. The corners of her mouth twitched and drooped; her step lost its springiness; and her figure appeared to give way at the waist and sink down for support into the stiff ripples of taffeta. Then, as quickly as her spirit had flagged, it recovered its energy and sprang back into poise. As the first whisper reached her, her tired features were transfigured by an arch and vivacious smile. Glancing up at the window, she waved gaily. Starry eyes, curving red lips, the transparent flush in her cheeks, even the delicate wings of her eyebrows—all seemed to be woven less of flesh than of some fragile bloom of desire. (21)

With her whole identity dependent on her looks, Eva worries about growing old, worries about losing her husband's love, fears losing her identity. She had had a beautiful voice in her youth, had had a chance for a career as a singer, but she had given that up to marry charming George Birdsong, "the least eligible of her suitors" (20). Now, she must constantly convince herself that their "'great passion'" (28) and the town's worship are enough to fulfill her. As she ages and her beauty diminishes, and as she sees her husband being attracted to younger women, convincing herself becomes harder and harder.

Whereas Eva's life demonstrates the burden of the cult of beauty on the beautiful woman, Etta Archbald's demonstrates its cruelty to the woman who lacks beauty. The daughter of General Archbald, Etta has the family status appropriate to a Southern belle, but the family name is not sufficient. She lives a life of misery because, being physically unattractive, she cannot succeed as a woman: "Her long, bleak face, tinged with the greenish pallor of the chronic invalid, broke out into wine-coloured splotches. . . . She had come into the world as a mistake of nature, defeated before she was born" (22).

The plain old maid is typically the object of an author's ridicule when she appears in fiction of the late-nineteenth and early-twentieth century, but Glasgow treats Etta with a depth that elicits the reader's understanding and sympathy. One of the most memorable and painful episodes in the novel depicts Etta's preparations for and attendance at a neighbor's dance party. Having spent hours trying to make herself attractive, Etta travels to the party with her father, wishing that someone will "'fall in love with me to-night for the sake of my sweet expression'" (104), her only alleged asset. As usual, however, Etta has no suitors—indeed, seems not to be noticed by the men. Glasgow presents Etta's plight through the eyes of her young niece Jenny Blair Archbald. "Oh, if only somebody, no matter how old and ugly, would ask poor Aunt Etta to dance! Perhaps this one will, at least he is ugly enough. . . . It can't be true. Yes, it is. He is really seeking her out. To be a man! Oh, the power, the glory, of being awaited in fear, of being hopefully awaited, in spite of the most unattractive appearance! But poor Aunt Etta will dance at last. . . . She will be saved from the fate of a wallflower." But Jenny Blair is wrong. The man "had passed Aunt Etta by and was boldly pursuing the prettiest and youngest girl on the floor." Meanwhile, "Aunt Etta was left sitting, with her sweet expression growing more false every minute, between Grandfather and Miss Abby Carter" (112–13).

What is a woman to do who cannot win a man—who

cannot succeed in the only acceptable avenue open to the woman of a good family? Without a home of her own, she becomes a hanger-on in her father's house and tries to save face, if not find fulfillment, by immersing herself in other interests. Glasgow suggests that church work has been one such face-saving outlet that the old maid has turned to, but Etta finds it a poor substitute for love.

> "I want love. I don't want any other interest. I want love."
> "But I thought you were doing so well with your church work."
> "I wasn't. I wasn't."
> "Etta, you must hold onto your pride." There was a stern accent in Mrs. Archbald's remonstrance. "After all, no woman can afford not to save her pride." (85)

Another outlet the powerless, unhappy woman may turn to is illnesses. Glasgow implies that Etta's chronic pains are as imaginary as real, that Etta unconsciously uses them to get attention and sympathy and also to excuse her failure to fulfill the ideal of Southern womanhood. Similarly, Eva Birdsong feigns illness to get her husband's attention and sympathy when she sees him take a stroll with a pretty young woman at the dance party. In another incident, Mrs. Archbald wishes she had advised her sister-in-law Isabella to try to hang onto her fiancé by going "'to bed and stay[ing] there until the scandal blew over'" (15).

As these examples illustrate, the cult of beauty, which has getting and keeping a husband as its end, turns women into false, artificial creatures. While she makes the reader understand why the women put such emphasis on appearance, Glasgow also tersely satirizes the lengths they will go to in that cause. Preparing for the dance party, Etta chooses a dress with ruffles that discreetly puff out her "flat, slightly stooping figure" in the right places. She draws her hair back "over a high, stiff roll, filled . . . with a substance that resembled the stuffing of sofas" (94). Glasgow particularly mocks the discomfort the women will endure for the sake of an hour-glass figure. Etta's waist is "smaller by two inches than the severely pinched waist" of her beautiful sister Isabella, who is "molded into a princess robe of pink satin spangled with sequins" (97, 96). What a relief bedtime must bring: "In the illuminated square of the doorway, [Jenny Blair] could see her mother's spreading figure, which was so much larger at night than in the daytime, attired in a starched cambric wrapper" (87).

The artificiality of the women's appearance is only the most visible evidence of—is, in fact, symbolic of—the falseness Glasgow sees throughout the society. In her autobiography, she explains: "I hated—I had always hated—the inherent falseness in much Southern tradition." Her career-long attempt to expose "the philosophy of evasive idealism" that she saw prevalent in the South's conversations, manners, customs, and literature[15] reaches its zenith in *The Sheltered Life*.

Whereas Eva Birdsong is frozen in the role of the Southern belle, expected to be forever young, vivacious, and beautiful, Cora Archbald has assumed the role of the society's other, more sedate ideal of womanhood, the Southern lady; she is gracious, kindhearted, generous, selfless, and totally devoted to her family and friends. She is also the perfect embodiment of the society's evasive idealism. Glasgow implies that the Southern lady's politeness, graciousness, consideration for others, all invite dishonesty and an evading of reality. The author actually uses the term *evasive idealism* in the text in describing Cora's attempt to cheer up her tired, depressed father-in-law, General Archbald. After Cora says to him, "'After all, you're only eight-three. Why, to look at you, any one would think you were still in the prime of life,'" Glasgow adds, "Usually her flattery succeeded; but to-night . . . he felt that he required a tonic more inspiriting than evasive idealism" (228).

Always smiling, full of platitudes for every occasion, Cora

glosses over pain, evil, and unscrupulous behavior. When her sister-in-law Etta, miserable and afraid because no man loves her, turns to her for comfort, Cora responds, "'But there isn't anything to be afraid of, dear. Take this bromide. . . . Try not to think of unpleasant things, and you'll go back to sleep'" (84), and later she adds, "'All women who haven't had love overestimate its importance'" (85). When her words do not stem Etta's misery, she advises Etta to pull herself together, to show some dignity and pride—to *pretend* she is not suffering. Appearance, she says, "'matters . . . more than anything in the world'" (86). In a humorous example of her deliberate blindness, she refuses to believe that her sister-in-law Isabella may be carrying on a romance with the carpenter Joseph Crocker because of their difference in class: "'With Joseph Crocker? No, my dear, how could she? Why, he wears overalls'" (26).

Glasgow repeatedly suggests a parallel between Cora as a purveyor of falseness and Cora as a Southern lady, as in these observations about her by General Archbald:

> He had often wondered how so good a woman could have so little regard for truth. There wasn't a kinder person on earth; but if she ever spoke the truth, it was by accident, or on one of those rare occasions when truth is more pleasant than fiction. . . . But because she was charitable and benign, her dissembling became, in some incredible fashion, the servant of goodness. How much innocent pleasure had she conferred, how much painful embarrassment had she relieved! Even when she had stood between him and happiness, he had never doubted that she was ruining his old age from the noblest motives. (234)

Only once is the reader allowed to see her without her pleasant Southern lady's mask. Having spent hours helping her daughter and sisters-in-law prepare for the dance party, she sinks down into an easy chair and, thinking no one is looking, relaxes "from the severe strain of keeping up an appearance": "Not her duty alone, but love, life, the world, the universe, God—all these had become suddenly too much for her. Stripped of her pleasant smile, stripped even of her sunny disposition, she was only a tired middle-aged woman, who rested . . . from the wearing endeavor to look on the bright side of things and hope for the best" (92).

In its implicitly critical exposure of the manners, conventions, and values of a society, *The Sheltered Life* fits the definition of a comedy of manners, or, as Glasgow called the novel, a history of manners. But the artistic success of the novel depends on the structure she gives her critique: rather than spotlighting her criticisms, she embeds them in a bildungsroman plot that follows innocent young Jenny Blair Archbald as she is educated in the ways of her world. Through this indirect approach, Glasgow avoids the didacticism of some of her early novels and prevents the satire from resulting in caricatures. She divides the bildungsroman into three sections, each of which advances the critique while also relating to Jenny Blair's movement from childhood to young adulthood, and from innocence to evasive idealism.

The first section of the novel presents Jenny Blair at age nine, the approximate age of first consciousness. As the novel opens, she is enchanted with the discovery of herself as a separate entity and is in love with life: "But all she knew was, 'I am this and not that.' All she felt was the sudden glory, the singing rhythm of life. Softly, without knowing why, she began crooning, 'I'm alive, alive, alive, and I'm Jenny Blair Archbald'" (4). A typical nine-year-old, she longs to be outside skating rather than sitting inside reading, at her mother's insistence, a book like *Little Women*, about such "poky old things" as Meg and Jo, "even if Mamma did form her character" on those heroines (3).

This opening scene shows Jenny Blair to be an innocent young girl who yearns for knowledge of the world: the real world outside her window, not the world to be discovered tediously through books. Her curiosity, common in children, is another illustration of her eagerness to know. She had asked her grandfather, "'When is time?'" and "'When is eternity?'" And she is curious about the world beyond her small world, "the world in which factories boomed, steam whistles blew, bad smells sprang up in the wind, and the new red touring cars buzzed through the streets" (12). With a child's desire for adventure and freedom to match her curiosity, she ventures into that larger world once her mother finally allows her to go out to play: "Nobody, least of all her mother, could understand the fascinated horror that drew her, like a tightened cord, toward the unknown and the forbidden. Nobody who had not been born with a rebel heart could share her impulse to skip and dance and flap her arms like fledgling wings as soon as she had broken away from the house and was sure none of them could run after her" (43).

At the beginning of the bildungsroman, then, Jenny Blair Archbald is, at nine years and seven months, a nearly blank page upon which the lessons of her society will be written. Her innocence, curiosity, and vitality are charming; she seems full of potential, and the reader has high hopes for her. Those hopes will be disappointed, however, when the reader discovers, in the last section of the novel, that Jenny Blair grows up to be a shallow young woman who, in the novel's climax, contributes to a tragedy, her chance for intellectual and moral development having been arrested by the lessons she learns along the way. Glasgow uses the first section of the novel not only to present Jenny Blair as a charming young girl full of potential but also to unfold the education of that young girl within the cult of beauty and the school of evasive idealism.

An only child living in a houseful of descendants of the Old South, and with her closest neighbors another adult couple of like background, Jenny Blair is continually exposed to the values and attitudes of the Old South. These people are virtually her only source for information about life. She eavesdrops on their conversations, as in the opening scene, and observes their actions. She is thus indirectly educated to their ideals and manners in almost every waking moment. Glasgow enhances the reader's recognition that this education is taking place by rendering this first section of the bildungsroman largely through Jenny Blair's perspective; the reader sees and hears what Jenny Blair sees and hears. For example, Jenny Blair overhears her mother when she tells Etta that appearance "matters . . . more than anything in the world," and she sees repeated evidence of the value the society places on beauty—and artificiality—in women. From the examples of Eva Birdsong and Aunts Isabella and Etta, she can't help but learn that a woman's one goal in life is to win the love of a man, that all is to be sacrificed to that goal, and that physical beauty is the surest route to the goal. But in addition to these implicit lessons, Jenny Blair frequently receives more direct instruction in the code of behavior of her society. Physical beauty and evasive idealism are the underlying themes of much of this instruction.

The lessons in the importance of physical beauty and appearance to the female are numerous. The first scene alone offers several. Twice in that scene, Mrs. Archbald calls Jenny Blair away from her reading and, in effect, instructs her in the greater importance of female beauty. The first time, she wants Jenny Blair to come try on a coat she is making, and in her daughter's hearing she then laments that, though Jenny Blair is much brighter than her playmate Bena Peyton, "'Bena has a nice plump little figure'" while, alas "'Jenny Blair is as straight as a pole'" (10). A few minutes later, Mrs. Archbald again invites her daughter to put aside her reading, this time to gaze out the window at the beautiful Eva Birdsong. It is clear, from her tone of voice and Jenny Blair's reaction, that Mrs. Archbald is offering the child a treat:

"Jenny Blair!" her mother called in an excited tone. "Jenny Blair, do you wish to see Mrs. Birdsong in her new violet toque?"

Springing to her feet, the child rushed into the library and flung herself between the red damask curtains. "Oh, Mamma, is she coming? Do you suppose she will speak to us?" (18)

The lesson is reinforced by Aunt Etta's reaction to the view from the window: "'How adorable she looks,' Etta sighed, with an emotion so intense that it was almost hysterical" (21). Jenny Blair can have no doubt that Mrs. Birdsong is the society's ideal, nor that her physical beauty is what has exalted her to that position.

That Jenny Blair, by age nine, has already taken such lessons to heart is illustrated in her reaction when George Birdsong, deliberately flattering her, tells her, "'You're old for your age, and you get better looking, too, every day. It won't surprise me if you grow up to be one of the prettiest girls in Queenborough.'" Glasgow describes Jenny Blair's reaction this way: "She drew in her breath sharply, as if all her thoughts were whistling a tune. Never before had any one held out the faintest hope that she might grow up to be pretty" (59). To be thought potentially beautiful is so important to her that she falls instantly in love with the man who speaks those words.

The lessons in evasive idealism are numerous also. The philosophy condones deception, often under the guise of consideration for others. Jenny Blair receives frequent instruction in the practice of this philosophy from her mother, Cora Archbald, the consummate evasive idealist, who is always looking on the bright side, seeing only what she wants to see. For example, after Aunt Isabella's fiancé calls off their engagement because of Isabella's indiscreet behavior, Mrs. Archbald carefully instructs her daughter in the acceptable—or prettified—version of this episode. "'Listen to me,

Jenny Blair.' Mrs. Archbald was speaking in her sternest tone. 'I have told you over and over that Aunt Isabella broke her engagement because she was not sure of the state of her feelings. Remember those words—the state of her feelings. If Bena Peyton ever says anything about it, that is what you are to tell her. Do you understand what I say?'" (92). Indeed, Jenny Blair does understand, perhaps better than her mother realizes. For even as a nine-year-old she has begun to catch on to the fact that words and reality need not match.

> "Run away now, and don't forget to tell Aunt Etta how sweet she is looking."
> "Is she really looking sweet, Mamma, or am I just to pretend?" (91)

Through such lessons, Jenny Blair is learning that deception is moral and civilized, that telling lies to make others feel better is good. Another version of that lesson is that telling lies, or keeping quiet, is good if telling the truth would hurt someone. George Birdsong is one of Jenny Blair's many instructors in this version of evasive idealism. When Jenny Blair falls and hurts herself while skating in forbidden territory, the chemical factory neighborhood, and George and his mistress Memoria, who lives nearby, come to her rescue, George strikes a pact of secrecy with her: "'It's better not to tell your mother you had a fall in Canal Street. It might make her feel worse, you know, and I've never found it did any good to make people feel worse'" (62). And Jenny Blair, who has obviously had previous experience in such presumably innocent deception, agrees: "'No, it never does any good. I always try not to tell Mamma anything I know will make her unhappy'" (62). To try not to make others unhappy is, of course, an admirable goal, but to use that goal to excuse one from taking responsibility for one's actions, as both George and Jenny do here, is not. Later in the novel, Jenny Blair will practice similar evasiveness and deception, with dire consequences.

Glasgow's title for this first section of the novel, "The Age of Make-Believe," links the bildungsroman and the critique of the Old South tradition. The title is a clear allusion to childhood, and hence to the section's role in the bildungsroman. The section portrays the protagonist as a child, a typical nine-year-old who is not only curious, innocent, and adventurous but also full of imagination. For example, when she gets bored sitting indoors reading, she imaginatively transforms the world outside her window: "Breathing hard, she shut her eyes tight and opened them quickly. This was a magic spell to make the world more surprising; and enchantment worked immediately upon the sky, the sycamore, and the rich bloom of the walled garden" (5). Later, she describes the charming Mrs. Birdsong's face as looking like "'a pink heart on a valentine,'" a comment that leads her mother to scold, "'Don't be silly. . . . You are letting your imagination run away with you again'" (23). The first section thus introduces the reader to the protagonist in the bildungsroman plot, an engaging child who, naturally, loves to make-believe. As the rest of the plot unfolds and the child grows up, the reader hopes to see her remain engaging yet adjust to and accept the real world.

The close reader will realize, however, that the title "The Age of Make-Believe" refers not only to the world of childhood but also the world of the Old South. Glasgow implies a parallel between the child's imaginativeness and love of make-believe, on the one hand, and the Old South's evasive idealism, on the other. In fact, she frequently uses language and incidents to suggest that the Queenborough remnants of the Old South are engaged in make-believe as much as is Jenny Blair.

Just as Jenny Blair squeezes her eyes tight shut and then opens them suddenly to find the world magically transformed, so do the adults in her world, as we have seen, close their eyes tight to anything they don't want to see and thus transform their world at will to what they want it to be. At one point, Glasgow describes Jenny Blair's mother, who ironically has just accused Jenny of letting her imagination run away with her, in this way: "Gradually, while the sheltered life closed in about her, she had retreated into the smiling region of phantasy. With much patience, she had acquired the capacity to believe anything and nothing" (24). Eva Birdsong has, all her married life, engaged in make-believe: she hides her feelings of insecurity, makes believe she is ecstatically happy, and puts on a smiling mask for the world. At the dance party, when she sees her husband with another woman, her world of make-believe begins to shatter, but her hostess, Mrs. Peyton, advises her to retain the facade:

> "But I saw them, Mary. I saw them with my own eyes——"
> "Hush, Eva. It is much wiser to pretend that you didn't. Even if you know, it is safer not to suspect anything." (117)

When Jenny Blair sees Mrs. Birdsong with her smiling mask momentarily removed, she is horrified by this revelation of reality beneath the adult world of smiling surfaces. Glasgow's language again associates the adults' custom of hiding true feelings with a game of pretense: "Then, watching the look in Mrs. Birdsong's face, the child was seized by the feeling of moral nakedness that came to her whenever the veil slipped away from life and even grown-up people stopped pretending. . . . she was scorched with shame, not for herself, but for Mrs. Birdsong. More than anything in the world, she hated to see her elders begin to crumble on the surface and let glimpses through of feelings that ought never to be exposed" (122).

At a happier moment during the adult dance party, Jenny Blair looks down on the romantically decorated Peyton garden and is enchanted, but she realizes, too, "'It isn't real. . . .

It isn't a bit more real than make-believe'" (119). And those
words, Glasgow hints, apply to the Old South tradition itself. The dance party has brought together the last of the
Old South, has created a romantic microcosm where
women can play once more the roles of Southern belles and
men those of gallant cavaliers, but this is only a party, it's
not the everyday real world: "No, it wasn't real. It wouldn't
last till to-morrow; but, oh, it was lovely, it was satisfying,
as long as you looked at it" (119). The Old South itself was
never so lovely as the romantic reminiscences would have it
be, but the remaining residents of Washington Street and a
few of their friends continue to try to hang onto that mythi-
cized world of graciousness, nobility, and happiness.

But to do so they have to resort to make-believe. They
have to ignore or whitewash those things they encounter
that conflict with graciousness, nobility, and happiness.
Near the end of section one, in a climactic instance of Jenny
Blair's receiving direct instruction in the practice of evasive
idealism, Mrs. Peyton whitewashes Eva Birdsong's jealous
hysteria: "'Go straight to bed, children, . . . and remember,
if any one asks you anything about Mrs. Birdsong, that she
had a sudden faintness and was obliged to leave early'"
(123). And Jenny Blair, unlike her realistic little friend Bena
Peyton, is happy to join the adult world of make-believe:
"'It *was* a sudden faintness,' she repeated firmly; for even at
her tender age she had not failed to perceive that you may
believe almost anything if you say it over often enough"
(124). With these words near the end of the first section of
the novel, Glasgow demonstrates that Jenny Blair's education in the school of evasive idealism is proving successful
indeed.

The second and much shorter section of the novel, titled
"The Deep Past," takes place eight years later, in 1914, and
is presented chiefly through General Archbald's perspective.
Throughout most of the section, Archbald, now eighty-
three, sits on a bench in the April sunlight reminiscing

about his life as he waits to be called into Eva Birdsong's hospital room. This section fleshes out the image of the general that Glasgow had introduced in the preceding section in the one chapter there that she had rendered through his perspective.

In reviewing his life, Archbald feels a great sense of loss—not, as is the usual case for Old South representatives in Southern literature, for things that once were but are no more, but for things that never were. Having adhered all his life to the Old South code expected of him, he has denied his own wishes, lost one and possibly two chances for love and happiness, and silently condoned policies and conventions contrary to his insights. The best he can say of his past is that it had been a "fair life": "Nothing that he wanted, but everything that was good for him" (163). He has fulfilled the role of the honorable, responsible, courtly Southern gentleman to perfection, but it has been a life of surfaces. "A surface! Yes, that, he realized now, was the flaw in the structure. Except for that one defeated passion in his youth, he had lived entirely upon the shifting surface of facts. He had been a good citizen, a successful lawyer, a faithful husband, an indulgent father; he had been, indeed, everything but himself. Always he had fallen into the right pattern; but the centre of the pattern was missing" (164).

Glasgow's critique of the Old South tradition here is stark and original. A gentle, sensitive, intelligent man, David Archbald is a reliable narrator, and for him to see his eighty-three years as only a stunted existence is poignant. But there is a double irony here. If the General has not been in his heart what he seems, the further irony is that, in spite of his heart, he has in fact been what he seems, for Glasgow implies that surfaces are everything to the Old South code: if one is from an acceptable family and acts like a Southern gentleman—if one "fall[s] into the right pattern"—one *is* a Southern gentleman.

The section also has a significant role, though a subtle

one, in the bildungsroman plot starring Jenny Blair. By revealing what the Old South system that Jenny is being educated to has done to one of its pillars—indeed, to one of her educators—it implicitly raises questions about Jenny's own future: What will become of the vibrant young girl who, the last time the reader saw her, seemed so alive and full of potential? Will she too be cowed and stunted, live "entirely upon the shifting surface of facts"?

The title of the section, "The Deep Past," is significant to both the critique of the Old South and the bildungsroman. It relates obviously to the former, in that in delving into his deep past Archbald necessarily delves into the Old South as an institution. His search is not nostalgic but painful. The term *the deep past* is also suggestive of death, which hangs over this middle section, both because of the operation Eva Birdsong faces and because of David Archbald's advanced age. Since Eva and the General are emblems of the Old South, Glasgow may also be suggesting that the Old South legacy is dying. But she is surely showing that the Old South's values and its code of behavior produce living deaths.

In relation to the bildungsroman, the title seems to suggest, and the action of the section illustrates, escape from the present. Admirably self-reflective about his past, Archbald recognizes—and has, for years—the shortcomings of the Old South tradition, but he does nothing to remedy them. He does not think about how he can make life better for his precious granddaughter, how he can give her better guidance and nurturing than he received in his youth—how he can help her avoid living a life of surfaces. He has been, as he says, an indulgent father, and he is an even more indulgent grandfather. Never does the reader see him offer Jenny Blair moral guidance or intellectual stimulation. As a guardian to his granddaughter, Archbald needs to be much involved in the present, but his thoughts and concerns (not only here but elsewhere in the novel) are much more about

Eva Birdsong, the ideal of the Old South, than about Jenny Blair. Indeed, he hardly knows Jenny Blair at all.

That Glasgow intended "The Age of Make-Believe" to suggest childhood, hope, and a beginning, and "The Deep Past" to be its counterpart, suggesting old age, apathy, and an end, is made clear by the direct parallels and contrasts between the last paragraphs of the two sections. At the end of "The Age of Make-Believe," Jenny Blair is so in love with life and feels so alive that she cannot stand still. Near the end of "The Deep Past," General Archbald sits unmoving, conscious of the approach of death and feeling that he has never really lived. Here is the ending of the first section:

> Then, without cause, without warning, . . . with the river breeze blowing in a sharp spray over her skin, she was visited by one of those swift flashes of ecstasy. Wordless, vast, encompassing, this extraordinary joy broke over her like an invisible shower. Without and within, she felt the rain of delight sprinkling her body and soul, trickling over her bare flesh, seeping down through her skin into the secret depths of her heart. "The world is so lovely," she cried, dancing round and round on her bare feet. "I'm alive, alive, alive, and I'm Jenny Blair Archbald!" (124–25)

What ecstasy, what hope and faith, innocent young Jenny Blair expresses! Near the end of section two, David Archbald almost arrives at that same sense of ecstasy and hope, but he cannot maintain the feeling, knowing life as he does.

> Suddenly, without warning, a wave of joy rose from the unconscious depths. Suppose that somewhere beyond, in some central radiance of being, he should find again that ecstasy he had lost without ever possessing. For one heartbeat, while the wave broke and the dazzling spray flooded

his thoughts, he told himself that he was immortal, that . . . he had found the confirmation of love, faith, truth, right, Divine goodness. Then, as swiftly as it had broken, the wave of joy spent itself. The glow, the surprise, the startled wonder, faded into the apathetic weariness of the end. He was only a old man warming his withered flesh in the April sunshine. "My life is nearly over," he thought, "but who knows what life is in the end?" (165)

The action of the third section of the novel takes place immediately after that of section two. The time is still 1914, Eva Birdsong is ill, and Jenny Blair Archbald is now seventeen. By late adolescence or young adulthood, the protagonist in a bildungsroman typically has been fully educated to the values and codes of his world (the protagonist is usually a "he"), and will soon go through a crucial experience or a spiritual crisis that leads him to evaluate who he is, perhaps to break from convention, and to arrive at maturity and individual identity. Having reached the threshold of early adulthood, Jenny Blair is fully educated to the values and codes of her world, and she will soon face a crucial experience that should make her see the world more realistically. However, she will fail that test. Another character in the novel, on the other hand, does go through a crisis that makes her question who she is and reach for a better way to live. Ironically, not young Jenny Blair but middle-aged Eva Birdsong is the character who arrives at awareness in this bildungsroman. In this last section of the novel, titled "The Illusion," Eva Birdsong confronts her romanticized identity and recognizes it as a destructive illusion. Like General Archbald, she realizes that she has been a victim of the Old South legacy. Unlike him, she attempts, though unsuccessfully, to throw off that legacy.

The crisis that brings on Eva's painful growth is a debilitating operation, probably a hysterectomy, and a long recuperation. Despite the pain she was suffering and the uncertainty she faced, Eva had entered the operating room with her smiling, vivacious Southern-belle mask intact. Afterwards, however, no longer able to disguise her declining health and fading beauty, she begins to question the role she has played for most of her forty-plus years. Early in the novel, Eva had instructed an admiring little Jenny Blair in the absoluteness of love and happiness for a woman: "'A great love doesn't leave room for anything else in a woman's life. It is everything'" (74) and "'you can never give up too much for happiness'" (77). Eight years later, however—eight years of solid stress and denial of George's unfaithfulness, and a few weeks after her operation—she advises Jenny Blair differently: "'I staked all my happiness on a single chance. I gave up all the little joys for the sake of the one greatest joy. Never do that, Jenny Blair.'" And she says, too, "'No fame on earth is so exacting as a reputation for beauty'" (284).

Like her caged canary, Ariel, Eva is imprisoned, her cage being society's expectations of women. The canary has been forced to live a stunted, unnatural life, and so has Eva. At one point, Eva seems to recognize the parallel between her beautiful caged bird and herself.

> "I sometimes wonder," she said, . . . "if it is fair to keep a single bird, even a canary, in a cage. If I let him out, what would become of him?"
>
> "He would fly away. You would never find him again."
>
> "Yes, when a bird flies away, you never find him again."
> (285)

But what if a woman were to fly away . . . , Eva seems to wonder. Near the end of the book, Eva does try to escape her cage. She takes to running impulsively out of the house to wander the neighborhood. "'I had to go. I couldn't stay in the house,'" she says (384). But she always comes back; she has nowhere else to light. In her flights, Eva is searching for the real Eva: "'Unless I go alone, I can never find myself. When you've never been yourself for forty years, you've forgotten what you are really'" (385). Several pages earlier, in another comparison of Eva to a bird seeking escape, Glasgow had suggested that she was destined to failure: "Then she struggled up, with a quiver of pain, like some bright winged creature fluttering helplessly on the earth, and gazed curiously about the room, as if she were in a strange place and could not remember whether she had ever seen it before" (365).

In the novel's climax, Eva apparently shoots her husband after discovering Jenny Blair in his arms. Though she has tried to find a true self behind the facade of the Southern belle, she does not find that missing center in time. It is the frustrated, insecure, aging Southern belle who shoots George. If she cannot be sure of George's love, she cannot be sure she is beautiful, and without love and beauty she is nothing.

The title "The Illusion" refers not only to Eva's shattered illusion but also to Jenny Blair's developing illusion. In this third section of her bildungsroman, Glasgow portrays the consequences of Jenny Blair's education in the philosophy and codes of the Old South tradition.

At age seventeen, Jenny Blair has decided she doesn't want to be a Southern belle; rather, she wants to be independent, go to New York, study to be an actress. She sees herself as a modern woman rejecting old-fashioned ways. The reader, however, recognizes her goals and her rebellion as romantic rather than principled. She has the naïveté and charm of youth, and the reader wants to like her, wants her to do well, escape harm, not harm others. But Jenny Blair, the self-professed rebel, has learned the lessons of her society all too well. During Eva Birdsong's hospitalization, she begins a flirtation with George Birdsong, a flirtation that she convinces herself is innocent and harmless, though immediately she loses her ambition to go to New York to be different and independent. She is naive and charming, yes, but Glasgow reveals her to be also a shallow, self-centered young woman who evades facing reality and who shows little sense of responsibility. Her education has not helped her to develop intellectually and morally; in a sense, she is still a child.

At age nine, she had learned that her society values beauty in a woman above all else, so at seventeen she is pleased to find herself attractive. Being beautiful and being loved are all that count. Her self-centeredness and shallowness are reflected in these thoughts: "Poor Aunt Etta, it must be dreadful to be like that. . . . It would be better to be young and pretty and work in a factory than to be old and ugly and tormented by a sinus infection. 'I'm glad I'm pretty,' she continued, flitting back to herself. 'I'm glad people love me because I'm pretty'" (344).

She is in love with George Birdsong, but she is also devoted to George's wife, Eva, who is now physically as well as emotionally ill; and she sees no inconsistency in these attitudes. In fact, she seems to feel that her devotion to Mrs. Birdsong excuses her love for Mrs. Birdsong's husband: she visits Eva often, feels sorry for her, gives her the beautiful kimono that she herself had received as a gift at Easter.

At first, she had treasured her one kiss from George and had told herself that it was harmless because no one would ever know about it. But, of course, the one kiss is not enough. She seeks George out and continues the flirtation, still arguing with herself that "'I couldn't bear to hurt [Mrs. Birdsong], . . . but how can it hurt her for me to feel this way in secret?'" (239). A product of her upbringing, she excuses her actions here much the way she had heard her mother, years before, excuse Isabella's flirtation with Joseph Crocker—Isabella didn't mean anything by it: "'She is only amusing herself'" and "'I don't believe there is any real harm in it'" (26). Her grandfather excuses George Birdsong's various infidelities similarly: "'Well, George has the kindest heart in the world. But even the kindest heart . . . sometimes fails to get the better of nature. All that side of his life has nothing more to do with his devotion to Eva than if—than if it were malaria from the bite of a mosquito'" (132). Jenny Blair seems to think her flirtation with George also has nothing to do with her devotion to Eva.

In the passage above, General Archbald indicates that George's infidelities are just a product of nature, that George can't be held responsible for them because he has no control over them. Later in the novel, Jenny Blair repeats her previous arguments and arrives at the same conclusion: "Since it was useless to deny her love, she could only remind her conscience . . . that she did not mean the slightest harm in the world. . . . 'Nothing could make me hurt her,' she thought passionately, 'but it can't harm her to have me love him in secret.' And, besides, even if she were to try with all her strength, she could not stop loving him. . . . 'When you can't help a thing, nobody can blame you'" (279).

These several but similar arguments allow the evasive idealist to avoid responsibility for his or her actions—and to excuse others for their actions. The arguments imply that no action is in and of itself immoral. How ironical that this same society holds people to a rigid code of manners and judges them severely on their appearance.

Jenny Blair may intend no harm by the flirtation, but harm does follow from it. Yet even in the face of Eva's apparent murder of her husband, Jenny Blair attempts to escape any responsibility for what has happened. She can only cry out, in the last words of the novel, "'Oh, Grandfather, I didn't mean anything. . . . I didn't mean anything in the world!'" (395), words that echo her thoughts, and evasion, after George first kissed her in the summerhouse: "'After all, it wasn't my fault . . . I didn't mean anything. I didn't mean anything in the world'" (222).

Jenny Blair might have experienced growth even yet, if

she had been forced to face and admit her role in the tragedy. But instantly the society closes ranks to protect its own.
John Welch, Mrs. Birdsong's cousin and the first on the
scene, who has suspected Jenny of carrying on a romance
with George, realizes immediately what has happened. Yet
the world will never hear that Eva Birdsong killed her husband or that Jenny Blair was in any way involved. John immediately comes up with a prettier version of the episode:
"'He shot himself. It was an accident'" (394). And General
Archbald, not surprisingly, accepts and supports that inter-
pretation.

John Welch's role here at the end of the bildungsroman
and the critique deserves comment. The reader may be surprised that John not only condones but authors the false
version of the tragedy. After all, twenty-five-year-old John
is a man of science, a young doctor, the one voice of the
new age in the book. He has criticized the society's evasive
idealism all along: "John, after the habit of all realists in every age, disliked sentimentality." Whereas others put the
best face on Mrs. Birdsong's illness and operation, John
speaks bluntly: "'She has a fifty-fifty chance. . . . Her heart
isn't quite so strong as it ought to be, but her kidneys are
sound'" (206). Yet John, the man of facts, the man who had
tried to get Jenny Blair to see and learn from the larger
world—he once told her she had a "'sparrow vision'" of
the world (296)—joins forces with the Old Order at the
end. His crossing the line may be Glasgow's way of re-
minding the reader that John, like Jenny Blair, has, after all,
been a child of that world himself, raised in the Birdsong
house. In his childhood, John, like Jenny Blair, had had a
child's natural curiosity, but unlike hers, his stayed with him:
at seventeen, Jenny Blair's current age, "his curiosity about
life was insatiable" (44) and would lead him to escape the
boundaries of the narrow and romanticizing world he was
reared in. At the end, however, he slips back into that world
to protect his beloved aunt Eva Birdsong and Jenny Blair.

Some critics have argued that John Welch the realist is Glasgow's spokesperson in this novel, but the irony of the ending—his joining forces with the romanticizers—shows that he certainly does not always speak for her. Indeed, his action at the end mocks his own words a few pages earlier, where, in a conversation with Jenny Blair, he in effect expresses the novel's theme and, in that instance, does speak for Glasgow: "'I suppose you call that view looking on the bright side; but that may be after all what is really the matter.'" Though Jenny Blair assumes John is speaking of Eva Birdsong's troubles, his further comments suggest he is not thinking of Mrs. Birdsong alone but of the society at large: "'I mean not facing things, trying to pretend that anything you don't wish to look at doesn't exist. It is a false attitude, of course, even if it is a noble one" (370). John and General Archbald's protecting Eva and Jenny Blair at the end may be noble, but it is false, and harmful, too, in that it allows Jenny Blair to continue not to face things, to pretend that anything she doesn't want to look at doesn't exist—to remain a sheltered child. Such is the final implication of Glasgow's bildungsroman—and her ultimate criticism of the Old South tradition.

The Sheltered Life has the marks of a masterful realist and artist. There are no shining heroes or dark villains here, no wasted words, no distracting intrusions by the author. Glasgow leads the reader to understand and sympathize with all of the characters by portraying them all as products of their upbringing and society. She has fully integrated the characters to her purpose of exposing a way of life. At the same time, the characterizations, especially of Jenny Blair Archbald and General David Archbald, transcend the particulars of place and time. In nine-year-old Jenny Blair, Glasgow has beautifully captured the consciousness, the words, the desires, the actions of a child; it is one of the most convincing portraits of childhood in literature. And rarely before has there appeared such a complex, realistic, and sympathetic portrait of old age as Glasgow presents in General Archbald.

The good General deserves a coda here, for many readers have seen him as the hero of the novel. Louis Auchincloss says "there's no question" that the author's sympathies lie with him,[16] and in her preface to the novel Glasgow herself describes him as "a lover of wisdom, a humane and civilized soul" (xix). Yet, as we have seen, Archbald, like all the characters, is the frequent object of the author's irony. The irony even becomes satirical at times. Such a proper old gentleman, such a "civilized soul" of the Old South, he thinks it improper, no matter how tired he is, not to be fully and formally attired whenever he is in public, even in the public areas of his own home. Once, his daughter-in-law persuades him to put on his slippers and lie down on a sofa in his library, with the doors closed, to rest, but there is a limit to how far he will go for comfort.

> "Wouldn't you be more comfortable if you loosened your collar?"
>
> He shook his head stubbornly, shrinking from so serious an infringement of habit. Though it was commendable to rebel in one's mind, it was imperative, he felt, to keep on one's collar. (262)

And no one, not even his daughter-in-law, Cora, whom he himself calls an evasive idealist, could be more of a romanticizer and evasive idealist than the good General himself. Of Eva Birdsong, he thinks, "'Even when she is dead, . . . her skeleton will have beauty'" (188).

Ellen Glasgow, realist, must have chuckled as she wrote those wonderfully romantic words.

Carol S. Manning

NOTES

1. Allen Tate to Donald Davidson, December 12, 1929, in *The Literary Correspondence of Donald Davidson and Allen Tate*, ed. John Tyree Fain and Thomas Daniel Young (Athens: Univ. of Georgia Press, 1974), 243; John Edward Hardy, "Ellen Glasgow," in *Southern Renascence: The Literature of the Modern South*, ed. Louis D. Rubin, Jr., and Robert D. Jacobs (Baltimore: Johns Hopkins Univ. Press, 1953), 248–49; Daniel Joseph Singal, *The War Within: From Victorian to Modernist Thought in the South, 1919–1945* (Chapel Hill: Univ. of North Carolina Press, 1982), xi.

2. Louis D. Rubin, Jr., Introduction to *Ellen Glasgow: Centennial Essays*, ed. M. Thomas Inge (Charlottesville: Univ. Press of Virginia, 1976), 4; Julius Rowan Raper, "Inventing Modern Southern Fiction: A Postmodern View," *The Southern Literary Journal* 22 (Spring 1990): 4.

3. Tate to Donald Davidson, December 12, 1929, in *Literary Correspondence*, 243.

4. Louis Auchincloss, "Ellen Glasgow," in his *Pioneers and Caretakers: A Study of Nine American Women Writers* (Boston: G. K. Hall and Co., 1985), 86.

5. Ibid., 88.

6. Louis D. Rubin, Jr. "The Road to Yoknapatawpha: George W. Cable and *John March, Southerner*," in his *Writers of the Modern South: The Faraway Country* (Seattle: Univ. of Washington Press, 1963), 21; and Rubin, Postscript, ibid., 232–33.

7. C. Vann Woodward, quoted in Rubin, Introduction to *Ellen Glasgow*, 4.

8. Thomas Daniel Young, "Introduction to Part III," in *The History of Southern Literature*, ed. Louis D. Rubin, Jr., et al. (Baton Rouge: Louisiana State Univ. Press, 1985), 262.

9. Carol S. Manning, "The Real Beginning of the Southern Renaissance," in *The Female Tradition in Southern Literature*, ed. Carol S. Manning (Urbana: Univ. of Illinois Press, 1993), 37–56.

10. Ellen Glasgow, *The Woman Within* (New York: Harcourt, Brace and Co., 1954), 42.

11. Ibid., 98.

12. Ibid.

13. Ibid., 129.

14. Ellen Glasgow, "The Dynamic Past," *Reviewer* 1 (March 15, 1921): 73, 78, 75.

15. Glasgow, *The Woman Within*, 97.

16. Auchincloss, "Ellen Glasgow," 81.